THE SACRED BOOKS OF THE EAST

F. MAX MULLER (ED.)

LIST OF THE 50 VOLUMES

1. Upanishads.
2. Sacred Laws of Aryas.
3. Texts of Confucianism.
4. Zend-Avesta.
5. Pahlavi Texts.
6. Qur'an.
7. Institutes of Vishnu.
8. Bhagavadgita, & c.
9. Qur'an.
10. (i) Dhammapada.
10. (ii) Sutta-Nipata.
11. Buddhist Suttas.
12. Satapatha-Brahmana.
13. Vinaya Texts.
14. Sacred Laws of Aryas.
15. Upanishads.
16. Texts of Confucianism.
17. Vinaya Texts.
18. Pahlavi Texts.
19. Fo-sho-hing-tsanking.
20. Vinaya Texts.
21. Saddharma Pundarika.
22. Gaina-Sutras.
23. Zend-Avesta.
24. Pahlavi Texts.
25. Laws of Manu.
26. Satapatha-Brahmana.
27. Texts of Confucianism (Li Ki).
28. Texts of Confucianism (Li Ki).
29. Grihya-Sutras.
30 Grihya-Sutras.
31. Zend-Avesta.
32. Vedic Hymns.
33. Minor Law-Books.
34. Vedanta-Sutras.
35. Milinda.
36. Milinda.
37. Pahlavi Texts.
38. Vedanta-Sutras.
39. Texts of Taoism
40. Texts of Taoism
41. Satapatha-Brahmana
42. Atharva-veda.
43. Satapatha-Brahmana.
44. Satapatha-Brahmana.
45. Gaina-Sutras.
46. Vedic Hymns.
47. Pahlavi Texts.
48. Vedanta-Sutras.
49. (i) Buddhakarita.
49. (ii) Mahayana Texts.
50. A General Index

The Sacred Books of the East, Vol. 11

BUDDHIST SUTTAS

Edited from Pali

F. MAX MULLER

Translated from Pali

T. W. RHYS DAVIDS

1. THE MAHA-PARINIBBANA SUTTANTA
2. THE DHAMMA-KAKKA-PPAVATTANA SUTTA
3. THE TEVIGGA SUTTANTA
4. THE AKANKHEYYA SUTTA
5. THE KETOKHILA SUTTA
6. THE MAHA-SUDASSANA SUTTANTA
7. THE SABBASAVA SUTTA

GYAN

Published by

GYAN

Gyan Publishing House
5, Ansari Road
Daryaganj, New Delhi-110002
Phone: 011-47034999, 9811692060
E-mail: books@gyanbooks.com

Distribution Network
gyanbooks.com
India, USA, Canada, UK, Australia, France

ISBN : 978-81-212-2937-1 (Set)
ISBN : 978-81-212-2407-9 (PB)
First Published, 1881

2nd Impression 2021

Printed at: Gyan Press, Delhi.

The Sacred Books of the East, Vol. 11

Buddhist Suttas
Edited by: F. Max Muller, Translated by: T. W. Rhys Davids

THE SACRED BOOKS OF THE EAST

TRANSLATED

BY VARIOUS ORIENTAL SCHOLARS

AND EDITED BY

F. MAX MÜLLER

VOL. XI

Oxford

AT THE CLARENDON PRESS

1881

BUDDHIST SUTTAS

TRANSLATED FROM PÂLI

BY

T. W. RHYS DAVIDS

1. THE MAHÂ-PARINIBBÂNA SUTTANTA
2. THE DHAMMA-*K*AKKA-PPAVATTANA SUTTA
3. THE TEVI*GG*A SUTTANTA
4. THE ÂKAṄKHEYYA SUTTA
5. THE *K*ETOKHILA SUTTA
6. THE MAHÂ-SUDASSANA SUTTANTA
7. THE SABBÂSAVA SUTTA

Oxford

AT THE CLARENDON PRESS

1881

CONTENTS.

GENERAL INTRODUCTION

TO THE

BUDDHIST SUTTAS.

ON being asked to contribute a volume of translations from the Pâli Suttas to the important series of which this work forms a part, the contributor has to face the difficulty of choosing from the stores of a nearly unknown literature—a difficulty arising from the embarrassment, not of poverty, but of wealth. I have endeavoured to make such a choice as would enable me to bring together into one volume a collection of texts which should be as complete a sample as one volume could afford of what the Buddhist scriptures, on the whole, contain. With this object in view I have refrained from confining myself to the most interesting books —those, namely, which deal with the Noble Eightfold Path, the most essential, the most original, and the most attractive part of Gotama's teaching; and I have chosen accordingly, besides the Sutta of the Foundation of the Kingdom of Righteousness (the Dhamma-*k*akka-ppavattana-Sutta), which treats of the Noble Path, six others which treat of other sides of the Buddhist system; less interesting perhaps in their subject matter, but of no less historical value.

These are—

1. The Book of the Great Decease (the Mahâ-parinibbâna-Suttanta), which is the Buddhist representative of what, among the Christians, is called a Gospel.

2. The Foundation of the Kingdom of Righteousness (the Dhamma-*k*akka-ppavattana-Sutta), containing the Four Noble Truths, and the Noble Eightfold Path which ends in Arahatship.

3. The Discussion on Knowledge of the Three Vedas (the Tevi*gg*a-Suttanta), which is a controversial dialogue on the right method of attaining to a state of union with Brahmâ.

4. The Sutta entitled 'If he should desire—' (Âkaṅkheyya-Sutta), which shows in the course of a very beautiful argument some curious sides of early Buddhist mysticism and of curiously unjustified belief.

5. The Treatise on Barrenness and Bondage (the *K*etokhila-Sutta), which treats of the Buddhist Order of Mendicants, from the moral, as distinguished from the disciplinary, point of view.

6. The Legend of the Great King of Glory (the Mahâ-sudassana-Suttanta), which is an example of the way in which previously existing legends were dealt with by the early Buddhists.

7. The Sutta entitled 'All the Âsavas' (the Sabbâsava-Sutta), which explains the signification of a constantly recurring technical term, and lays down the essential principles of Buddhist Agnosticism.

The Discipline of the Buddhist Mendicants, the Rules of their Order—probably the most influential, as it is the oldest, in the world—will be fully described, down to its minutest details, in the translation of the Vinaya Pi*t*aka, which will appropriately form a subsequent part of this Series of Translations of the Sacred Books of the East. There was therefore no need to include any Sutta on this subject in the present volume: but of the rest of the matters discussed in the Buddhist Sacred Books—of Buddhist legend, gospel, controversial theology, and ethics—the works selected will I trust give a correct and adequate, if necessarily a somewhat fragmentary, idea.

The age of these writings can be fixed, without much uncertainty, at about the latter end of the fourth or the beginning of the third century before the commencement of the Christian era. This is the only hypothesis which seems, at present, to account for the facts known about them. It should not however be looked upon as anything more than a good working hypothesis to be accepted until all the texts of the Buddhist Pâli Suttas shall have been properly edited. For it depends only on the fact that one of the texts now translated contains several statements, and one very significant silence, which afford ground for chronological argument. That argument amounts only to probability, not to certainty; and it might scarcely be worth while to put it forward were it not that the course of the enquiry will be found to raise several questions of very considerable interest.

The significant silence to which I refer occurs in the account of the death of Gotama at the end of the Mahâ-parinibbâna-Sutta[1]; and I cannot do better than quote Dr. Oldenberg's remarks upon it at p. xxvi of the able Introduction to his edition of the text of the Mahâ-vagga.

'The Tradition regarding the Councils takes up the thread of the story where the accounts of the life and work of Buddha, given in the Sutta Pi*t*aka, end. After the death of the Master—so it is related in the *K*ulla-vagga—Subhadda, the last disciple converted by Buddha shortly before his death[2], proclaimed views which threatened the dissolution of the community.

'"Do not grieve, do not lament," he is said to have said to the believers. "It is well that we have been relieved of the Great Master's presence. We were oppressed by him when he said, 'This is permitted to you, this is not permitted.' In future we can do as we like, and not do as we do not like."

'In opposition to Subhadda,—the tradition goes on to relate,—there came forward one of the most distinguished and oldest of Buddha's disciples, the great Kassapa, who proposed that five hundred of the most eminent members of the community should assemble at Râ*g*agaha, the royal residence of the ruler of Magadha, in order to collect the Master's precepts in an authentic form. It has already been said above, how, during the seven months' sitting of

[1] Translated below, pp. 112–135.

[2] This is a mistake. The Subhadda referred to is quite a different person from the last convert. See my note below, p. 127.

the assembly, Kassapa as president fixed the Vinaya with the assistance of Upâli, and the Dhamma with the assistance of Ânanda.

'This is the story as it has come down to us. What we have here before us is not history, but pure invention; and, moreover, an invention of no very recent date. Apart from internal reasons that might be adduced to support this, we are able to prove it by comparing another text which is older than this story, and the author of which cannot yet have known it. I allude to the highly important Sutta, which gives an account of the death of Buddha, and the Pâli text of which has recently been printed by Professor Childers. This Sutta gives[1] the story—in long passages word for word the same as in the *K*ulla-vagga—of the irreverent conduct of Subhadda, which Kassapa opposes by briefly pointing to the true consolation that should support the disciples in their separation from the Master. Then follows the account of the burning of Buddha's corpse, of the distribution of his relics among the various princes and cities, and of the festivals which were instituted in honour of these relics. Everything that the legend of the First Council alleges as a motive for, and as the background to, the story about Kassapa's proposal for holding the Council, is found here altogether, except that there is no allusion to the proposal itself, or to the Council. We hear of those speeches of Subhadda, which, according to the later tradition, led Kassapa to make his proposal, but we do not hear anything of the proposal itself. We hear of the great assembly that meets for the distribution of Buddha's relics, in which—according to the later tradition—Kassapa's proposal was agreed to, but we do not hear anything of these transactions. It may be added that we hear in this same Sutta[2] of the precepts which Buddha delivered to his followers shortly before his death, concerning doubts and differences of opinion that might arise, among the members of the community, with regard to the Dhamma and the Vinaya, and with regard to

[1] Pages 67, 68 in the edition of Childers.
[2] Pages 39, 60, 61, ibid.

the treatment of such cases when he should no longer be with them. If anywhere, we should certainly have expected to find here some allusion to the great authentic depositions of Dhamma and Vinaya after Buddha's death, which, according to the general belief of Buddhists, established a firm standard according to which differences could be judged and have been judged through many centuries. There is not the slightest trace of any such allusion to the Council. This silence is as valuable as the most direct testimony. It shows that the author of the Mahâ-parinibbâna-Sutta did not know anything of the First Council.'

The only objection which it seems to me possible to raise against this argument is that the conclusion is worded somewhat too absolutely; and that it is rather a begging of the question to state, in the very first words referring to the Mahâ-parinibbâna-Sutta, that it is older than the story in the *K*ulla-vagga, and that its author could not have known that work. But no one will venture to dispute the accuracy of Dr. Oldenberg's representation of the facts on which he bases his conclusion; and the conclusion that he draws is, at least, the easiest and readiest way of explaining the very real discrepancy that he has pointed out. We shall be quite safe if we only say that we have certain facts which lend strong probability to the hypothesis that the author of the Mahâ-parinibbâna-Sutta did not know that account of the First Council which we find in the *K*ulla-vagga.

We do not know for certain the time at which that part of the *K*ulla-vagga, in which that account occurs, was composed. I think it quite possible that it was as late as the Council of Patna (B.C. 250), though Dr. Oldenberg places it somewhat earlier[1]. But even if we put the conclusion of the *K*ulla-vagga as late as the year I have mentioned, it is still in the highest degree improbable that the Mahâ-parinibbâna-Sutta, supposing it to be an older work, can have been composed very much later than the fourth century B.C.—a provisional date sufficient at present for practical purposes.

[1] Mahâ-vagga, p. xxxviii.

This conclusion, however, is only almost, and not quite certain. It is just possible that the author of the Book of the Great Decease omitted all mention of the First Council at Râgagaha, not because he did not know of it, but because he considered it unnecessary to mention an event which had no bearing on the subject of his work. He was describing the death of the Buddha, and not the history of the Canon or of the Order.

I must confess however that I only mention this as a possibility from a desire rather to understate than to overstate my case. For, firstly, it should be remembered that the writer does not merely omit to mention an occurrence subsequent to and unconnected with the Great Decease. He does more: he gives an account of the Subhadda incident which is inconsistent and irreconcilable with the legend or narrative of the Râ*g*agaha Council as related in the *K*ulla-vagga. Had that narrative, as we now have it, been received in his time among the Brethren, he would scarcely have done this.

And, secondly, he does not, after all, close his book, as he might well have done, with the Great Decease itself. It will be seen from the translation below[1] that there was a point in his narrative, the exclamations of sorrow at the death of the Buddha, which would have formed, had he desired to omit all unnecessary details, a very fitting conclusion to his narrative. The Book of the Great King of Glory, the Mahâ-sudassana-Sutta, closes with the very exclamation our author puts, at this point, into the mouth of Sakka. The Mahâ-parinibbâna was then over, and the Mahâ-parinibbâna-Sutta might have then been closed. But he goes on and describes in detail the cremation, the distribution of the relics, and the feasts celebrated in their honour. It is not necessary for my point to show that it was in the least degree unnatural to do so. It is sufficient to be able to point out that the author having done so,—having gone on to the arrival of Kassapa, who was afterwards (in the *K*ulla-vagga) said to have held the Council; having mentioned the very incident which, according to the

[1] See below, Chap. VI, § 21.

other narrative, gave rise to the holding of the Council; and having referred to events which took place after the Council,—it is scarcely a tenable argument to say that he, knowing of it, did not refer, even incidentally and in half a sentence, to so important an event, simply because it did not come, necessarily, within the subject of his work. And when we find that in other works on the death of the Buddha, referred to below[1], the account of the Council of Râ*g*agaha has, in fact, been included in the story, it is difficult to withhold our assent to the very great probability of the hypothesis, that it would have been included also in the Pâli Book of the Great Decease had the belief in the tradition of the Council been commonly held at the time when that book was put into its present shape. At the same time we must hold ourselves quite prepared to learn that some other explanation may turn out to be possible. The argument, if it applied to writers of the nineteenth century, would be conclusive. But we know too little about the mode in which the Pâli Pi*t*akas were composed to presume at present to be quite certain.

The Mahâ-parinibbâna-Sutta was then probably composed before the account of the First Council of Râ*g*agaha in the concluding part of the *K*ulla-vagga. It was also almost certainly composed after Pâ*t*aliputta, the modern Patna, had become the capital city of the kingdom of Magadha; after the worship of relics had become common in the Buddhist church; and after the rise of a general belief in the *K*akkavatti theory, in the ideal of a sacred king, a supreme overlord in India.

The first of these last three arguments depends on the prophecy placed in Gotama's mouth as to the future greatness of Pâ*t*aliputta—a prophecy found in the Mahâ-vagga as well as in the Mahâ-parinibbâna-Sutta. It is true that the guess may actually have been made, and that it required no great boldness to hazard a conjecture so vaguely expressed. The words simply are—

'And among famous places of residence and haunts of

---

[1] See p. xxxviii.

busy men, this will become the chief, the city of Pâṭaliputta, a centre for interchange of all kinds of wares. But there will happen three disasters to Pâṭaliputta, one of fire, and one of water, and one of dissension[1].'

But it is, to say the least, improbable that the conjecture would have been recorded until after the event had proved it to be accurate: and it would scarcely be too hazardous to maintain that the tradition of the guess having been made would not have arisen at all until after the event had occurred.

What was the event referred to may also be questioned, as the words quoted do not, in terms, declare that the city would become the actual capital. But we know, not only from Buddhist, but from Greek historians, that it did, and this is most probably the origin of the prophecy.

Now the Mâlâlaṅkâravatthu, a Pâli work of modern date, but following very closely the more ancient books, has been translated, through the Burmese, by Bishop Bigandet; and it says,

'That monarch [Susunâga], not unmindful of his mother's origin, re-established the city of Vesâlî, and fixed in it the royal residence. From that time Râǵagaha lost her rank of royal city, which she never afterwards recovered. He died in 81' [that is, of the Buddhist era reckoned from the Great Decease][2]. . . .

Relying on similar authority Bishop Bigandet afterwards himself says:

'King Kâḷâsoka left Râǵagaha, and removed the seat of his empire to Palibothra [the Greek name for Pâṭaliputta], near the place where the modern city of Patna stands[2].'

---

[1] See below, Chap. I, § 28. I have translated Puṭabhedanam, 'a centre for the interchange of all kinds of wares,' in accordance with the commentary, which is clearly based on a derivation from puṭa, 'a bag or bundle.' But I see that Trenckner in his Pâli Miscellany renders nânâpuṭabhedanam by 'surrounded by a number of dependent towns.'

At the end the text has 'from fire or from water or from dissension;' on which Buddhaghosa says that or stands here for and; and the comment is correct enough, not of course philologically, but exegetically. But in either case the last clause is of very little importance for the present argument.

[2] Bigandet's 'Legend of the Burmese Budha,' third edition, vol. ii. pp. 115, 183. I have altered the spelling only of the proper names.

It would seem therefore that, according to the tradition followed by this writer, Susunâga first removed the capital to Vesâli, and his successor Kâ*l*âsoka, who died, in the opinion of the writer in question, in 118 after the Great Decease, finally fixed it at Pâ*t*aliputta.

If we therefore apply this date to the prophecy we must come to the conclusion that the Book of the Great Decease was put into its present form at least 100 years after the Buddha's death, and probably a little more. But the authority followed by Bishop Bigandet is very late; and no mention of these occurrences is found either in the Dîpava*m*sa or in the Mahâva*m*sa. I think indeed that the whole account of these two kings, as at present accepted in Ceylon and Birma, is open to grave doubt[1] (in which connection it should be noticed that the oldest account of the Council of Vesâli, in the *K*ulla-vagga, Book XII, makes no mention of Kâ*l*âsoka).

We have next to consider the reference to the relics in the concluding sections of Chapter VI as a possible basis for chronological argument. These sections are almost certainly older than the time when especial sanctity was claimed for Buddhist dâgabas on the ground that they contained particular relics of the Blessed One (such as a tooth, or the bowl, or the neck bone); for if such special relics were accepted as objects of worship when the Book of the Great Decease was put together, they would naturally have been mentioned in the course of Chapter VI.

It is even almost certain that when the sections were put into their present form no Buddhist dâgaba was in existence except at the eight places mentioned in them; and the words are quite consistent with the belief that those eight had themselves then ceased to have any very widespread and acknowledged sanctity. So in Chapter V, § 13, where four places are spoken of 'which the believing man should visit with feelings of reverence and of awe,' there is no mention of dâgabas at all; and in Chapter V, § 16, it is

[1] See my 'Ancient Coins and Measures of Ceylon,' p. 50.

clearly implied that only one dâgaba, or memorial burial mound, should be erected in honour of a Tathâgata, just as one memorial mound should be erected in honour of a king of kings.

When we recollect that in the first and second, and perhaps in the third century before Christ, dâgabas had already been erected in honour of the Buddha in distant parts of the continent of India, and had rapidly become famous as places of pilgrimage, the reasonable conclusion to be drawn from these passages is that the Book of the Great Decease is older than them all; or, at the least, that it was written before any of them had become famous.

On the other hand, there is evidently an exaggerated belief as to the respect in which the Buddha was held by his contemporaries underlying the concluding and other sections of the book. It is probable enough that Gotama was held in deep respect by the simple people among whom he lived and moved about as a religious teacher and reformer. It may well be that the inhabitants of the village where he died gave him a sort of public funeral. But that the neighbouring clans should have vied one with the other for the possession of his remains is quite inconsistent with the position that he can reasonably be supposed to have held among them. It must have taken some time for this belief to spring up, and be received without question.

In a similar way a considerable interval must have elapsed before the beautiful parable in the last section of Chapter I could have given rise to the belief in the miracle (the solitary miracle ascribed to the Buddha, so far as I know, in the Sutta Pi*t*aka) recorded in the previous section.

So also the comparison drawn between the Buddha and a *K*akkavatti Râ*g*a or King of Kings in Chapter V, § 37, and Chapter VI, § 33, can scarcely have arisen till the rise of a lord paramount in the valley of the Ganges had familiarised the people with the idea of a Universal Monarch. Now it was either just before or just after the well-known Councils at Vesâli, of which mention has been made above, that that important revolution took place which raised a low-caste adventurer to be the first *K*akkavatti Râ*g*a[1]. To the people of that time *K*andragupta seemed to be lord of the world, for to them India was the world—just as European writers even now talk complacently of 'the world' while ignoring three-fourths of the human race.

'Is it surprising,' as I have asked elsewhere, 'that this unity of power in one man made a deep impression upon them? Is it surprising that, like Romans worshipping Augustus, or like Greeks adding the glow of the sun-myth to the glory of Alexander, the Indians should have formed an ideal of their *K*akkavatti, and have transferred to this new ideal many of the dimly sacred and half-understood traits of the Vedic heroes? Is it surprising that the Buddhists should have found it edifying to recognise in their hero "the *K*akkavatti of Righteousness;" and that the story of the Buddha should have become tinged with the colouring of these *K*akkavatti myths?'

In point of fact we know that in later works the attraction of this poetic ideal led to the almost complete disregard of the simpler narrative which seemed so poor and meagre in comparison; and M. Senart has shown how large a proportion of the later poem called the Lalita Vistara is inspired by it. When, in isolated passages of the Book of the Great Decease, we find the earliest germs of this fruitful train of thought, we are I think safe in concluding that it assumed its present form after the notorious career of *K*andragupta had made him supreme in the valley of the Ganges.

All the above arguments tend in one direction; namely, that the final redaction of the Book of the Great Decease must be assigned to the latter part of the fourth century before Christ, or to the earlier part of the following century. And so much alike are it and all the other Suttas translated in this volume in their form, in their views of life, and in

[1] I have ventured in my 'Ancient Coins and Measures of Ceylon,' p. 51, to point out that the Councils of Vesâli were very possibly held just at the time when Nanda was defeated by *K*andragupta. Târanâtha, the Tibetan historian, while placing the Councils, like all the later authorities, under an Asoka (probably *K*andragupta), says (p. 41 of Wassilief's German translation) that the assembled brethren were fed by Nanda.

the religious doctrines they lay down, that, though it may be possible hereafter to show that some are a little older or a little younger than the others, every one will I think admit that they must all be assigned to about the same period of time. There is not the least reason to believe that either of them is older than the Book of the Great Decease; and the argument has only been confined to it because it alone deals with the kind of subject which can give foundation to chronological conclusions. When the whole of the literature of the Pâli Pi*t*akas has been fully explored, we may perhaps be able to reach a more definite conclusion.

We are in absolute ignorance as to the actual author of any of the texts I have translated. It is quite evident that they are not the work of Gotama himself; and it is difficult to believe that even his immediate disciples could have spoken of him in the exaggerated terms in which occasionally he is here described. On the other hand, the history of similar religious movements teaches us how quickly such notions spring up concerning the omniscience and sinlessness of the founder of the movement; and it would be better to reserve our judgment as to the impossibility, on this account alone, of those Suttas having been composed even by the very earliest disciples.

It would be of less importance who composed the Suttas if we could be sure that they gave an accurate account of the teachings of the great thinker and reformer whose words they purport to preserve. But though, like all other writings of a similar character, they are doubtless based upon traditions older than the time of their authors or final redactors, they cannot unfortunately be depended upon as entirely authentic. And it will be always difficult, even when the whole of the Suttas have been published, to attempt to discriminate between the original doctrine of Gotama, and the later accretions to, or modifications of it.

But we can already make some steps towards such a discrimination, without much fear of being contradicted.

There can be little doubt but that the doctrines of the Four Noble Truths and of the Noble Eightfold Path, the 'Foundation of the Kingdom of Righteousness,' were not only the teaching of Gotama himself, but were the central and most essential part of it. I am aware that no method can be more misleading, or more uncritical, than first to form a theory regarding the personal character of the author of a new religious movement—as some later critics of the Gospel History have done—and then to adopt those passages in the sacred books which fit in with that character, and to reject those which oppose it. We cannot begin by postulating that Gotama was a man of high moral earnestness, and of great intellectual acuteness; and then disregard all the passages in which erroneous, and even puerile, opinions or sayings are placed in his mouth. But it does not follow that we are obliged either altogether to reject the evidence of the Buddhist Scriptures as to what Gotama did actually teach, or altogether to accept it.

It will be acknowledged that the Suttas have preserved for us at least the belief of the earliest Buddhists—the Buddhists in India—as to what the original doctrines, taught by the Buddha himself, had been. We have in the Vinaya Pi*t*aka an invaluable and indisputable record of the mental characteristics and capabilities of these earliest followers of the Buddhist faith. Sanskrit scholars are engaged in elucidating the history of the beliefs in which Gotama was brought up, and which though often modified and frequently denied, still underlie, throughout, all that he is represented to have taught. We have therefore reliable evidence of the system out of which, and we know the system into which, Gotama's teaching was developed. This being so, it will be impossible to refrain, in despair, from the attempt to solve one of the most interesting problems which the history of the Âryan race presents to us. Scholars will never be unanimously agreed on all points; but they will agree in ascribing some parts of the early Buddhist Dharma or doctrine only to the early disciples; and after allowing for all reasonable doubts, they will agree in ascribing other parts to the great Teacher himself. I venture to think that not only the Four Noble Truths, but the whole of the Seven Jewels of the Law, may already be placed, with certainty, in the latter category[1].

The form, in which these Suttas have been preserved, deserves careful attention. Every reader will be struck at once with the constant repetitions. These repetitions are not essential, and are merely designed to facilitate the learning of the Suttas by heart. Writing was unknown in the age of the Buddha, and probably for long after his time. In all probability indeed, just as the Indians learnt from the Greeks, not the art of coinage, but the custom of issuing a legally authorised coinage[2]; so it was from the Greeks that they acquired, if not their earliest alphabet, at least the knowledge of the utility of writing. But even for some time after writing was generally known, it was considered a desecration to make use of it for the preservation of the sacred books. This feeling naturally passed away much sooner among the adherents of the popular religious faith of Buddhism, than it did among their conservative opponents. With the latter it is by no means extinct even now, and the first record we have of the Buddhist Scriptures being reduced into writing is the well-known passage in the Dîpava*m*sa, which speaks of their being recorded in books in Ceylon towards the beginning of the first century before the commencement of our era. And as all our copies of the Buddhist Pi*t*akas are, at present, derived from those then in use in Ceylon, we are practically concerned only with those thus referred to in the Dîpava*m*sa[3].

The date of the Dîpava*m*sa may be placed approximately in the fourth century of our era; but its author reproduces the continued tradition of the monasteries in

---

[1] They will be found enumerated, and shortly described, in a note below (pp. 62, 63). I am glad to learn that my friend Dr. Morris is preparing a full account of them, drawn from various parts of the Sutta Pi*t*aka, for his forthcoming work to be accordingly entitled 'The Seven Jewels of the Law.'

[2] See my 'Ancient Coins and Measures of Ceylon' (Part VI of Numismata Orientalia), p. 13.

[3] Dîpava*m*sa XX, vv. 20, 21, quoted in the Mahâva*m*sa, p. 207.

which he dwelt, and he is more probably correct, than not, in the assertion I have quoted. It would follow that the Buddhist Scriptures were, till then, handed down by word of mouth only; and no one who is acquainted with the wonderful powers of memory possessed by Indian priests, who can devote their whole lives to the task of acquiring and repeating their sacred books by heart, will doubt for a moment the possibility of this having been the case.

Two methods were adopted in India to aid this power of memory. One, adopted chiefly by the grammarians, was to clothe the rules to be remembered in very short enigmatical phrases (called sûtras or threads), which taxed the memory but little, while they required elaborate commentaries to render them intelligible. The other, the method adopted in the Buddhist writings (both Sutta and Vinaya), was, firstly, the use of stock phrases, of which the commencement once given, the remainder followed as a matter of course; and secondly, the habit of repeating whole sentences, or even paragraphs, which in our modern books would be understood or inferred, instead of being expressed.

The stock phrases, which must be distinguished from the repetitions, belong certainly to a very early period of Buddhism, and many of them recur in Sanskrit as well as in Pâli texts[1]. One result of these numerous repetitions of phrases and paragraphs is that the preservation of the text, when once established, was rendered very easy; and that mistakes in the MSS. can now be easily rectified when they occur in such repeated passages. To edit the text of such portions of a Pâli Sutta is therefore a comparatively easy task; and it may be said of all the Suttas here translated, that they have thus acquired a valuable protection against that danger of corruption from various readings which often renders uncertain the text of important passages of works written on the very different and simpler system

[1] Several examples of such passages occur in the present volume in the Âkaṅkheyya- and Mahâ-sudassana-Suttas, where they are pointed out in the notes.

to which we are accustomed. On the other hand, however, the catchwords may sometimes have given rise to serious interpolations.

It is open to much doubt whether, in the numerous passages where such stock phrases and repetitions occur, the best mode of translation is to follow word for word the expressions found in the original (but only inserted there to perform a service no longer necessary), or to make use of contractions, the fact of their being so being duly pointed out, either in notes, or by some typographical expedient. Where, for instance, a long paragraph is devoted to what an elder of the Buddhist Order of Mendicants should do, or be, under certain given circumstances, and the whole paragraph is then repeated word for word, of an ordinary member, and of a nun, and of a lay-disciple (upâsaka), or of a religious woman (upasîkâ)[1], it would be possible to convey the whole sense intended, by translating that an elder of the Order, and an ordinary member, and a nun, and a lay-disciple of either sex, should do, or be, such and such things.

But every case of repetition is not so simple as this; such curtailing destroys at least the form and the emphasis of the originals; and it seemed more in accordance with the rules laid down in the prospectus to the Series of Translations from the Sacred Books of the East, of which this volume forms a part, to adhere in all cases strictly to the text. With the exception of the earlier chapters in the Book of the Great Decease, in which a few such contractions will be found mentioned in the notes, I have therefore reproduced almost all the repetitions. The result will not, I trust, be embarrassing to the reader who keeps constantly in mind the aim and origin of these stock phrases and repetitions, and does not allow the wearisome form in which they are presented to shut out from his view the logical sequence of the sometimes very striking ideas which these Suttas contain. I venture to go further and to maintain that it is not necessary or

[1] See below, Book of the Great Decease, Chap. III, §§ 7, 8.

even correct to read through the whole of passages which were never intended to be read. We shall do wisely when coming to a phrase which we already know, to make use of a little judicious skipping, and, noting the course of the argument, to pass on, with even mind, to the next paragraph.

I send forth the following translations with very great diffidence. It is not too much to say that the discovery of early Buddhism has placed all previous knowledge of the subject in an entirely new light; and has turned the flank, so to speak, of most of the existing literature on Buddhism. I use the term 'discovery' advisedly, for though the Pâli texts have existed for many years in our public libraries, they are only now beginning to be understood; and the Buddhism of the Pâli Pi*t*akas is not only a quite different thing from Buddhism as hitherto commonly received, but is antagonistic to it. I cannot hope that the renderings of the many technical terms, now for the first time submitted to the judgment of students of early Buddhism, will all stand the test of time. So perfectly dovetailed is the old Buddhist system, so utterly different from European Christianity are the ideas involved, so pregnant are the expressions used with deep and earnest religious feelings resting on a foundation completely apart from our own, that the translation of each term becomes a problem of great difficulty and delicacy. Where Gogerly or Burnouf has dealt with any word, the process has been easier: but there are many words they have not touched, and while Gogerly had no sympathy with these ancient beliefs, Burnouf has confined himself chiefly to later phases of Buddhism. There are several paragraphs—such as the one at Chapter I, § 12 of the Book of the Great Decease—which have cost me more time and trouble than the reader of the few words they contain will easily believe; and it would be impossible to add a note to every word justifying the rendering which was finally adopted to convey the Buddhist idea, without involving at the same time some misleading implication.

In order to call attention to the fact, when a word in the original Pâli is one of these technical terms of the Buddhist system of self-training, and when therefore the English expression must be taken in that technical sense, I have throughout written the technical terms with capital letters; and I would invite the special notice of the reader to the words thus distinguished[1].

Apart, too, from the necessity of great care in the rendering of single words, I have felt bound to make some attempt, however inadequate, to reproduce the style and tone of the Buddhist author, or authors. A mere word-for-word translation, though much easier to make, and perhaps more useful to those engaged in the study of the language would not only fail to do justice to the original, but would even convey a wrong impression to those who are interested in these works from the point of view of the comparative history of religious belief. There is a very real, though peculiar, eloquence in a considerable number of the prose passages, and more especially in the closing sections of each chapter; not the mere rhetorical eloquence of a clever word-painter, but the unconscious eloquence which springs from deep religious emotion. So also in the verses scattered through the Book of the Great Decease, while there is occasional doggrel, there are also one or two passages (such as I, 34; IV, 56; VI, 15–18, and 63) where the rhythm of the Pâli verses is exceedingly beautiful, and the thoughts expressed not devoid of fancy. The translation of such passages has been beset with difficulty; and I am only too conscious how small has been the success attained. But I must ask the reader constantly to bear in mind that words, dull and bare to us, are full of meaning to the Buddhist. 'The Blessed Master came to the Mango-grove' is a very plain statement of supposed fact: but to the earnest Buddhist the mention of 'the Master' calls up to his mind

[1] I regret to say that the printer has very frequently omitted to reproduce these capitals; but they still remain in some places, and the paragraph which explains them is therefore retained.

his highest ideal of what is wise and great and kind; and the Mango-grove is surrounded to him with all the poetry, and is associated with all the tender memories which to the devout and earnest Christian are wrapped up in such names as Bethany or the Mount of Olives. While impressed therefore with the knowledge of having come far short of my ideal, I feel there is for these reasons some justification in asking a kindly consideration for this first volume of English translations from the prose portions of the Pâli Pi*t*akas.

T. W. RHYS DAVIDS.

BRICK COURT, TEMPLE,
August, 1880.

MAHÂ-PARINIBBÂNA-SUTTANTA.

INTRODUCTION

TO THE

BOOK OF THE GREAT DECEASE.

In translating this Sutta I have followed the text published by my friend the late Mr. Childers, first in the Journal of the Royal Asiatic Society, and afterwards separately. In the former the text appeared in two instalments, the first two sheets, with many various readings in the foot-notes, in the volume for 1874; and the remainder, with much fewer various readings, in the volume for 1876. The reprinted text omits most of the various readings in the first two sheets, and differs therefore slightly in the paging. The letters D, S, Y, and Z, mentioned in the notes, refer to MSS. sent to Mr. Childers from Ceylon by myself, Subhûti Unnânse, Yâtramulle Unnânse, and Mudliar de Zoysa respectively. The MS. mentioned as P (in the first two sheets quoted only in the separate edition) is, no doubt, the Dîgha Nikâya MS. of the Phayre collection in the India Office Library. The other four are now I believe in the British Museum.

The Hon. George Turnour of the Ceylon Civil Service published an analysis of this work in the Journal of the Bengal Asiatic Society for 1839; but as he unfortunately skips, or only summarises, most of the difficult passages, his work, though a most valuable contribution for the time, now more than half a century ago, has not been of much service for the present purpose. Of much greater value was Buddhaghosa's commentary contained in the Sumaṅgala Vilâsinî[1]; but the great fifth-century commen-

[1] I have used the copy made for Turnour, and now in the India Office Collection.

tator wrote of course for Buddhists, and not for foreign scholars; and his edifying notes and long exegetical expansions of the text (quite in the style of Matthew Henry) often fail to throw light on the very points which are most interesting, and most doubtful, to European readers.

The Mâlâlankâra-vatthu, a late Pâli work by a Burmese author of the eighteenth century[1], is based, in that part of it relating to the last days of the Buddha, almost exclusively on the Book of the Great Decease, and on Buddhaghosa's commentary upon it. Bishop Bigandet's translation into English of a Burmese translation of this work, well known under the title of 'The Life or Legend of Gaudama the Budha of the Burmese,' affords evidence therefore of the traditional explanations of the text. In the course either of the original author's recasting, or of the double translation, so many changes have taken place, that its evidence is frequently ambiguous and not always quite trustworthy: but with due caution, it may be used as a second commentary.

The exact meaning which was originally intended by the title of the book is open to doubt. 'Great-Decease-Book' may as well mean 'the Great Book of the Decease,' as 'the Book of the Great Decease.' This book is in fact longer than any other in the collection, and the epithet 'Great' is often opposed in titles to a 'Short' Sutta of (otherwise) the same name[2]. But the epithet is also frequently intended, without doubt, to qualify the immediately succeeding word in the title[3]; and, though the phrase 'Great Decease,' as applied to the death of the Buddha, has not been found elsewhere, it is, I think, meant to do so here[4].

[1] See 'The Life or Legend,' &c., third edition, vol. ii. p. 149. The date there given (1134 of the Burmese era = 1773 A.D.) is evidently the date of the original work, and not of the translation. Nothing is said in the book itself or in Bishop Bigandet's notes of the name of the author, or of the name or date of the Burmese translator.

[2] There are several such pairs in the Ma*gg*h*i*mâ Nikâya; and the Mahâ-Satippa*tth*âna-Sutta in the Dîgha is the same as the Satipa*tth*âna-Sutta in the Ma*gg*h*i*ma.

[3] E.g. in the Mahâ-padhâna-Sutta and Mahâ-sudassana-Sutta.

[4] Childers seems to have been of the same opinion, vide Dict. I, 268.

The division of the Book into chapters, or rather Portions for Recitation, is found in the MSS.; the division of these chapters into sections has been made by myself. It will be noticed that a very large number of the sections have already been traced, chiefly by Dr. Morris and myself, in various other parts of the Pâli Pi*t*akas: whole paragraphs or episodes, quite independent of the repetitions and stock phrases above referred to, recurring in two or more places. The question then arises whether (1) the Book of the Great Decease is the borrower, whether (2) it is the original source, or whether (3) these passages were taken over, both into it, and into the other places where they recur, from earlier sources. It will readily be understood that, in the present state of our knowledge, or rather ignorance, of the Pâli Pi*t*akas, this question cannot as yet be answered with any certainty. But a few observations may even now be made.

Generally speaking the third of the above possible explanations is not only more probable in itself, but is confirmed by parallel instances in literatures developed under similar conditions, both in the valley of the Ganges and in the basin of the Mediterranean.

It is quite possible that while some books—such as the Mahâ-vagga, the *K*ulla-vagga, and the Dîgha Nikâya—usually owe their resemblances to older sources now lost or absorbed; others—such as the Sa*m*yutta and the Aṅguttara—are always in such cases simply borrowers from sources still existing.

At the time when our Book of the Great Decease was put into its present shape, and still more so when a Book of the Great Decease was first drawn up, there may well have been some reliable tradition as to the events that took place, and as to the subjects of his various discourses, on the Buddha's last journey. He had then been a public Teacher for forty-five years; and his system of doctrine, which is really, on the whole, a very simple one, had already been long ago elaborated, and applied in numerous discourses to almost every conceivable variety of circumstances. What he then said would most naturally be, as it is represented to have been, a final recapitulation of the most important and characteristic tenets of his religion. But these are, of course, precisely those subjects which are most fully and most frequently dealt with in other parts of the Pâli Pitakas. No record of his actual words could have been preserved. It is quite evident that the speeches placed in the Teacher's mouth, though formulated in the first person, in direct narrative, are only intended to be summaries, and very short summaries, of what was said on these occasions. Now if corresponding summaries of his previous teaching had been handed down in the Order, and were in constant use among them, at the time when the Book of the Great Decease was put together, it would be a safe and easy method to insert such previously existing summaries in the historical account as having been spoken at the places where the Teacher was traditionally believed to have spoken on the corresponding doctrines. In the historical book the simple summaries would sufficiently answer every purpose; but when each particular matter became the subject of a separate book or division of a book, the same summaries would be included, but would be amplified and elucidated. And this is in fact the relation in which several of the recurring passages, as found in the Book of the Great Decease, stand to the same passages when found elsewhere.

On the other hand, some of the recurring passages do not consist of such summaries, but are actual episodes in the history. As an instance of these we may take the long extract at the end of the first, and the beginning of the second chapter (I, 20–II, 3, and again II, 16–II, 24), which is found also in the Mahâ-vagga. The words are (nearly[1]) identical in both places, but in the Book of the Great Decease the account occurs in its proper place in the middle of a connected narrative, whereas in the Mahâ-vagga, a treatise on the Rules and Regulations of the Order, it seems strangely out of place. So the passage, also a long one, with which the Book of the Great

[1] On the difference see the note at II, 16. It affects only a few localising phrases in a narrative occupying (in the translation) thirteen pages.

Decease commences (on the Seven Conditions of Welfare), seems to have been actually borrowed by the Aṅguttara Nikâya from our work.

The question of these summaries and parallel passages cannot be adequately treated by a discussion of the instances found in any one particular book. It must be considered as a whole, and quite apart from the allied question of the 'stock phrases' above alluded to, in a discussion of all the instances that can be found in the Pâli Pi*t*akas. For this purpose tabulated statements are essential, and as a mere beginning such a statement is here annexed (including the passages, marked with an asterisk, which have every appearance of belonging to the same category).

BOOK OF THE GREAT DECEASE.				OTHER BOOKS.
Chap. I	(34 sections)	§§ 1–10	..	Aṅguttara (Sutta-nipâta).
"	"	§ 11	..	" (*Kh*a-nipâta).
"	"	§§ 16, 17[1]	..	Dîgha (Sampasâdaniya) and Sa*m*yutta (Satippa*tth*âna-vagga).
"	"	§§ 20–34	..	Mahâ-vagga VI, 28.
"	"	§§ 1, 2, 3	..	Mahâ-vagga VI, 29.
Chap. II	(35 sections)	§§ 13, 14, 15	..	Dîgha (Satippa*tth*âna). Ma*ggh*ima ". Sa*m*yutta ". Vibhaṅga ".
"	"	§§ 16–24	..	Mahâ-vagga VI, 30.
"	"	§§ 27–35	..	Sa*m*yutta (Satippa*tth*âna-vagga).
Chap. III	(66 sections)	§§ 1–10	..	Sa*m*yutta (Iddhipâda-vagga). Aṅguttara (A*tth*a-nipâta).
"	"	§§ 11–20	..	Aṅguttara (A*tth*a-nipâta).
"	"	§§ 21–23*	..	? Eight Assemblies.
"	"	§§ 24–32 [1]	..	Aṅguttara (A*tth*a-nipâta).
"	"	§§ 33–42	..	Aṅguttara (A*tth*a-nipâta).
Chap. IV	(58 sections)	§§ 2, 3	..	Aṅguttara (*K*atuka-nipâta).
		§§ 7–11 *	..	" "

[1] Omitted in Po-fa-tsu. See below, p. xxxviii.

BOOK OF THE GREAT DECEASE.			OTHER BOOKS.
Chap. V (69 sections)	§ 10	..	Aṅguttara (Duka-nipâta).
" "	§§ 16–22 [1]	..	" (*K*atuka-nipâta).
" "	§§ 27–31* [1]	..	" "
" "	§ 36	..	Sa*m*yutta (Satippa*tth*âna-vagga).
" "	§§ 41–44	..	Dîgha (Mahâ-sudassana-Sutta).
" "	§ 60	..	*K*ulla-vagga V, 8, 1.
" "	§ 63	..	Mahâ-vagga I, 38, 1.
" "	§ 68	..	*K*ulla-vagga XI, 1, 15.
Chap. VI (62 sections)	§ 16	..	Dîgha (Mahâ-sudassana-Sutta).
" "	§§ 36–41	..	*K*ulla-vagga XI, 1, 1.

No Sanskrit work has yet been discovered giving an account of the last days of Gotama; but there are several Chinese works which seem to be related to ours. Of one especially, named the Fo Pan-ni-pan King (apparently Buddha-Parinibbâna-Sutta, but such an expression is unknown in Pâli), Mr. Beal says[2]:

'This appears to be the same as the Sûtra known in the South. . . . It was translated into Chinese by a Shaman called Fa-tsu, of the Western Tsin dynasty, circa 200 A.D.'

I do not understand this date. The Western Tsin dynasty is placed by Mr. Beal himself on the fly-leaf of the Catalogue at 265–313 A.D. And whether the book referred to is really the same work as the Book of the Great Decease seems to me to be very doubtful. At p. 160 of his 'Catena of Buddhist Scriptures from the Chinese' Mr. Beal says, that another Chinese work 'known as the Mahâ Parinirvâ*n*a Sûtra' 'is evidently the same as the Mahâ Parinibbâna Sutta of Ceylon,' but it is quite evident from the extracts which he gives that it is an entirely different and much later work.

On this book there would seem further to be a translated commentary, Ta Pan-ni-pan King Lo, mentioned

[1] Omitted by Po-fa-tsu. See below, p. xxxviii.

[2] Catalogue of Buddhist Chinese Books in the India Office Library, p. 95.

at p. 100 of the same Catalogue, and there assigned to Chang-an of the Tsin dynasty (589-619 A.D.).

At pp. 12-13 of the same Catalogue we find no less than seven other works, and an eighth on p. 77, not indeed identified with the Book of the Great Decease, but bearing titles which Mr. Beal represents in Sanskrit as Mahâparinirvâ*n*a Sûtra. They purport to be translated respectively—

	A. D.
1. By Dharmaraksha of the Northern Liang dynasty .	502-555
2. By Dharmaraksha " "	
3. By Fa Hian and Buddhabhadra of the Eastern Tsin dynasty	317-419
4. By *Gñ*ânabhadra and others of the Eastern Tang dynasty	620-904
5. By Dharmagupta and others of the Western Tsin dynasty	265-313
6. By Fa Hian of the Eastern Tsin dynasty . .	317-419
7. Unknown.	
8. By Dharmabodhi of the Former Wei dynasty . .	circa 200
Indian author, Vasubandhu.	

Whether Nos. 1 and 2, and again 3 and 6 are the same is not stated; and in the Indian Antiquary for 1875 Mr. Beal gives an account of another undated work, as existing in the India Office Collection, bearing a different title from any of the above, but which he also translates as Mahâparinibbâna Sutta. It purports to be the very oldest of the Vaipulya Sûtras, whereas the book quoted in the Catena is there said to be 'one of the latest of the expanded Sûtras.'

'The general outline,' says Mr. Beal[1], 'is this. Buddha, on a certain occasion, proceeded to Kinsinagara (sic), and entering a grove of Sâla trees, there reposed. He received a gift of food from Chanda, an artisan of the neighbouring town. After partaking of the food he was seized with illness. He discoursed through the night with his disciples, and disputed with certain heretical teachers. At early dawn he turned on his right side with his head to the north, and died. The Sâla trees bent down to form a canopy over his head. The account then proceeds to relate

[1] Indian Antiquary, vol. iv. p. 90.

the circumstances of his cremation, and the subsequent disputes, between the Mallas and others, for his ashes.'

There is a curious echo here of some of the sections translated below; though each particular item of the summary is really in contradiction with the corresponding part of the Pâli book. There is perhaps another Chinese work on the death of Buddha, of the existence of which I have been informed, through the kind intervention of Professor Max Müller, by Mr. Kasawara. It was translated by Po-fa-tsu between 290 and 306 A. D. It seems to be the same as the first mentioned above, but it contains a good deal of matter not found in the Mahâ-parinibbâna-Sutta (notably an account of the Râ*g*agaha Council, the mention of which is so conspicuously absent from the Pâli work); and it omits many of the sections found in the Pâli. Mr. Kasawara has been kind enough to send me the following details regarding those omissions, and they are of peculiar interest as compared with the table given above[1]:

Chapters in the Pâli.	Sections wanting in Chinese.
1st Chapter . .	15–18.
3rd Chapter . .	21–42.
4th Chapter . .	53–56.
5th Chapter . .	4–6; 16–23; 27–31; 48–51.
6th Chapter . .	27; 48–50.

There is no evidence to show that any of the above works are translations of our Sutta, or in any sense the same work. No reliance, in fact, can be placed upon the mere similarity of title in order to show that a Chinese work and an Indian one are really the same: and I regret that attempts should have been made to fix the date of Indian works by the fact that Chinese translations bearing similar titles are said to have been made in a certain period. But the above-mentioned works on the Great Decease will, when published, throw valuable light on the traditions of different, though no doubt later, schools of Buddhist thought; and a detailed comparison would probably throw a very interesting light on the way in which

[1] On p. xxxvi.

religious legends of this kind vary and grow; and the existence of these Chinese translations affords ground for the hope that we may some day discover an earlier Sanskrit work on the same subject[1].

The cremation ceremonies described in the sixth chapter are not without interest. It would be natural enough that Gotama should have been buried without any of those ritualistic forms the usefulness of which he denied, and without any appeal to gods whose power over men he ignored. But the tone of the narrative makes it at least possible that there was not really anything unusual in the method of his cremation; and that the elaborate rites prescribed in the Brâhmanical books for use at a funeral[2] were not, in practice, observed in the case of the death of any person other than a wealthy Brâhman, or some layman of rank who was a devoted adherent of the Brâhmans.

In the same way we find that in those countries where the more ancient form of Buddhism still prevails, there are a few simple forms to be used in the case of the cremation of a distinguished Bhikkhu or Upâsaka; but in ordinary cases bodies are buried without any ceremony.

So in Ceylon, Robert Knox—whose rare and curious work, one of the most trustworthy books of travels extant, deserves more notice than it has received, and who was a captive there for many years before the natives were influenced by any contact with Europeans—says[3],

'It may not be unacceptable to relate how they burn their dead. As for persons of inferior quality, they are interred in some convenient places in the woods (there being no set places for burial), carried thither by two or three of their friends, and buried without any more ado. They lay them on their backs, with their heads to the West, and their feet to the East, as we do. Then these people go and wash: for they are unclean by handling the dead.

---

[1] I have not been able to trace any reference to either of these Chinese works in Mr. Edkins's 'Chinese Buddhism.'

[2] See Max Müller in Z. D. M. G., vol. ix.

[3] Knox's 'Historical Relation of Ceylon,' Part III, Chap. xi.

'But persons of greater quality are burned, and that with ceremony. When they are dead they lay them out, and put a cloth over their privy parts; and then wash the body, by taking half a dozen pitchers of water and pouring upon it. Then they cover him with a linen cloth, and so carry him forth to burning. This is when they burn the body speedily. But otherwise they cut down a tree that may be proper for their purpose, and hollow it like a hog-trough, and put the body, being disembowelled and embalmed, into it, filling up all about with pepper, and so let it lie in the house until it be the king's command to carry it out to the burning. For that they dare not do without the king's order if the person deceased be a courtier. Sometimes the king gives no order in a great while; it may be not at all: therefore, in such cases, that the body may not take up house-room or annoy them, they dig a hole in the floor of their house, and put hollowed tree and all in, and cover it. If afterwards the king commands to burn the body, they take it up again, in obedience to the king—otherwise there it lies.

'Their order for burning is this: if the body be not thus put into a trough or hollow tree, it is laid upon one of his bedsteads, which is a great honour among them. This bedstead with the body on it, or hollowed tree with the body in it, is fastened with poles, and carried upon men's shoulders unto the place of burning, which is some eminent place in the fields, or highways, or where else they please. There they lay it upon a pile of wood some two or three feet high;—then they pile up more wood upon the corpse, lying thus on the bedstead or in the trough. Over all they have a kind of canopy built (if he be a person of very high quality), covered at top, hung about with painted cloth, and bunches of cocoa-nuts, and green boughs; and so fire is put to it. After all is burnt to ashes, they sweep together the ashes into the manner of a sugar-loaf, and hedge the place round from wild beasts breaking in, and they will sow herbs there. Thus I saw the king's uncle, the chief tirinanx[1] (who was, as it were, the chief primate of all the

[1] Knox's way of spelling Terunnânsê, that is, Thera.

nation), burned upon a high place, that the blaze might be seen a great way[1].'

I myself saw an Unnânsê burned very much in this way near the Weyangoda Court-house; and there is a long account in the native newspaper, the Lak-riwi-kirana (Ceylon Sunbeam), of the 12th March, 1870, of the cremation of a Weda-râla, or native doctor. Bishop Bigandet relates in a note in his 'Life or Legend of Gautama' the corresponding ceremonies still in use in Burma, of which he has been a witness[2]; but cremation is apparently as seldom resorted to in Burma as it is in Ceylon.

The unceremonious mode of burying the dead referred to by Knox is not adopted in the more settled districts on the sea coast. When at Galle I enquired into the funeral customs there prevalent, with the following result[3]:

A few hours after a man has died, the relations wash the corpse, shave it; and, having clothed it with a strip of clean white cloth, place it on a bedstead covered with white cloth, and under a canopy (wiyana) also of white cloth. They then place two lamps, one to burn at the head, and the other at the foot of the corpse, and use perfumes.

A coffin is then prepared, covered with black cloth; and the body is placed on the coffin, and is then sprinkled over with lavender or rose-water. The women meanwhile bow backwards and forwards with their hands behind their heads, uttering loud wailings over the deceased.

Then the male relatives carry the coffin to the grave, which is dug in one of their own cocoa-nut topes near by, and over which is raised a more or less elaborate canopy or arch of cloths and evergreens (ge*d*i-ge), adorned with the tender leaves and flowers of the cocoa-nut. Along the path also from the house to the grave young cocoa-nut leaves and flowers are sometimes hung, and the pathway itself is often spread with clean white cloths.

The tom-tom beaters go first; and the dull monotonous

---

1 In the older editions of Knox there is a curious engraving of a body being thus burnt.

2 Third edition, vol. ii. pp. 78, 79.

3 See the Ceylon Friend for 1870, pp. 109 and following.

sound of their instruments of music is appropriate enough. Then follow some Buddhist mendicants, in number according to the wealth or influence of the deceased, and walking under a portable canopy of white cloth. Then the coffin is carried by the nearest male relatives, and followed by other male relatives and relations—no females, even the widowed mother of an only son, taking part in this last sad procession.

Three times the coffin is carried round the grave: then it is placed on two sticks placed across the mouth of the pit; and one end of a roll of white cloth is placed on the coffin, the other end being held by all the Unnânsês (Bhikkhus) whilst the people repeat three times in Pâli the well-known formula of the Refuges (the simple Nicene Creed of the Buddhists):

'I take my refuge in the Buddha,
I take my refuge in the Dhamma,
I take my refuge in the Order[1].'

Then the priests respond, thrice repeating in Pâli the well-known verse discussed below[2]:

'How transient are all component things!
Their nature's to be born and die;
Coming, they go; and then is best,
When each has ceased, and all is rest!'

Then the Unnânsês let go the roll of white cloth, and whilst water is poured from a goblet into a cup placed on a plate until the cup is full to the brim[3], they again chaunt three times in Pâli the following verses:—

'As rivers, when they fill, must flow,
And reach, and fill the distant main;

---

[1] Buddha*m* sara*n*a*m* ga*kkh*âmi
Dhamma*m* sara*n*a*m* ga*kkh*âmi
Sa*m*gha*m* sara*n*a*m* ga*kkh*âmi.

[2] Ani*kk*â vata sa*m*khârâ uppâdavaya-dhammino
Uppa*gg*itvâ niru*ggh*anti tesa*m* vûpasamo sukho.

See 'Book of the Great Decease,' VI, 16, and the 'Legend of the Great King of Glory,' II, 42.

[3] This ceremony is called Pæ*m* wadanawâ.

So surely what is given here
Will reach and bless the spirits there!

If you on earth will gladly give
Departed ghosts will gladly live!

As water poured on mountain tops
Must soon descend, and reach the plain;
So surely what is given here
Will reach and bless the spirits there[1]!'

The relations then place the coffin in the grave, and each throws in a handful of earth. The Unnânsês then go away, taking the roll or rolls of cloth, one end of which was placed upon the coffin. The grave is filled in. Two lights, one at the head of it, and one at the foot, are left burning. And then the friends and relations return to the house.

The funeral now being over, is followed by a feast; for though nothing may be cooked in a house or hut in which there is a corpse, yet plenty of food has been brought in from neighbouring tenements by the relations of the deceased.

There is, however, yet another very curious ceremony to be gone through. Three or seven days—whichever, according to the rules of astrology, is a lucky day—after the deceased person died, an Unnânsê is duly invited to the house in which the deceased died. He arrives in the evening; reads bana (that is, the Word, passages from the sacred books) throughout the night; and in the morning is presented with a roll of white cloth, and is asked to partake of food, chiefly of course curries, of those different kinds of which the deceased had been most particularly fond.

---

1 Yathâ vârivahâ pûrâ paripûrenti sâgara*m*
Evam eva ito dinna*m* petânam upakappati.

Ito dinnena yâpenti petâ kâlakatâ tahi*m*.

Unname udaka*m* va*tt*am yathâ ninna*m* pavattati
Evam eva ito dinna*m* petâna*m* upakappati.

These verses occur in the Tiroku*dd*a-Sutta of the Khuddaka-Pâ*th*a, but in a different order.

This ceremony is called Mataka Dânaya (Gift for the Dead), and the previous feast is called Mataka Bhatta (Feast in honour of the Dead): the two combined taking the place of an ancient rite observed in pagan, pre-Buddhistic, times, and then also called Mataka Bhatta, in which offerings were made to the Petas; that is, to the manes, or departed ghosts, of ancestors and near relations. Such offerings are of course forbidden to Buddhists[1], and it is a very instructive instance of a survival in belief, of the effect of the natural reluctance to make much change in the mode of paying the customary funeral respect to deceased friends, that the kind of food supposed to be most appreciated by the dead should still be used in the Buddhist funeral rites.

Another part of the ceremony, that part where one end of a roll of cloth is placed on the coffin while the other end is held by all the assembled Unnânsês[2], is a fragment of ritualistic symbolism which deserves attention. The members of the Buddhist Order of Mendicants were enjoined to avoid all personal decoration of any kind; and to attire themselves in cloths of no value, such as might be gathered from a dust heap (Pa*m*su-kûla), or even from a cemetery. This was a principle to be followed, not a literal rule to be observed; and therefore from the first presents of strips of plain white cotton cloth, first torn in pieces to deprive them of any commercial value, then pieced together again and dyed a dull orange colour to call to mind the colour of old worn out linen, were the material from which the mendicants' clothing was actually made. But the duty of contempt for dress (called Pa*m*su-kûlikaṅga, from the dust heap) was never lost sight of, and advantage was taken of the gifts given by the faithful at funerals to impress this duty upon the minds of the assembled Bhikkhus.

Nothing is known of any religious ceremony having been performed by the early Buddhists in India, whether the person deceased was a layman, or even a member of the

[1] Compare the Mataka-Bhatta-*G*âtaka (No. 18), translated in 'Buddhist Birth Stories,' vol. i. pp. 226 and following.

[2] See p. xlii.

Order. The Vinaya Piṭaka, which enters at so great length into all the details of the daily life of the recluses, has no rules regarding the mode of treating the body of a deceased Bhikkhu. It was probably burnt, and very much in the manner described in the last chapter of our Sutta —that is to say, it was reverently carried out to some convenient spot, and there simply cremated on a funeral pyre without any religious ritual, a small tope being more often than not erected over the ashes. Though funerals are, naturally, not unfrequently mentioned in the historical books, and in the Birth Stories, there is nowhere any reference to a recognised mode of performing any religious ceremony[1].

The date of the Great Decease is not quite certain. The dwellers in the valley of the Ganges, for many generations after Gotama's death, were a happy people, who had no need of dates; and it was only long afterwards, and in Ceylon, that the great event became used as the starting-point for chronological calculations, as the Buddhist era.

The earliest use of the Buddha's Parinibbâna as such an era is in an Inscription of King Nissaṅka Malla's, of the twelfth century A.D., published by me in the Journal of the Royal Asiatic Society for 1875. Both in the historical records of Ceylon, and in those passages of the Purâṇas which are the nearest approach to historical records in India, the chronology is usually based on the lists of kings, just as it is in the Old Testament. Only by adding together the lengths of the reigns of the intermediate kings is it possible to calculate the length of the time that is said to have elapsed between any two given events.

If these lists of kings had been accurately kept from

---

[1] Compare Mahâvaṃsa, pp. 4, 125, 129, 199, 223–225, and Chap. 39, verse 28; Gâtaka I, 166, 181, 402; II, 6; Dasaratha Gâtaka, pp. 1, 21, 22, 26, &c.; Dhammapada Commentary, pp. 94, 205, 206, 222, 359; Hatthavana-galla-vihâra-vaṃsa, Chap. IX; Hardy, 'Eastern Monachism,' pp. 322–324.

The words Saddhaṃ, Uddhadehikaṃ, and Nivâpo, given in Childers, refer to pagan rites.

On funerals among Buddhists in Japan, see Miss Bird's 'Unbeaten Tracks,' vol. i.

Gotama's time to the time when the existing chronicles were compiled, we should be able, if we could fix the date of any one of the kings, to calculate the date of the Buddha's death. This last we can do; for the date of *K*andragupta, and the date of his grandson Asoka, can be independently fixed within a few years by the aid of the Greek historians. But unfortunately the earlier parts of the otherwise reliable Ceylon chronicles are, like the earlier parts of Livy's otherwise reliable history of Rome, full of inconsistencies and impossibilities.

According to the Râ*g*a-paramparâ, or line of kings, in the Ceylon chronicles, the date of the Great Decease would be 543 B.C., which is arrived at by adding to the date 161 B.C. (from which the reliable portion of the history begins) two periods of 146 and 236 years. The first purports to give the time which elapsed between 161 B.C. and the great Buddhist church Council held under Asoka, and in the eighteenth year of his reign, at Patna; and the second to give the interval between that Council and the Buddha's death.

It would result from the first calculation that the date of Asoka's coronation would be 325 B.C. (146 + 161 + 18). But we know that this must contain a blunder or blunders, as the date of Asoka's coronation can be fixed, as above stated, with absolute certainty within a year or two either way of 267 B.C.

Would it then be sound criticism to accept the other, earlier, period of 236 years found in those chronicles—a period which we cannot test by Greek chronology—and by simply adding the Ceylon calculation of 236 years to the European date for the eighteenth year of Asoka (that is circa 249 B.C.) to conclude that the Buddha died in or about 485 B.C.?

I cannot think so. The further we go back the greater does the probability of error become, not less. The most superficial examination of the details of this earlier period shows too, that they are unreliable; and what reliance would it be wise to place upon the total, apart from the details, when we find it mentioned for the first time in a work, the Dîpava*m*sa, written eight centuries after the date it is proposed to fix?

If further proof were needed, we have it in the fact that the Dîpava*m*sa actually contains the details of another calculation—based not on the lists of kings (Râ*g*a-parampar*â*), but on a list of Theras (Thera-paramparâ) stretching back from Asoka's time to the time of the great Teacher—which contradicts this calculation of 236 years.

The Thera-paramparâ gives the name of the member of the Buddhist Order of Mendicants, that is, the Thera, who ordained Mahinda (the son of Asoka), then the name of the Thera who ordained that Thera, and so on. There are only five of them from Upâli, who was ordained sixteen years after Buddha's death, down to Mahinda inclusive. This would account not for 236, but only for about 150 years.

For let the reader take the case of any clergyman in the present day. The Bishop who ordains him would have been ordained thirty or forty years before; and four such intervals would fill out, not 236 years, but about a century and a half; and a similar argument applies with reasonable certainty to the case in point.

An examination of the details of the List of Theras confirms this conclusion strongly on every essential point. An examination also of the List of Kings shows that the period of 236 years is wrong by being too long. The shorter period of 150 years between Asoka and the Great Decease agrees much better with what we know of the literary history of Buddhism during that interval. And it also agrees with the tradition of the northern Buddhists as preserved by Hiouen Thsang, and in Kashmîr and Tibet[1]. In the 'Questions of Milinda' also—a work of unknown date, preserved only in its Pâli form, but

[1] Julien's translation of Hiouen Thsang, 'Mémoires sur les contrées occidentales,' vol. i. p. 172; Kahla*n*a's Râ*g*a-tara*n*gin*î*, Book I; and Csoma Körösi in 'Asiatic Researches,' vol. xx. pp. 92, 297. They place the Great Decease 400 years before Kanishka, whose Council was held shortly after the commencement of our era.

possibly derived from a northern Buddhist Sanskrit work—the date of the Buddha's death is fixed at five hundred years before the time of Milinda[1], who certainly reigned about a century after Christ. I am, therefore, of opinion that the hitherto accepted date of the Buddha's death should be modified accordingly.

This would make the date of the Great Decease about 420–400 B.C. (very possibly a year or two later), and the date of Gotama's birth therefore eighty years earlier, or in round numbers about 500 B.C.

I have discussed the whole question at full length in my 'Ancient Coins and Measures of Ceylon,' written in amplification of a paper read in 1874 before the Royal Asiatic Society; and to that work I must refer any reader, who may take interest in these chronological discussions, for ampler details. I have been able here to present only a summary of an argument which is in so far of little importance, inasmuch as the rectification which I have ventured to propose only differs by a little more than half a century from the earliest date which can in any case be suggested as approximately correct (that is about 485 B.C.). The date 543 B.C., still unfortunately accepted outside the circle of students of Buddhism[2], is now acknowledged to be too early by all scholars who have seriously considered the subject.

---

[1] Trenckner, p. 3. Mr. Trenckner says in his preface that Buddhaghosa quotes this work, but unfortunately he does not give any reference. See the note below on our Sutta, Chap. VI, § 3.

[2] See, for instance, Max Duncker, 'History of Antiquity,' vol. iv. p. 364. On the dated Edict, ascribed by some to Asoka, see my note loc. cit., and Oldenberg, 'Introd. to the Mahâ-vagga,' p. xxxviii.

THE BOOK

OF THE

GREAT DECEASE.

MAHÂ-PARINIBBÂNA-SUTTA.

CHAPTER I.

1[1]. Thus have I heard. The Blessed One was once dwelling in Râ*g*agaha, on the hill called the Vulture's Peak. Now at that time A*g*âtasattu, the son of the queen-consort of Videha origin[2], the king of Magadha, was desirous of attacking the Va*gg*ians; and he said to himself, 'I will root out these Va*g*-

---

[1] Sections 1–10, inclusive, recur in the Va*gg*i Vagga of the Sutta Nipâta in the Aṅguttara Nikâya; and there is a curiously incorrect version of § 3 in the Fa Kheu Pi Hu, translated from the Chinese by Mr. Beal, under the title of 'The Dhammapada from the Buddhist Canon,' pp. 165, 166.

[2] A*g*âtasattu Vedehiputto. The first word is not a personal name, but an official epithet, 'he against whom there has arisen no (worthy or equal) foe;' the second gives us the maiden family, or tribal (not personal) name of his mother. Persons of distinction are scarcely ever mentioned by name in Indian Buddhist books, a rule applying more especially to kings, but extended not unfrequently to private persons. Thus Upatissa, the earnest and thoughtful disciple whom the Buddha himself declared to be 'the second founder of the kingdom of righteousness,' is referred to either as Dhamma-senâpati or as Sâriputta; epithets of corresponding origin to those in the text. By the *G*ains A*g*âtasattu is called Kû*n*ika or Ko*n*ika, which again is probably not the name given to him at the rice-eating (the ceremony corresponding to infant baptism), but a nickname acquired in after life.

*g*ians, mighty and powerful[1] though they be, I will destroy these Va*gg*ians, I will bring these Va*gg*ians to utter ruin!'

2. So he spake to the Brâhman Vassakâra, the prime-minister of Magadha, and said:

'Come now, O Brâhman, do you go to the Blessed One, and bow down in adoration at his feet on my behalf, and enquire in my name whether he is free from illness and suffering, and in the enjoyment of ease and comfort, and vigorous health. Then tell him that A*g*âtasattu, son of the Vedehi, the king of Magadha, in his eagerness to attack the Va*gg*ians, has resolved, "I will root out these Va*gg*ians, mighty and powerful though they be, I will destroy these Va*gg*ians, I will bring these Va*gg*ians to utter ruin!" And bear carefully in mind whatever the Blessed One may predict, and repeat it to me. For the Buddhas speak nothing untrue!'

3. Then the Brâhman Vassakâra hearkened to the words of the king, saying, 'Be it as you say.' And ordering a number of magnificent carriages to be made ready, he mounted one of them, left Râ*g*agaha with his train, and went to the Vulture's Peak, riding as far as the ground was passable for car-

[1] Evammahiddhike evammahânubhâve. There is nothing supernatural about the iddhi here referred to. Etena tesaṅ samagga-bhâvan kathesi says the commentator simply: thus referring the former adjective to the power of union, as he does the second to the power derived from practice in military tactics (hatthisippâdîhi). The epithets are, indeed, most commonly applied to the supernatural powers of Devatâs, Nâgas, and other fairy-like beings; but they are also used, sometimes in the simple sense of this passage, and sometimes in the other sense, of Buddhas and of other Arahats. See M. P. S. 12, 43; M. Sud. S. 49–53; *G*ât. I, 34, 35, 39, 41.

riages, and then alighting and proceeding on foot to the place where the Blessed One was. On arriving there he exchanged with the Blessed One the greetings and compliments of friendship and civility, sat down respectfully by his side [and then delivered to him the message even as the king had commanded [1]].

4. Now at that time the venerable Ânanda was standing behind the Blessed One, and fanning him. And the Blessed One said to him: 'Have you heard, Ânanda, that the Va*gg*ians hold full and frequent public assemblies?'

'Lord, so I have heard,' replied he.

'So long, Ânanda,' rejoined the Blessed One, 'as the Va*gg*ians hold these full and frequent public assemblies; so long may they be expected not to decline, but to prosper.'

[And in like manner questioning Ânanda, and receiving a similar reply, the Blessed One declared as follows the other conditions which would ensure the welfare of the Va*gg*ian confederacy [2].]

'So long, Ânanda, as the Va*gg*ians meet together in concord, and rise in concord, and carry out their undertakings in concord—so long as they enact nothing not already established, abrogate nothing that has been already enacted, and act in accordance with the ancient institutions of the Va*gg*ians as established in former days—so long as they honour and esteem and revere and support the Va*gg*ian elders, and hold it a point of duty to hearken to their words—so long as no women or girls

---

[1] § 2 repeated.

[2] In the text there is a question, answer, and reply with each clause.

belonging to their clans are detained among them by force or abduction—so long as they honour and esteem and revere and support the Vaggian shrines[1] in town or country, and allow not the proper offerings and rites, as formerly given and performed, to fall into desuetude—so long as the rightful protection, defence, and support shall be fully provided for the Arahats among them, so that Arahats from a distance may enter the realm, and the Arahats therein may live at ease—so long may the Vaggians be expected not to decline, but to prosper.'

5. Then the Blessed One addressed Vassakâra the Brâhman, and said:

'When I was once staying, O Brâhman, at Vesâli at the Sârandada Temple[2], I taught the Vaggians these conditions of welfare; and so long as those conditions shall continue to exist among the Vaggians, so long as the Vaggians shall be well instructed in those conditions, so long may we expect them not to decline, but to prosper.'

'We may expect then,' answered the Brâhman, 'the welfare and not the decline of the Vaggians when they are possessed of any one of these conditions of welfare, how much more so when they are possessed of all the seven. So, Gotama, the Vaggians cannot be overcome by the king of Magadha; that is, not in battle, without diplomacy or breaking up their alliance[3]. And now, Gotama, we must go; we are busy, and have much to do.'

---

[1] *K*etiyâni, which Sum. Vil. explains as Yakkha-*k*etiyâni.

[2] The commentator adds that this was a vihâra erected on the site of a former temple of the Yakkha Sârandada.

[3] 'Overcome' is literally 'done' (akara*n*îyâ), but the word evidently has a similar sense to that which 'done' occasionally has

'Whatever you think most fitting, O Brâhman,' was the reply. And the Brâhman Vassakâra, delighted and pleased with the words of the Blessed One, rose from his seat, and went his way.

---

6. Now soon after he had gone the Blessed One addressed the venerable Ânanda, and said: 'Go now, Ânanda, and assemble in the Service Hall such of the Brethren[1] as live in the neighbourhood of Râgagaha.'

---

in colloquial English. The Sum. Vil. (fol. *ñ*) says akara*n*îyâ, akatabbâ agahetabbâ: yadidaṁ, nipâta-mattaṁ: yuddhassâti, kara*n*atthe sâmi-va*k*anaṁ, abhimukhena yuddhena gahetuṁ na sakkâ ti attho. Upalâpanâ, which I have only met with here, must mean 'humbug, cajolery, diplomacy;' see the use of the verb upa-lâpeti, at Mahâ Vagga V, 2, 21; *G*ât. II, 266, 267; Pât. in the 70th Pâ*k*. Sum. Vil. explains it, at some length, as making an alliance, by gifts, with hostile intent, which comes to much the same thing. The root I think is lî.

[1] The word translated 'brethren' throughout is in the original bhikkhû, a word most difficult to render adequately by any word which would not, to Christians and in Europe, connote something different from the Buddhist idea. A bhikkhu, literally 'beggar,' was a disciple who had joined Gotama's order; but the word refers to their renunciation of worldly things, rather than to their consequent mendicancy; and they did not really beg in our modern sense of the word. Hardy has 'priests;' I have elsewhere used 'monks' and sometimes 'beggars' and 'members of the order.' This last is, I think, the best rendering; but it is too long for constant repetition, as in this passage, and too complex to be a really good version of bhikkhu. The members of the order were not priests, for they had no priestly powers. They were not monks, for they took no vow of obedience, and could leave the order (and constantly did so and do so still) whenever they chose. They were not beggars, for they had none of the mental and moral qualities associated with that word. 'Brethren' connotes very much the position in which they stood to one another; but I wish there were a better word to use in rendering bhikkhu.

And he did so; and returned to the Blessed One, and informed him, saying:

'The company of the Brethren, Lord, is assembled, let the Blessed One do as seemeth to him fit.'

And the Blessed One arose, and went to the Service Hall; and when he was seated, he addressed the Brethren, and said:

'I will teach you, O mendicants, seven conditions of the welfare of a community. Listen well and attend, and I will speak.'

'Even so, Lord,' said the Brethren, in assent, to the Blessed One; and he spake as follows:

'So long, O mendicants, as the brethren meet together in full and frequent assemblies—so long as they meet together in concord, and rise in concord, and carry out in concord the duties of the order — so long as the brethren shall establish nothing that has not been already prescribed, and abrogate nothing that has been already established, and act in accordance with the rules of the order as now laid down—so long as the brethren honour and esteem and revere and support the elders of experience and long standing, the fathers and leaders of the order, and hold it a point of duty to hearken to their words—so long as the brethren fall not under the influence of that craving which, springing up within them, would give rise to renewed existence[1]—so long as the brethren delight in a life of solitude—so long as the brethren so train their minds[2] that good and holy men shall come to them, and those who have come shall dwell at ease

[1] 'Ponobhavikâ' punabbhava-dâyikâ. (S. V. fol. *t*û.)

[2] 'Pa*kk*atta*m* yeva sati*m* upa*tth*âpessantî' ti attano abbhantarc sati*m* upa*tth*âpessanti. (S. V. fol. *t*û.)

—so long may the brethren be expected, not to decline, but to prosper. So long as these seven conditions shall continue to exist among the brethren, so long as they are well-instructed in these conditions, so long may the brethren be expected not to decline, but to prosper.'

7. 'Other seven conditions of welfare will I teach you, O brethren. Listen well, and attend, and I will speak.'

And on their expressing their assent, he spake as follows:

'So long as the brethren shall not engage in, or be fond of, or be connected with business—so long as the brethren shall not be in the habit of, or be fond of, or be partakers in idle talk—so long as the brethren shall not be addicted to, or be fond of, or indulge in slothfulness—so long as the brethren shall not frequent, or be fond of, or indulge in society—so long as the brethren shall neither have, nor fall under the influence of, sinful desires—so long as the brethren shall not become the friends, companions, or intimates of sinners—so long as the brethren shall not come to a stop on their way [to Nirvâ*n*a [1]] because they

[1] 'Oramattakenâ' ti avaramattakena appamattakena. 'Antarâ' ti arahatta*m* appatvâ 'va etth' antare. 'Vosânan' ti.... osakkanam ida*m* vutta*m* hoti. Yâva sîla-pârisuddhi-mattena vâ vipassanâ-mattena vâ sotâpanna-bhâva-mattena vâ sakadâgâmi-bhâva-mattena vâ anâgâmi-bhâva-mattena vâ 'vosâna*m*' na 'âpa*gg*issanti' nâma 'vuddhi yeva bhikkhûna*m* pâ*t*ika*m*khâ no parihâni.' S. V. (fol. *tri*). This is an interesting analogue to Philippians iii. 13: 'I count not myself to have apprehended: but this one thing I do, forgetting those things which are behind, and reaching forth unto those things which are before, I press toward the mark,' &c. See also below, Chap. V, § 68.

have attained to any lesser thing—so long may the brethren be expected not to decline, but to prosper.

'So long as these conditions shall continue to exist among the brethren, so long as they are instructed in these conditions, so long may the brethren be expected not to decline, but to prosper.'

8. 'Other seven conditions of welfare will I teach you, O brethren. Listen well, and attend, and I will speak.'

And on their expressing their assent, he spake as follows:

'So long as the brethren shall be full of faith, modest in heart, afraid of sin[1], full of learning, strong in energy, active in mind, and full of wisdom, so long may the brethren be expected not to decline, but to prosper.

'So long as these conditions shall continue to exist among the brethren, so long as they are instructed in these conditions, so long may the brethren be expected not to decline, but to prosper.'

9. 'Other seven conditions of welfare will I teach you, O brethren. Listen well, and attend, and I will speak.'

And on their expressing their assent, he spake as follows:

---

[1] The exact distinction between hiri and ottappa is here explained by Buddhaghosa as follows:

'Hirimanâ' ti pâpa-*g*igu*kkh*ana-lakkha*n*âya hiriyâ yutta*k*ittâ. 'Ottâpî' ti pâpato bhaya-lakkha*n*ena ottappena samannâgatâ: that is, loathing sin as contrasted with fear of sin. But this is rather a gloss than an exact and exclusive definition. Ahirikâ is shamelessness, anotappa*m* frowardness. At *G*ât. I, 207 we find hiri described as subjective, and ottappa as objective, modesty of heart as contrasted with decency in outward behaviour.

'So long as the brethren shall exercise themselves in the sevenfold higher wisdom, that is to say, in mental activity, search after truth, energy, joy, peace, earnest contemplation, and equanimity of mind, so long may the brethren be expected not to decline, but to prosper.

'So long as these conditions shall continue to exist among the brethren, so long as they are instructed in these conditions, so long may the brethren be expected not to decline, but to prosper.'

10. 'Other seven conditions of welfare will I teach you, O brethren. Listen well, and attend, and I will speak.'

And on their expressing their assent, he spake as follows:

'So long as the brethren shall exercise themselves in the sevenfold perception due to earnest thought, that is to say, the perception of impermanency, of non-individuality[1], of corruption, of the danger of sin, of sanctification, of purity of heart, of Nirvâ*n*a, so long may the brethren be expected not to decline, but to prosper.

'So long as these conditions shall continue to exist among the brethren, so long as they are instructed in these conditions, so long may the brethren be expected not to decline, but to prosper.'

11. 'Six conditions of welfare will I teach you, O brethren. Listen well, and attend, and I will speak.'

And on their expressing their assent, he spake as follows:

---

[1] For a further explanation of the meaning of anatta*m* see Gotama's second discourse in the Mahâ Vagga I, 6: 38–47. Buddhaghosa makes no special comment here on either of the seven perceptions.

'So long as the brethren shall persevere in kindness of action, speech, and thought amongst the saints, both in public and in private—so long as they shall divide without partiality, and share in common with the upright and the holy, all such things as they receive in accordance with the just provisions of the order, down even to the mere contents of a begging bowl—so long as the brethren shall live among the saints in the practice, both in public and in private, of those virtues which (unbroken, intact, unspotted, unblemished) are productive of freedom [1], and praised by the wise; which are untarnished by the desire of future life, or by the belief in the efficacy of outward acts [2]; and which are conducive to high and holy thoughts—so long as the brethren shall live among the saints, cherishing, both in public and in private, that noble and saving faith which leads to the complete destruction of the sorrow of him who acts according to it—so long may the brethren be expected not to decline, but to prosper.

'So long as these six conditions shall continue to

---

[1] Buddhaghosa takes this in a spiritual sense, 'tâni pan' etâni (sîlâni) ta*n*hâ-dâsavyato mo*k*etvâ bhu*g*issa-bhâva-kara*n*ato bhu*g*issâni:' that is, 'These virtues are bhu*g*issâni because they bring one to the state of a free man by delivering him from the slavery of craving.'

[2] Ta*n*hâ-di*tth*îhi aparâma*tth*attâ, ida*m* nâma tva*m* âpannapubbo ti kena*k*i parama*tth*u*m* asakku*n*eyyattâ *k*a, 'aparâma*tth*âni' (S.V. fol. *t*û), that is, 'These virtues are called aparâma*tth*âni because they are untarnished by craving or delusion, and because no one can say of him who practices them, "you have been already guilty of such and such a sin."' Craving is here the hope of a future life in heaven, and delusion the belief in the efficacy of rites and ceremonies (the two nissayas) which are condemned as unworthy inducements to virtue.

exist among the brethren, so long as they are instructed in these six conditions, so long may the brethren be expected not to decline, but to prosper.'

---

12. And whilst the Blessed One stayed there at Râ*g*agaha on the Vulture's Peak he held that comprehensive religious talk with the brethren on the nature of upright conduct, and of earnest contemplation, and of intelligence. 'Great is the fruit, great the advantage of earnest contemplation when set round with upright conduct. Great is the fruit, great the advantage of intellect when set round with earnest contemplation. The mind set round with intelligence is freed from the great evils, that is to say, from sensuality, from individuality, from delusion, and from ignorance[1].'

---

[1] This paragraph is spoken of as if it were a well-known summary, and it is constantly repeated below. The word I have rendered 'earnest contemplation' is samâdhi, which occupies in the Pâli Pi*t*akas very much the same position as faith does in the New Testament; and this section shows that the relative importance of samâdhi, paññâ, and sîla played a part in early Buddhism just as the distinction between faith, reason, and works did afterwards in Western theology. It would be difficult to find a passage in which the Buddhist view of the relation of these conflicting ideas is stated with greater beauty of thought, or equal succintness of form.

The expression 'set round with' is in Pâli paribhâvita, which Dr. Morris holds to be etymologically exactly parallel to our phrase 'perfected by,' on the ground that facio is a causal of the Latin representative of the Sanskrit root bhû. In the *K*etokhila Sutta of the Ma*gg*h*ima Nikâya eggs are said to be paribhâvitâni by a brooding hen. Buddhaghosa says simply sîla-paribhâvito ti âdesu yamhi sîle *th*atvâ magga-samâdhi*m* nibbattenti so tena sîlena paribhâvito. 'The samâdhi belonging to the (Noble Eightfold) Path is said to be paribhâvito by that virtue, in which they (that is, the converted) are steadfast whilst they practice the samâdhi.'

13. Now when the Blessed One had sojourned at Râ*g*agaha as long as he pleased, he addressed the venerable Ânanda, and said: 'Come, Ânanda, let us go to Ambala*tth*ikâ.'

'So be it, Lord!' said Ânanda in assent, and the Blessed One, with a large company of the brethren, proceeded to Ambala*tth*ikâ.

14. There the Blessed One stayed in the king's house and held that comprehensive religious talk with the brethren on the nature of upright conduct, and of earnest contemplation, and of intelligence. 'Great is the fruit, great the advantage of earnest contemplation when set round with upright conduct. Great is the fruit, great the advantage of intellect when set round with earnest contemplation. The mind set round with intelligence is freed from the great evils, that is to say, from sensuality, from individuality, from delusion, and from ignorance.'

---

15. Now when the Blessed One had stayed as long as was convenient at Ambala*tth*ikâ, he addressed the venerable Ânanda, and said: 'Come, Ânanda, let us go on to Nâlandâ.'

'So be it, Lord!' said Ânanda, in assent, to the Blessed One.

Then the Blessed One proceeded, with a great company of the brethren, to Nâlandâ; and there, at Nâlandâ, the Blessed One stayed in the Pâvârika mango grove.

16. [1] Now the venerable Sâriputta came to the

[1] This conversation is given at length in the Sampasâdaniya Sutta of the Dîgha Nikâya, and also in the Satipa*tth*âna Vagga of the Sa*m*yutta Nikâya. I have compressed mere repetitions at the places marked with [ ] where the preceding clauses are, in the text, repeated in full.

place where the Blessed One was, and having saluted him, took his seat respectfully at his side, and said: 'Lord! such faith have I in the Blessed One, that methinks there never has been, nor will there be, nor is there now any other, whether Sama*n*a or Brâhman, who is greater and wiser than the Blessed One, that is to say, as regards the higher wisdom.'

'Grand and bold are the words of thy mouth, Sâriputta: verily, thou hast burst forth into a song of ecstasy! of course then thou hast known all the Blessed Ones who in the long ages of the past have been Arahat Buddhas, comprehending their minds with yours, and aware what their conduct was, what their doctrine, what their wisdom, what their mode of life, and what salvation they attained to?'

'Not so, O Lord!'

'Of course then thou hast perceived all the Blessed Ones who in the long ages of the future shall be Arahat Buddhas comprehending [in the same manner their whole minds with yours]?'

'Not so, O Lord!'

'But at least then, O Sâriputta, thou knowest me as the Arahat Buddha now alive, and hast penetrated my mind [in the manner I have mentioned]!'

'Not even that, O Lord!'

'You see then, Sâriputta, that you know not the hearts of the Arahat Buddhas of the past and of the future. Why therefore are your words so grand and bold? Why do you burst forth into such a song of ecstasy?'

17. 'O Lord! I have not the knowledge of the hearts of the Arahat Buddhas that have been, and are to come, and now are. I only know the lineage

of the faith. Just, Lord, as a king might have a border city, strong in its foundations, strong in its ramparts and tora*n*as, and with one gate alone; and the king might have a watchman there, clever, expert, and wise, to stop all strangers and admit only friends. And he, on going over the approaches all round the city, might not so observe all the joints and crevices in the ramparts of that city as to know where even a cat could get out. That might well be. Yet all living things of larger size that entered or left the city, would have to do so by that gate. Thus only is it, Lord, that I know the lineage of the faith. I know that the Arahat Buddhas of the past, putting away all lust, ill-will, sloth, pride, and doubt; knowing all those mental faults which make men weak; training their minds in the four kinds of mental activity; thoroughly exercising themselves in the sevenfold higher wisdom, received the full fruition of Enlightenment. And I know that the Arahat Buddhas of the times to come will [do the same]. And I know that the Blessed One, the Arahat Buddha of to-day, has [done so] now[1].'

---

18. There in the Pavârika mango grove the Blessed One held that comprehensive religious talk

---

[1] The tertium quid of the comparison is the completeness of the knowledge. Sâriputta acknowledges that he was wrong in jumping to the wide conclusion that his own lord and master was the wisest of all the teachers of the different religious systems that were known to him. So far—after the cross-examination by the Buddha—he admits that his knowledge does not reach. But he maintains that he does know that which is, to him, after all the main thing, namely, that all the Buddhas must have passed through the process here laid down as leading up to Buddhahood. The Pâli of 'the full fruition of Enlightenment' is anuttara*m* sammâ-sambodhi*m*, which might be rendered 'Supreme Buddhahood.'

with the brethren on the nature of upright conduct, and of earnest contemplation, and of intelligence. 'Great is the fruit, great the advantage of earnest contemplation when set round with upright conduct. Great is the fruit, great the advantage of intellect when set round with earnest contemplation. The mind set round with intelligence is freed from the great evils, that is to say, from sensuality, from individuality, from delusion, and from ignorance.'

---

19. Now when the Blessed One had stayed as long as was convenient at Nâlandâ, he addressed the venerable Ânanda, and said: 'Come, Ânanda, let us go on to Pâ*t*aligâma.'

'So be it, Lord!' said Ânanda, in assent, to the Blessed One.

Then the Blessed One proceeded, with a great company of the brethren, to Pâ*t*aligâma.

20. [1]Now the disciples at Pâ*t*aligâma heard of his arrival there, and they went to the place where he was, took their seats respectfully beside him, and invited him to their village rest house. And the Blessed One signified, by silence, his consent.

21. Then the Pâ*t*aligâma disciples seeing that he had accepted the invitation, rose from their seats, and went away to the rest house, bowing to the Blessed One and keeping him on their right as they past him[2]. On arriving there they made the rest

---

[1] From this sentence down to the end of the verses at Chap. II, § 3, is, with a few unimportant variations, word for word the same as Mahâ Vagga VI, 28, 1, to VI, 29, 2.

[2] It would be very rude to have left him otherwise. So in Europe a similar custom is carried still further, persons leaving the royal presence being expected to go out backwards.

house fit in every way for occupation[1], placed seats in it, set up a water-pot, and fixed an oil lamp. Then they returned to the Blessed One, and bowing, stood beside him, and said: 'All things are ready, Lord! It is time for you to do what you deem most fit.'

22. And the Blessed One robed himself, took his bowl and other things, went with the brethren to the rest house, washed his feet, entered the hall, and took his seat against the centre pillar, with his face towards the east. And the brethren also, after washing their feet, entered the hall, and took their seats round the Blessed One, against the western wall, and facing the east. And the Pâ*t*aligâma disciples too, after washing their feet, entered the hall, and took their seats opposite the Blessed One, against the eastern wall, and facing towards the west.

23. [2]Then the Blessed One addressed the Pâ*t*aligâma disciples, and said: 'Fivefold, O householders, is the loss of the wrong-doer through his want of rectitude. In the first place the wrong-doer, devoid of rectitude, falls into great poverty through sloth; in the next place his evil repute gets noised abroad; thirdly, whatever society he enters—whether of Brâhmans, nobles, heads of houses, or Sama*n*as—

---

[1] With reference to Oldenberg's note at Mahâ Vagga, p. 384, it may be mentioned that Buddhaghosa says here, 'sabba-santharin' ti yathâ sabba*m* santhata*m* yeva. (S. V. fol. *te*.)

[2] The following sentences contain a synopsis of what was merely the elementary righteousness, the Âdi-brahma-*k*ariya*m*, quite distinct from, and not for a moment to be compared in glory with the Magga-brahma-*k*ariya*m*, the system developed in the Noble Eightfold Path. It will have been seen above, § 11, that the latter, to be perfect, must be untarnished by the attraction of the hope of heaven or the fear of hell.

he enters shyly and confused; fourthly, he is full of anxiety when he dies; and lastly, on the dissolution of the body, after death, he is reborn into some unhappy state of suffering or woe[1]. This, O householders, is the fivefold loss of the evil-doer!'

24. 'Fivefold, O householders, is the gain of the well-doer through his practice of rectitude. In the first place the well-doer, strong in rectitude, acquires great wealth through his industry; in the next place, good reports of him are spread abroad; thirdly, whatever society he enters—whether of nobles, Brâhmans, heads of houses, or members of the order—he enters confident and self-possessed; fourthly, he dies without anxiety; and lastly, on the dissolution of the body, after death, he is reborn into some happy state in heaven. This, O householders, is the fivefold gain of the well-doer.'

25. When the Blessed One had thus taught the disciples, and incited them, and roused them, and gladdened them, far into the night with religious discourse, he dismissed them, saying, 'The night is far spent, O householders. It is time for you to do what you deem most fit.' 'Even so, Lord!' answered the disciples of Pâtaligâma, and they rose from their seats, and bowing to the Blessed One, and keeping him on their right hand as they passed him, they departed thence.

And the Blessed One, not long after the disciples

[1] Four such states are mentioned, apâya, duggati, vinipâto, and nirayo, all of which are temporary states. The first three seem to be synonyms. The last is one of the four divisions into which the first is usually divided, and is often translated hell; but not being an eternal state, and not being dependent or consequent upon any judgment, it cannot accurately be so rendered.

of Pâtaligâma had departed thence, entered into his private chamber.

---

26. At that time Sunîdha and Vassakâra, the chief ministers of Magadha, were building a fortress at Pâtaligâma to repel the Vaggians, and there were a number of fairies who haunted in thousands the plots of ground there. Now, wherever ground is so occupied by powerful fairies, they bend the hearts of the most powerful kings and ministers to build dwelling-places there, and fairies of middling and inferior power bend in a similar way the hearts of middling or inferior kings and ministers.

27. And the Blessed One, with his great and clear vision, surpassing that of ordinary men, saw thousands of those fairies haunting Pâtaligâma. And he rose up very early in the morning, and said to Ânanda: 'Who is it then, Ânanda, who is building a fortress at Pâtaligâma?'

'Sunîdha and Vassakâra, Lord, the chief ministers of Magadha, are building a fortress there to keep back the Vaggians.'

28. They act, Ânanda, as if they had consulted with the Tâvatimsa angels. [And telling him of what he had seen, and of the influence such fairies had, he added]: 'And among famous places of residence and haunts of busy men, this will become the chief, the city of Pâtali-putta, a centre for the interchange of all kinds of wares. But three dangers will hang over Pâtali-putta, that of fire, that of water, and that of dissension[1].'

---

[1] This paragraph is of importance to the orthodox Buddhist as proving the Buddha's power of prophecy and the authority of the

29. Now Sunîdha and Vassakâra, the chief ministers of Magadha, proceeded to the place where the Blessed One was. And when they had come there they exchanged with the Blessed One the greetings and compliments of friendship and civility, and stood there respectfully on one side. And, so standing, Sunîdha and Vassakâra, the chief ministers of Magadha, spake thus to the Blessed One:

'May the venerable Gotama do us the honour of taking his meal, together with the company of the brethren, at our house to-day.' And the Blessed One signified, by silence, his consent.

30. Then when Sunîdha and Vassakâra, the chief ministers of Magadha, perceived that he had given his consent, they returned to the place where they dwelt. And on arriving there, they prepared sweet dishes of boiled rice, and cakes; and informed the Blessed One, saying:

Buddhist scriptures. To those who conclude that such a passage must have been written after the event that is prophesied, it is valuable evidence of the age both of the Mahâ Vagga and of the Mahâparinibbâna Sutta;—evidence, however, that cannot as yet be applied to its full extent, as the time at which Pâ*t*ali-gâma had grown into the great and important city of Pâ*t*ali-putta is not as yet known with sufficient certainty. The late Burmese tradition on this point given in Bigandet's Legend of the Burmese Buddha, vol. ii, p. 183, can scarcely be depended upon, though it doubtless rests on older documents, and is mentioned also by Hiouen Thsang.

The curious popular belief as to good and bad fairies haunting the sites of houses gave rise to a quack science, akin to astrology, called vatthu-vi*gg*â, which Buddhaghosa explains here at some length, and which is frequently condemned elsewhere in the Pâli Pi*t*akas. See, for instance, § 1 of the Mahâ-sîla*m*, translated below in the Tevi*gg*a Sutta. The belief is turned to ridicule in the edifying legend, No. 40, in my 'Buddhist Birth Stories,' pp. 326–334.

'The hour of food has come, O Gotama, and all is ready.'

And the Blessed One robed himself early, took his bowl with him, and repaired with the brethren to the dwelling-place of Sunîdha and Vassakâra, and sat down on the seat prepared for him. And with their own hands they set the sweet rice and the cakes before the brethren with the Buddha at their head, and waited on them till they had had enough. And when the Blessed One had finished eating his meal, the ministers brought a low seat, and sat down respectfully at his side.

31. And when they were thus seated the Blessed One gave thanks in these verses:—

'Wheresoe'er the prudent man shall take up his abode
Let him support there good and upright men of self-control.
Let him give gifts to all such deities as may be there.
Revered, they will revere him: honoured, they honour him again;
Are gracious to him as a mother to her own, her only son.
And the man who has the grace of the gods, good fortune he beholds [1].'

[1] This passage gives Buddhaghosa a good deal of difficulty, as it apparently inculcates offerings to the gods, which is contrary not only to both the letter and spirit of Buddhism, but also to the practice of Buddhists. He explains away the gifts to the deities by saying they are gifts of merit only (patti)—the giver giving the four necessaries to Bhikkhus, and then expressing a wish that the Devatâs should share in his puñña. I am inclined to think, on the authority of the Deva-dhamma *G*âtaka (No. 9 in 'Buddhist

32. And when he had thanked the ministers in these verses he rose from his seat and departed thence. And they followed him as he went, saying, 'The gate the Sama*n*a Gotama goes out by to-day shall be called Gotama's gate, and the ferry at which he crosses the river shall be called Gotama's ferry.' And the gate he went out at was called Gotama's gate.

---

33. But the Blessed One went on to the river. And at that time the river Ganges was brimful and overflowing[1]; and wishing to cross to the opposite bank, some began to seek for boats, some for rafts of wood, while some made rafts of basket-work[2]. Then the Blessed One as instantaneously as a strong man would stretch forth his arm, or draw it back again when he had stretched it forth, vanished from this side of the river, and stood on the further bank with the company of the brethren.

34. And the Blessed One beheld the people looking for boats and rafts, and as he beheld them he brake forth at that time into this song:—

'They who cross the ocean drear
Making a solid path across the pools—

Birth Stories'), that by the deities are here meant the 'good and upright men of self-control,' mentioned in the previous clause. The verses were perhaps originally non-Buddhistic.

[1] Samatittikâ kâkapeyyâ. See the note on Teviggâ Sutta I, 19, translated below, where the same expression occurs.

[2] Ulumpan ti pâra*m* gamanatthâya â*n*iyo-ko*tt*etvâ kata*m*; kullan ti valli-âdîhi bandhitvâ katabba*m*, says Buddhaghosa. The spelling u*l*umpa*m* would correspond better to the Sanskrit form u*d*upa, and has been chosen by Childers in his dictionary, and by Oldenberg in his transliteration of this passage (Mahâ Vagga VI, 28 : 11, 12).

Whilst the vain world ties its basket rafts—
These are the wise, these are the saved indeed[1]!'

End of the First Portion for Recitation.

---

[1] That is, those who cross the 'ocean drear' of ta*n*hâ, or craving; avoiding, by means of the 'dyke' or causeway of the Noble Path, the 'pools' or shallows of lust, and ignorance, and delusion (comp. Dhp. v. 91), whilst the vain world looks for salvation from rites, and ceremonies, and gods,—'these are the wise, these are the saved indeed!'

How the metre of the verses in the text fell into the confusion in which it at present stands is not easy to see. One would expect—

Ye visa*gg*a pallalâni taranti a*nn*ava*m* sara*m*
Kulla*m* hi *g*ano bandhati ti*nn*â medhâvino *g*anâ.

That a gloss can creep into the text, even in verses, is clear from the indisputable instance at *G*âtaka II, 35; and the words setu*m* katvâna would have been a very natural gloss had the passage once stood as above. Then supposing that a copyist or reciter had found the words ye visa*gg*a pallalâni setu*m* katvâna taranti a*nn*ava*m* sara*m*, he might have corrected, as he thought, the order of the words so as to avoid any possibility of the words being taken to mean that the setu, the solid causeway, was made over the a*nn*ava*m* sara*m*, the vastly deep, which would be palpably absurd. Buddhaghosa found setu*m* katvâna in the text, but it is not possible to tell in what order he found the words. The Turnour MS. of the Sumangala Vilâsinî has pabandhati, but a Ceylon copy of the Samanta Pâsâdikâ confirms the Burmese reading bandhati at Mahâ Vagga VI, 28, 13. I need scarcely say that the translation follows the printed text. We know too little about the history of the Pâli Suttas to be able to do more than make a passing note of such curiosities.

On vanishing away from a place, comp. below, III, 22.

CHAPTER II.

1. Now the Blessed One addressed the venerable Ânanda, and said: 'Come, Ânanda, let us go on to Ko*t*igâma.'

'So be it, Lord!' said Ânanda, in assent, to the Blessed One.

The Blessed One proceeded with a great company of the brethren to Ko*t*igâma; and there he stayed in the village itself[1].

2. And at that place the Blessed One addressed the brethren, and said: 'It is through not understanding and grasping four Noble Truths, O brethren, that we have had to run so long, to wander so long in this weary path of transmigration, both you and I!'

'And what are these four?'

'The noble truth about sorrow; the noble truth about the cause of sorrow; the noble truth about the cessation of sorrow; and the noble truth about the path that leads to that cessation. But when these noble truths are grasped and known the craving for existence is rooted out, that which leads to renewed existence is destroyed, and then there is no more birth!'

3. Thus spake the Blessed One; and when the Happy One had thus spoken, then again the Teacher said:

---

[1] As will be observed from the similar passages that follow, there is a regular sequence of clauses in the set descriptions of the Buddha's movements. The last clause should specify the particular grove or house where the Blessed One stayed; but it is also (in this and one or two other cases) inserted with due regularity even when it adds nothing positive to the sense.

'By not seeing the four Noble Truths as they
really are,
Long is the path that is traversed through many
a birth;
When these are grasped, the cause of birth is
then removed,
The root of sorrow rooted out, and there is no
more birth.'

---

4. There too, while staying at Ko*t*igâma, the Blessed One held that comprehensive religious discourse with the brethren on the nature of upright conduct, and of earnest contemplation, and of intelligence. 'Great is the fruit, great the advantage of earnest contemplation when set round with upright conduct. Great is the fruit, great the advantage of intellect when set round with earnest contemplation. The mind set round with intelligence is freed from the great evils,—that is to say, from sensuality, from individuality, from delusion, and from ignorance.'

---

5. Now when the Blessed One had remained as long as was convenient at Ko*t*igâma, he addressed the venerable Ânanda, and said: 'Come, Ânanda, let us go on to the villages of Nâdika.'

'So be it, Lord!' said Ânanda, in assent, to the Blessed One.

And the Blessed proceeded to the villages of Nâdika with a great company of the brethren; and there, at Nâdika, the Blessed One stayed at the Brick Hall[1].

---

[1] At first Nâdika is (twice) spoken of in the plural number; but then, thirdly, in the last clause, in the singular. Buddhaghosa

6. And the venerable Ânanda went to the Blessed One and paid him reverence and took his seat beside him. And when he was seated, he addressed the Blessed One, and said: 'The brother named Sâ*lh*a has died at Nâdika, Lord. Where has he been reborn, and what is his destiny? The sister named Nandâ has died, Lord, at Nâdika. Where is she reborn, and what is her destiny?' And in the same terms he enquired concerning the devout Sudatta, and the devout lady Su*g*âtâ, the devout Kakudha, and Kâlinga, and Nika*t*a, and Ka*t*issabha, and Tu*tth*a, and Santu*tth*a, and Bhadda, and Subhadda.

7. 'The brother named Sâ*lh*a, Ânanda, by the destruction of the great evils has by himself, and in this world, known and realised and attained to Arahatship, and to emancipation of heart and to emancipation of mind. The sister named Nandâ, Ânanda, has, by the complete destruction of the five bonds that bind people to this world, become an inheritor of the highest heavens, there to pass entirely away, thence never to return. The devout Sudatta, Ânanda, by the complete destruction of the three bonds, and by the reduction to a minimum of lust, hatred, and delusion has become a Sakadâgâmin, who on his first return to this world will make an end of sorrow. The devout woman Su*g*âtâ, Ânanda, by the complete destruction of the three bonds, has become converted, is no longer liable to be reborn in a state of suffering, and is assured of final salva-

explains this by saying that there were two villages of the same name on the shore of the same piece of water. On the public resting-place for travellers, which in this instance bore the proud title of Brick Hall, see 'Buddhist Birth Stories,' pp. 280–285.

tion[1]. The devout Kakudha, Ânanda, by the complete destruction of the five bonds that bind people to these lower worlds of lust, has become an inheritor of the highest heavens, there to pass entirely away, thence never to return. So also is the case with Kâlinga, Nika*t*a, Ka*t*issabha, Tu*tth*a, Santu*tth*a, Bhadda, and Subhadda, and with more than fifty devout men of Nâdika. More than ninety devout men of Nâdika, who have died, Ânanda, have by the complete destruction of the three bonds, and by the reduction of lust, hatred, and delusion, become Sakadâgâmins, who on their first return to this world will make an end of sorrow. More than five hundred devout men of Nâdika who have died, Ânanda, have by the complete destruction of the three bonds become converted, are no longer liable to be reborn in a state of suffering, and are assured of final salvation.

8. 'Now there is nothing strange in this, Ânanda, that a human being should die, but that as each one does so you should come to the Buddha, and enquire about them in this manner, that is wearisome to the Buddha. I will, therefore, teach you a way of truth, called the Mirror of Truth, which if an elect disciple possess he may himself predict of himself, "Hell is destroyed for me, and rebirth as an animal, or a ghost, or in any place of woe. I am converted, I am no longer liable to be reborn in a state of suffering, and am assured of final salvation."

9. 'What then, Ânanda, is this mirror of truth? It is the consciousness that the elect disciple is in this world possessed of faith in the Buddha—

[1] See 'Buddhism,' pp. 108–110, and below, VI, 9.

believing the Blessed One to be the Holy One, the Fully-enlightened One, Wise, Upright, Happy, World-knowing, Supreme, the Bridler of men's wayward hearts, the Teacher of gods and men, the Blessed Buddha. And that he (the disciple) is possessed of faith in the Truth—believing the truth to have been proclaimed by the Blessed One, of advantage in this world, passing not away, welcoming all, leading to salvation, and to be attained to by the wise, each one for himself. And that he (the disciple) is possessed of faith in the Order—believing the multitude of the disciples of the Blessed One who are walking in the four stages of the noble eightfold path, the righteous, the upright, the just, the law-abiding — believing this church of the Buddha to be worthy of honour, of hospitality, of gifts, and of reverence; to be the supreme sowing ground of merit for the world; to be possessed of the virtues beloved by the good, virtues unbroken, intact, unspotted, unblemished, virtues which make men truly free, virtues which are praised by the wise, are untarnished by the desire of future life or by the belief in the efficacy of outward acts, and are conducive to high and holy thought[1].'

10. 'This, Ânanda, is the way, the mirror of truth, which if an elect disciple possess he may himself predict of himself: "Hell is destroyed for me; and rebirth as an animal, or a ghost, or in any place of woe. I am converted; I am no longer liable to be reborn in a state of suffering, and am assured of final salvation."'

---

11. There, too, at the Brick Hall at Nâdika the

[1] See above, § I, 11.

Blessed One addressed to the brethren that comprehensive religious discourse on the nature of upright conduct, and of earnest contemplation, and of intelligence.

'Great is the fruit, great the advantage of earnest contemplation when set round with upright conduct. Great is the fruit, great the advantage of intellect when set round with earnest contemplation. The mind set round with intelligence is freed from the great evils, that is to say, from sensuality, from individuality, from delusion, and from ignorance.'

---

12. Now when the Blessed One had remained as long as he wished at Nâdika, he addressed Ânanda, and said: 'Come, Ânanda, let us go on to Vesâli.'

'So be it, Lord!' said Ânanda, in assent, to the Blessed One.

Then the Blessed One proceeded, with a great company of the brethren, to Vesâli; and there at Vesâli the Blessed One stayed at Ambapâli's grove.

13. Now there the Blessed One addressed the brethren, and said: 'Let a brother, O mendicants, be mindful and thoughtful; this is our instruction to you.'

14. 'And how does a brother become mindful?'

'Herein, O mendicants, let a brother, as he dwells in the body, so regard the body that he, being strenuous, thoughtful, and mindful, may, whilst in the world, overcome the grief which arises from bodily craving—while subject to sensations, let him continue so to regard the sensations that he, being strenuous, thoughtful, and mindful, may, whilst in the world, overcome the grief arising from the craving which follows our sensation—and so also as he thinks or reasons or feels let him overcome the grief which arises from the craving due to ideas, or reasoning, or feeling.'

15. 'And how does a brother become thoughtful?'

'He acts, O mendicants, in full presence of mind whatever he may do, in going out and coming in, in looking and watching, in bending in his arm or stretching it forth, in wearing his robes or carrying his bowl, in eating and drinking, in consuming or tasting, in walking or standing or sitting, in sleeping or waking, in talking and in being silent.

'Thus let a brother, O mendicants, be mindful and thoughtful; this is our instruction to you[1].'

---

[1] This doctrine of being 'mindful and thoughtful'—sato sampa*g*âno—is one of the lessons most frequently inculcated in the Pâli Pi*t*akas, and is one of the 'Seven Jewels of the Law.' It is fully treated of in each of the Nikâyas, forming the subject of the Mahâ Satippa*tth*âna Sutta in the Dîgha Nikâya, and the Satipa*tth*âna Sutta of the Ma*gg*h*ima Nikâya, and the Satippa*tth*âna Vaggo of the Sa*m*yutta Nikâya, as well as of various passages in the Aṅguttara Nikâya and of the work called Vibhaṅga in the Abhidhamma Pi*t*aka. I am glad to learn that Dr. Morris intends to collect and compare all these passages in his forthcoming work on the 'Seven Jewels of the Law.' These sections of the Mahâparinibbâna Sutta and the treatment in the Vibhaṅga have preserved, in Dr. Morris's opinion, the oldest form of the doctrine. Compare Chap. II, § 34.

Buddhaghosa has no comment here on the subject itself, reserving what he has to say for the comment on the Suttas devoted entirely to it; but he observes in passing that the reason why the Blessed One laid stress, at this particular time and place, on the necessity of being 'mindful and thoughtful,' was because of the imminent approach of the beautiful courtezan in whose grove they were staying. The use of the phrase sati upa*tth*âpetabbâ below, Chap. V, § 13 (text, p. 51), in reference to the way in which women should be treated, is quite in accordance with this explanation. But see the next note.

16. [1] Now the courtezan Ambapâli heard that the Blessed One had arrived at Vesâli, and was staying at her mango grove. And ordering a number of magnificent vehicles to be made ready, she mounted one of them, and proceeded with her train towards her garden. She went in the carriage as far as the ground was passable for carriages; there she alighted; and she proceeded on foot to the place where the Blessed One was, and took her seat respectfully on one side. And when she was thus seated the Blessed One instructed, aroused, incited, and gladdened her with religious discourse.

17. Then she—instructed, aroused, incited, and gladdened with his words—addressed the Blessed One, and said:

'May the Blessed One do me the honour of taking his meal, together with the brethren, at my house to-morrow.'

And the Blessed One gave, by silence, his consent. Then when Ambapâli the courtezan saw that the Blessed One had consented, she rose from her seat and bowed down before him, and keeping him on her right hand as she past him, she departed thence.

[1] From this point down to the words 'he rose from his seat,' in § II, 24, is, with a few unimportant variations, word for word the same as Mahâ Vagga VI, 30, 1, to VI, 30, 6. But the passage there follows immediately after the verses translated above, § I, 34, so that the events here (in §§ 16–22) localised at Vesâli, are there localised at Ko*t*igâma. Our section II, 5 is then inserted between our sections II, 22 and II, 23; and our section II, 12 does not occur at all, the Blessed One only reaching Ambapâli's grove when he goes there (as in our section II, 23) to partake of the meal to which he had been invited. Buddhaghosa passes over this discrepancy in silence.

18. Now the Li*kkh*avis of Vesâli heard that the Blessed One had arrived at Vesâli, and was staying at Ambapâli's grove. And ordering a number of magnificent carriages to be made ready, they mounted one of them and proceeded with their train to Vesâli. Some of them were dark, dark in colour, and wearing dark clothes and ornaments: some of them were fair, fair in colour, and wearing light clothes and ornaments: some of them were red, ruddy in colour, and wearing red clothes and ornaments: some of them were white, pale in colour, and wearing white clothes and ornaments.

19. And Ambapâli drove up against the young Li*kkh*avis, axle to axle, wheel to wheel, and yoke to yoke, and the Li*kkh*avis said to Ambapâli the courtezan, 'How is it, Ambapâli, that thou drivest up against us thus?'

'My Lords, I have just invited the Blessed One and his brethren for their morrow's meal,' said she.

'Ambapâli! give up this meal to us for a hundred thousand,' said they.

'My Lords, were you to offer all Vesâli with its subject territory[1], I would not give up so honourable a feast!'

Then the Li*kkh*avis cast up their hands[2], exclaiming, 'We are outdone by this mango girl! we are out-reached by this mango girl[3]!' and they went on to Ambapâli's grove.

20. When the Blessed One saw the Li*kkh*avis

---

[1] Sâhâran ti sa-*g*anapadan. (S. V. *t*au.)

[2] Angulî po*th*esu*m*. Childers translates this phrase 'to snap the fingers as a token of pleasure;' but Buddhaghosa says, angulî po*th*esun ti angulî *k*âlesu*m*. (S. V. *t*au.)

[3] Ambapâli means mango grower, one who looks after mangoes.

approaching in the distance, he addressed the brethren, and said:

'O brethren, let those of the brethren who have never seen the Tâvati*m*sa gods, gaze upon this company of the Li*kkh*avis, behold this company of the Li*kkh*avis, compare this company of the Li*kkh*avis—even as a company of Tâvati*m*sa gods [1].'

21. And when they had ridden as far as the ground was passable for carriages, the Li*kkh*avis alighted there, and then went on on foot to the place where the Blessed One was, and took their seats respectfully by his side. And when they were thus seated the Blessed One instructed and roused and incited and gladdened them with religious discourse [2].

22. Then they instructed and roused and incited and gladdened with his words, addressed the Blessed One, and said, 'May the Blessed One do us the honour of taking his meal, together with the brethren, at our house to-morrow?'

'O Li*kkh*avis, I have promised to dine to-morrow with Ambapâli the courtezan,' was the reply.

[1] The Tâvati*m*sa-devâ are the gods in the heaven of the Great Thirty-Three, the principal deities of the Vedic Pantheon. Buddhaghosa says, 'Ima*m* Li*kkh*avi-parisa*m* tumhâka*m* *k*ittena Tâvati*m*sa-parisa*m* upasa*m*haratha upanetha alliyâpetha: Yath' eva hi Tâvati*m*sâ abhirûpa pâsâdikâ nîlâdi-nâna-va*nn*â evañ *k*' ime Li*kkh*avi-râ*g*âno pîti. Tâvati*m*sehi samake katvâ passathâ ti attho.'

[2] The Mâlâlaṅkâra-vatthu gives the substance of the discourse on this occasion. 'The princes had come in their finest and richest dress; in their appearance they vied in beauty with the nats (or angels). But foreseeing the ruin and misery that was soon to come upon them all, the Buddha exhorted his disciples to entertain a thorough contempt for things that are dazzling to the eyes, but essentially perishable and unreal in their nature.'—Bigandet, 2nd ed. p. 260.

Then the Li*kkh*avis cast up their hands, exclaiming, 'We are outdone by this mango girl! we are outreached by this mango girl!' And expressing their thanks and approval of the words of the Blessed One, they rose from their seats and bowed down before the Blessed One, and keeping him on their right hand as they past him, they departed thence.

23. And at the end of the night Ambapâli the courtezan made ready in her mansion sweet rice and cakes, and announced the time to the Blessed One, saying, 'The hour, Lord, has come, and the meal is ready!'

And the Blessed One robed himself early in the morning, and took his bowl, and went with the brethren to the place where Ambapâli's dwelling-house was: and when he had come there he seated himself on the seat prepared for him. And Ambapâli the courtezan set the sweet rice and cakes before the order, with the Buddha at their head, and waited upon them till they refused any more.

24. And when the Blessed One had quite finished his meal, the courtezan had a low stool brought, and sat down at his side, and addressed the Blessed One, and said: 'Lord, I present this mansion to the order of mendicants, of which the Buddha is the chief.' And the Blessed One accepted the gift; and after instructing, and rousing, and inciting, and gladdening her with religious discourse, he rose from his seat and departed thence[1].

[1] Bishop Bigandet says: 'In recording the conversion of a courtezan named Apapalika, her liberality and gifts to Budha and his disciples, and the preference designedly given to her over princes and nobles, who, humanely speaking, seemed in every respect better entitled to attentions—one is almost reminded of

25. While at Ambapâli's mango grove the Blessed One held that comprehensive religious discourse with the disciples on the nature of upright conduct, and of earnest contemplation, and of intelligence.

'Great is the fruit, great the advantage of earnest contemplation when set round with upright conduct. Great is the fruit, great the advantage of intellect when set round with earnest contemplation. The mind set round with intelligence is freed from the great evils, that is to say, from sensuality, from individuality, from delusion, and from ignorance.'

---

26. Now when the Blessed One had remained as long as he wished at Ambapâli's grove, he addressed Ânanda, and said: 'Come, Ânanda, let us go on to Beluva[1].'

'So be it, Lord,' said Ânanda, in assent, to the Blessed One.

Then the Blessed One proceeded, with a great company of the brethren, to Beluva, and there the Blessed One stayed in the village itself.

---

27. Now the Blessed One there addressed the brethren, and said: 'O mendicants, do you take up your abode round about Vesâli, each according to the place where his friends, intimates, and close companions may live, for the rainy season of vassa. I shall enter upon the rainy season here at Beluva.'

---

the conversion of "a woman that was a sinner," mentioned in the Gospels' (Legend of the Burmese Budha, 2nd ed. p. 258).

[1] Beluva-gâmako ti Vesâli-samîpe pâda-gâmako, 'a village on a slope at the foot of a hill near Vesâli,' says Buddhaghosa. (S. V. *in loc.*)

'So be it, Lord!' said those brethren, in assent, to the Blessed One. And they entered upon the rainy season round about Vesâli, each according to the place where his friends or intimates or close companions lived: whilst the Blessed One stayed even there at Beluva.

---

28. Now when the Blessed One had thus entered upon the rainy season, there fell upon him a dire sickness, and sharp pains came upon him, even unto death. But the Blessed One, mindful and self-possessed, bore them without complaint.

29. Then this thought occurred to the Blessed One, 'It would not be right for me to pass away from existence without addressing the disciples, without taking leave of the order. Let me now, by a strong effort of the will, bend this sickness down again, and keep my hold on life till the allotted time be come[1].'

30. And the Blessed One, by a strong effort of the will, bent that sickness down again, and kept his hold on life till the time he fixed upon should come. And the sickness abated upon him.

---

31. Now very soon after the Blessed One began to recover; when he had quite got rid of the sickness, he went out from the monastery, and sat down behind the monastery on a seat spread out there. And the venerable Ânanda went to the place where the Blessed One was, and saluted him, and took a seat respectfully on one side, and addressed the

[1] The commentary on *gîvita-saṅkhâram adhitthâya vihareyyan* is not quite clear, but the general meaning of the words cannot be very different from the version given in the text.

Blessed One, and said: 'I have beheld, Lord, how the Blessed One was in health, and I have beheld how the Blessed One had to suffer. And though at the sight of the sickness of the Blessed One my body became weak as a creeper, and the horizon became dim to me, and my faculties were no longer clear[1], yet notwithstanding I took some little comfort from the thought that the Blessed One would not pass away from existence until at least he had left instructions as touching the order.'

32. 'What, then, Ânanda? Does the order expect that of me? I have preached the truth without making any distinction between exoteric and esoteric doctrine: for in respect of the truths, Ânanda, the Tathâgata has no such thing as the closed fist of a teacher, who keeps some things back[2]. Surely, Ânanda, should there be any one who harbours the thought, "It is I who will lead the brotherhood," or, "The order is dependent upon me," it is he who

---

[1] Madhuraka-*g*âto viyâ ti sa*ñg*âta-garubhâvo sa*ñg*âta*tth*abhâvo (sic) sûle uttâsita-sadiso: na pakkhâyantî ti na pakâsenti nânâkâra*n*â na upa*tth*ahanti: Dhammâ pi ma*m* na ppa*t*ibhantî ti sati-ppa*tth*ânâ dhammâ mayha*m* pâka*t*â na honti. (S.V. fol. *t*âm.) As the first clause is corrupt, I have translated madhuraka-*g*âto independently of it. Childers's reading na*m* na ppa*t*ibhanti is clearly incorrect. My own MS. of the Dîgha Nikâya and the Turnour MS. of the Samyutta Nikâya agree with Buddhaghosa.

[2] Na tatth' Ânanda Tathâgatassa dhammesu â*k*ariyamu*tth*i; on which Buddhaghosa says, Â*k*ariya-mu*tth*î (MS. vu*tth*î) ti yathâ bâhirakâna*m* â*k*ariya-mu*tth*i nâma hoti: daharakâle kassa*k*i akathetvâ pa*kkh*ima-kâle mara*n*a-ma*ñk*e nipannâ piya-manâpassa antevâsikassa kathenti: evam Tathâgatassa ida*m* mahallaka-kâle pa*kkh*ima-*tth*âne kathessâmî ti mu*tth*i*m* (MS. vu*tth*i*m*) katvâ pariharitvâ *th*apita*m* ki*ñk*i n'atthî ti. (S. V. *t*âm.) Comp. *G*âtaka II, 221, 250.

should lay down instructions in any matter concerning the order. Now the Tathâgata, Ânanda, thinks not that it is he who should lead the brotherhood, or that the order is dependent upon him. Why then should he leave instructions in any matter concerning the order? I too, O Ânanda, am now grown old, and full of years, my journey is drawing to its close, I have reached my sum of days, I am turning eighty years of age; and just as a worn-out cart, Ânanda, can only with much additional care be made to move along, so, methinks, the body of the Tathâgata can only be kept going with much additional care[1]. It is only, Ânanda, when

[1] Vegha-missakena, the meaning of which is not clear. The Mâlâlaṅkâra-vatthu, as rendered by Bigandet, has 'repairs.' The Sumangala Vilâsinî says, Veghamissakenâ ti bâha-bandhana-*k*akka-bandhanâdinâ pa*t*isaṅkhara*n*ena veghamissakena; thus giving the same meaning, but in such a way as to throw no light on the derivation of the word. The whole episode from § II, 27 to the end of the chapter occurs also word for word in the Satipa*tth*âna Vagga of the Sa*m*yutta Nikâya, and the Burmese Phayre MS. there reads vekhamissakena, as the Burmese MS. does here. My Dîgha Nikâya confirms Childers's reading, which no doubt correctly represents the uniform tradition of the Ceylon MSS. The Sumangala Vilâsinî goes on, mañ*ñ*e ti *g*ara-saka*t*a*m* viya meghamissakena mañ*ñ*e yâpeti arahatta-phala-veghanena *k*atu-iriyâpatha-kappana*m* Tathâgatassa hoti nidasseti. Here the reading megha of the Turnour MS. must be a copyist's slip of the pen for vegha, and veghanena is no clearer than veghamissakena. On the use of the word missaka at the end of a compound see *G*âtaka II, 8, 420, 433. I have translated on what seems to me the only solution at present possible, namely, that an initial *a* has been dropt, and that veghâ or vekhâ = avekshâ, 'attention, foresight, care.' In the same way though avala*ñg*eti does occur (*G*âtaka I, 111), the more usual form in Pâli, and the only one given by Childers, is vala*ñg*eti.

the Tathâgata, ceasing to attend to any outward thing, or to experience any sensation, becomes plunged in that devout meditation of heart which is concerned with no material object—it is only then that the body of the Tathâgata is at ease.

33. 'Therefore, O Ânanda, be ye lamps unto yourselves. Be ye a refuge to yourselves. Betake yourselves to no external refuge. Hold fast to the truth as a lamp. Hold fast as a refuge to the truth. Look not for refuge to any one besides yourselves. And how, Ânanda, is a brother to be a lamp unto himself, a refuge to himself, betaking himself to no external refuge, holding fast to the truth as a lamp, holding fast as a refuge to the truth, looking not for refuge to any one besides himself?

34. 'Herein, O Ânanda, let a brother, as he dwells in the body, so regard the body that he, being strenuous, thoughtful, and mindful, may, whilst in the world, overcome the grief which arises from bodily craving—while subject to sensations let him continue so to regard the sensations that he, being strenuous, thoughtful, and mindful, may, whilst in the world, overcome the grief which arises from the sensations—and so, also, as he thinks, or reasons, or feels, let him overcome the grief which arises from the craving due to ideas, or to reasoning, or to feeling.

35. 'And whosoever, Ânanda, either now or after I am dead, shall be a lamp unto themselves, and a refuge unto themselves, shall betake themselves to no external refuge, but holding fast to the truth as their lamp, and holding fast as their refuge to the truth, shall look not for refuge to any one besides themselves—it is they, Ânanda, among my

bhikkhus, who shall reach the very topmost Height!—but they must be anxious to learn[1].'

End of the Second Portion for Recitation.

---

[1] Tamatagge me te Ânanda bhikkhû bhavissanti ye ke*k*i sikkhâkâmâ. The Burmese MSS. for me te read p'ete, which is a little easier. Buddhaghosa says, Tamatagge ti tamagge. Ma*ggh*e takâro padasandhivasena vutto. Ida*m* vutta*m* hoti ime aggatamâ ime aggamâ ti: eva*m* sabba*m* tamayoga*m* *kh*inditvâ ativiya agge uttama-bhâve te Ânanda mama*m* bhikkhû bhavissanti. Kesa*m* ati-agge bhavissanti? Ye ke*k*i sikkhâkâmâ sabbesa*m* te *k*atu-sati-ppa*t*-*th*âna-go*k*arâ *k*a bhikkhû agge bhavissantî ti. Arahatta-tikû*t*ena desa*n*am ga*n*hati, 'Tamatagge is for tamagge. The t in the middle is used for euphony. This word means, "these are the most pre-eminent, the very chief." Having, as above stated, broken every bond of darkness (tama) those bhikkhus of mine, Ânanda, will be at the very top, in the highest condition. They will be at the very top of whom? Those bhikkhus who are willing to learn, and those who exercise themselves in the four ways of being mindful and thoughtful, they shall be at the top of all (the rest). Thus does he make Arahatship the three-peaked height of his discourse' (compare on this last phrase Nibbânena desanâkû*t*am ga*n*hati, *G*âtaka I, 275, 393, 401; and see also I, 114). Uttama, the highest (scil. bhâva, condition), is used absolutely of Arahatship or Nirvâ*n*a at *G*âtaka I, 96; Aggaphala occurs in the same sense at *G*âtaka I, 114; and even Phalagga at Mah. 102. The last words, 'but they must be anxious to learn,' seem to me to be an after thought. It is only those who are thoroughly determined to work out their own salvation, without looking for safety to any one else, even to the Buddha himself, who will, whilst in the world, enter into and experience Nirvâ*n*a. But, of course, let there be no mistake, merely to reject the vain baubles of the current superstitious beliefs is not enough. There is plenty to learn and to acquire, of which enough discourse is elsewhere. For aggamâ in the comment we must read aggatamâ. If one could read amatagge in the text, all difficulty would vanish; but this would be too bold, and neither do I see how the use of anamatagge can help us.

CHAPTER III.

1[1]. Now the Blessed One robed himself early in the morning, and taking his bowl in the robe, went into Vesâli for alms, and when he returned he sat down on the seat prepared for him, and after he had finished eating the rice he addressed the venerable Ânanda, and said: 'Take up the mat, Ânanda; I will go to spend the day at the *K*âpâla *K*etiya.'

'So be it, Lord!' said the venerable Ânanda, in assent, to the Blessed One. And taking up the mat he followed step for step behind the Blessed One.

2. So the Blessed One proceeded to the *K*âpâla *K*etiya, and when he had come there he sat down on the mat spread out for him, and the venerable Ânanda took his seat respectfully beside him. Then the Blessed One addressed the venerable Ânanda, and said: 'How delightful a spot, Ânanda, is Vesâli, and the Udena *K*etiya, and the Gotamaka *K*etiya, and the Sattambaka *K*etiya, and the Bahuputta *K*etiya, and the Sârandada *K*etiya, and the *K*âpâla *K*etiya.

3. 'Ânanda! whosoever has thought out, developed, practised, accumulated, and ascended to the very heights of the four paths to Iddhi[2], and so

---

[1] The whole of this passage down to the end of § 10 recurs in the Iddhipâda Vagga of the Sa*m*yutta Nikâya.

[2] Iddhi. The four paths are, 1. will, 2. effort, 3. thought, and 4. investigation, each united to earnest thought and the struggle against sin. The Iddhi reached by them is supposed in works on Buddhism to be a bodily condition (power of flying, &c.), by which the body rose superior to all the ordinary limitations of

mastered them as to be able to use them as a means of (mental) advancement, and as a basis for edification, he, should he desire it, could remain in the same birth for a kalpa, or for that portion of the kalpa which had yet to run. Now the Tathâgata has thought them out, and thoroughly practised and developed them [in all respects as just more fully described], and he could, therefore, should he desire it, live on yet for a kalpa, or for that portion of the kalpa which has yet to run.'

4. But even though a suggestion so evident and a hint so clear were thus given by the Blessed One, the venerable Ânanda was incapable of comprehending them; and he besought not the Blessed One, saying, 'Vouchsafe, Lord, to remain during the kalpa! Live on through the kalpa, O Blessed One! for the good and the happiness of the great multitudes, out of pity for the world, for the good and the gain and the weal of gods and men!' So far was his heart possessed by the Evil One[1].

---

matter—a bodily condition corresponding to the mental condition of exaltation and power by which it was reached. On this curiously perverted exaggeration of the real influence of the mind over the body see, further, the translator's 'Buddhism,' pp. 174–177. Two of the string of participles—yânikatâ, which may possibly mean 'made use of as a vehicle,' and susamâraddhâ, 'most thoroughly ascended up to'—might seem to allude to Iddhi as a power of flying bodily through the air. But the whole set of participles is used elsewhere of conditions of mind highly esteemed among the Buddhists, and incapable of giving support to any such allusion. So, for instance, of universal love (mettâ) at *G*âtaka II, 61.

[1] Yathâ ta*m* Mârena pariyu*tth*ita*k*itto. Here ta*m* is the indeclinable particle, yathâ ta*m* introducing an explanation. My MS. of the Dîgha Nikâya and the Turnour MS. of the Sumangala Vilasinî read pari*v*u*tth*ita, and either spelling is correct. The

5. A second and a third time did the Blessed One [say the same thing, and a second and a third time was Ânanda's heart thus hardened].

6. Now the Blessed One addressed the venerable Ânanda, and said: 'You may leave me, Ânanda, awhile, and do whatever seemeth to thee fit.'

'So be it, Lord!' said the venerable Ânanda, in assent, to the Blessed, and rising from his seat he saluted the Blessed One, and passing him on the right, sat down at the foot of a certain tree not far off thence.

---

7. Now not long after the venerable Ânanda had been gone, Mâra, the Evil One, approached the Blessed One, and stood beside him. And so standing there, he addressed the Blessed One in these words:

'Pass away now, Lord, from existence; let the Blessed One now die. Now is the time for the Blessed One to pass away—even according to the

fact is that the *y* or *v* in such cases is even less than euphonic; it is an assistance not to the speaker, but merely to the writer. Thus in the Siṅhalese duwanawâ, 'to run,' the spoken word is duanawâ, and the *w* is written only to avoid the awkward use in the middle of a word of the initial sign for the sound *a*. That the speakers of Pâli found no difficulty in pronouncing two vowels together is abundantly proved by numerous instances. The writers of Pâli, in those cases in which the second vowel begins a word, use without hesitation the initial sign; but in the middle of the word this would be so ungainly that they naturally prefer to insert a consonantal sign to carry the vowel sign. The varying readings I have pointed out are a strong confirmation of the correctness of the pronunciation of modern native scholars; and we may the more readily adopt it as the question is not really one concerning the pronunciation of Pâli, but concerning the use which modern native copyists make of their own alphabet. I would pronounce therefore pari-u*tth*ita-*k*itto.

word which the Blessed One spoke when he said[1]: "I shall not die, O Evil One! until the brethren and sisters of the order, and until the lay-disciples of either sex[2] shall have become true hearers, wise and well-trained, ready and learned, versed in the Scriptures, fulfilling all the greater and the lesser duties, correct in life, walking according to the precepts—until they, having thus themselves learned the doctrine, shall be able to tell others of it, preach it, make it known, establish it, open it, minutely explain it and make it clear—until they, when others start vain doctrine, shall be able by the truth to vanquish and refute it, and so to spread the wonder-working truth abroad!"'

8. 'And now, Lord, the brethren and sisters of the order and the lay-disciples of either sex have become [all this], are able to do [all this]. Pass away now therefore, Lord, from existence; let the Blessed One now die! The time has come for the Blessed One to pass away—even according to the word which he spake when he said, "I shall not die, O Evil One! until this pure religion of mine shall have become successful, prosperous, widespread, and popular in all its full extent—until, in a word, it shall have been well proclaimed to men." And now, Lord, this pure religion of thine has become [all this]. Pass away now therefore, Lord, from

---

[1] The words here quoted were spoken by the Buddha, after he had been enjoying the first bliss of Nirvâna, under the shepherd's Nigrodha tree (see my 'Buddhist Birth Stories,' pp. 109–111). The Evil One then also tempted him to die (see below, paragraph III, 43), and this was his reply.

[2] The whole paragraph is repeated, here and below, for each of these classes of persons.

existence; let the Blessed One now die! The time has come for the Blessed One to pass away!'

9. And when he had thus spoken, the Blessed One addressed Mâra, the Evil One, and said: 'O Evil One! make thyself happy, the final extinction of the Tathâgata shall take place before long. At the end of three months from this time the Tathâgata will die!'

---

10. Thus the Blessed One while at the *K*âpâla *K*etiya deliberately and consciously rejected the rest of his allotted sum of life. And on his so rejecting it there arose a mighty earthquake, awful and terrible, and the thunders of heaven burst forth. And when the Blessed One beheld this, he broke out at that time into this hymn of exultation:

'His sum of life the sage renounced,
The cause of life immeasurable or small;
With inward joy and calm, he broke,
Like coat of mail, his life's own cause!'

---

11. Now the following thought occurred to the venerable Ânanda: 'Wonderful indeed and marvellous is it that this mighty earthquake should arise, awful and terrible, and that the thunders of heaven should burst forth! What may be the proximate, what the remote cause of the appearance of this earthquake?'

12. Then the venerable Ânanda went up to the place where the Blessed One was, and did obeisance to the Blessed One, and seated himself respectfully at one side, and said: 'Wonderful indeed and marvellous is it that this mighty earthquake should arise, awful and terrible, and that the thunders of

heaven should burst forth! What may be the proximate, what the remote cause of the appearance of this earthquake?'

13. 'Eight are the proximate, eight the remote causes, Ânanda, for the appearance of a mighty earthquake. What are the eight? This great earth, Ânanda, is established on water, the water on wind, and the wind rests upon space. And at such a time, Ânanda, as the mighty winds blow, the waters are shaken by the mighty winds as they blow, and by the moving water the earth is shaken. These are the first causes, proximate and remote, of the appearance of a mighty earthquake.

14. 'Again, Ânanda, a Sama*n*a or a Brâhman of great (intellectual) power, and who has the feelings of his heart well under his control; or a god or fairy (devatâ[1]) of great might and power,—when such a

[1] Devatâ is a fairy, god, genius, or angel. I am at a loss how to render this word without conveying an erroneous impression to those not familiar with ancient ideas, and specially with ancient Buddhist ideas, of the spirit world. It includes gods of all sorts; tree and river nymphs; the kindly fairies or ghosts who haunt houses (see my 'Buddhist Birth Stories,' Tale No. 40); spirits in the ground (see above, § I, 26); the angels who minister at the great renunciation, the temptation, and the death of the Buddha; the guardian angels who watch over men, and towns, and countries; and many other similar beings. 'Celestial being' would be wholly inapplicable, for instance, to the creatures referred to in the curious passage above (§ I, 26). 'Superhuman being' would be an inaccurate rendering; for all these light and airy shapes come below, and after, man in the Buddhist order of precedence. 'Spirit' being used of the soul inside the human body, and of the human soul after it has left the body, and figuratively of mental faculties—none of which are included under devatâ—would suggest ideas inconsistent with that of the Pâli word. As there is therefore no appropriate general word I have chosen, for each passage where the expression occurs, the word used in English of the special class

one by intense meditation of the finite idea of earth or the infinite idea of water (has succeeded in realising the comparative value of things[1]) he can make this earth move and tremble and be shaken violently. These are the second causes, proximate or remote, of the appearance of a mighty earthquake.

15. 'Again, Ânanda, when a Bodhisatta consciously and deliberately leaves his temporary form in the heaven of delight and descends into his mother's womb, then is this earth made to quake and tremble and is shaken violently. These are the third causes, proximate or remote, of the appearance of a mighty earthquake[2].

more particularly referred to in the passage of the text. Here all kinds of devatâs being referred to, and there being no word in English for them all, I have ventured to put the word devatâ into my version, and to trouble the reader with this note.

[1] Yassa parittâ pa*th*avi-sa*ññ*â bhâvitâ hoti appamâ*n*â âposa*ññ*â, on which Buddhaghosa says simply, Parittâ ti dubbalâ: appamâ*n*â ti balavâ, and then goes on, as a note to kampeti, to tell a long story how Sangharakkhita Sâma*n*era, the nephew of Nâga Thera, attained Arahatship on the day of his admission to the order; and at once proceeded to heaven, and standing on the pinnacle of the palace of the king of the gods, shook the whole place with his big toe; to the great consternation and annoyance of the exalted dwellers therein! There is no doubt a real truth in the idea that deep thought can shake the universe, and make the palaces of the gods to tremble, just as faith is said in Matthew xxi. 21 to be able to remove mountains, and cause them to be cast into the sea. But these figurative expressions have, in Buddhism, become a fruitful soil for the outgrowth of superstitions and misunderstandings; and the train of early Buddhist speculation in this field has yet to be elucidated. There is much about it in the Mahâ Padhâna Sutta of the Dîgha Nikâya, where Chap. III, §§ 11–20 recur.

[2] The Bodhisatta's voluntary incarnation is looked upon by the Buddhists as a great act of renunciation, and curious legends have

16. 'Again, Ânanda, when a Bodhisatta deliberately and consciously quits his mother's womb, then the earth quakes and trembles and is shaken violently. This is the fourth cause, proximate and remote, of the appearance of a mighty earthquake.

17. 'Again, Ânanda, when a Tathâgata arrives at the supreme and perfect enlightenment, then this earth quakes and trembles and is shaken violently.

---

gathered about it. One is that on the night when she conceived his mother dreamt that a white elephant entered her side. The account will be found at length in my 'Buddhist Birth Stories' (pp. 62–64), and the earthquake is there mentioned in terms identical with those in the text. The sacred event is also one of those represented on the ancient bas-reliefs round the Bharhut Thûpa, a full description of which will be found in General Cunningham's most interesting work, 'The Stupa of Bharhut.' General Cunningham says of the description placed above this sculpture: 'Above it in large characters is inscribed Bhagavato rûkdanta, which may perhaps be translated, "Buddha as the sounding elephant," from ru, to sound, to make a particular sort of sound.' Now the first word of the inscription is in the genitive case, so that if the second word could mean an elephant, the whole would signify, 'The Buddha's elephant.' But the characters which General Cunningham reads rûkdanta are, I venture to suggest, okkanti (? ûkkanti); and the inscription simply says, 'The descent of the blessed One.' As I have pointed out in 'Buddhism' (p. 184), the white elephant legend is one of those hallowed sun stories by which half-converted Hindus have striven to embellish the life story of the Teacher whose followers they had become. In the Lalita Vistara (Calc. ed. p. 63) the entrance of the elephant into Mâyâ precedes the dream; but though the ignorant may have therefore accepted it as a fact, it is of course only a figure of speech—and I venture to think from the Hindu standpoint, a beautiful figure of speech—to express the incarnation of divine mildness and majesty in a human form. The use of such a figure is not confined to India. In the earliest of the Apocryphal Gospels, the Gospel according to the Hebrews, the incarnation of the divine gentleness and love is expressed by saying that a dove from heaven 'entered into' the human form.

This is the fifth cause, proximate and remote, of the appearance of a mighty earthquake.

18. 'Again, Ânanda, when a Tathâgata founds the sublime kingdom of righteousness, then this earth quakes and trembles and is shaken violently. This is the sixth cause, proximate and remote, of the appearance of a mighty earthquake.

19. 'Again, Ânanda, when a Tathâgata consciously and deliberately rejects the remainder of his life, then this earth quakes and trembles and is shaken violently. This is the seventh cause, proximate and remote, of the appearance of a mighty earthquake.

20. 'Again, Ânanda, when a Tathâgata passes entirely away with that utter passing away in which nothing whatever is left behind, then this earth quakes and trembles and is shaken violently. This is the eighth cause, proximate and remote, of the appearance of a mighty earthquake.

---

21. 'Now of eight kinds, Ânanda, are these assemblies. Which are the eight[1]? Assemblies of nobles, Brâhma*n*as, householders, and Sama*n*as, and the angel hosts of the Guardian Angels, the Great Thirty-Three, Mâra, and Brahma.

22. 'Now I call to mind, Ânanda, how when I used to enter into an assembly of many hundred nobles, before I had seated myself there or talked to them or started a conversation with them, I used to become in colour like unto their colour, and in voice like unto their voice. Then with religious discourse

[1] The connection, or rather want of connection, between this and the last paragraph seems to me to be very suggestive as to the way in which the Sutta was composed. The narrative is resumed at paragraph III, 43. On vanishing away, comp. I, 33.

I used to instruct, incite, and quicken them, and fill them with gladness. But they knew me not when I spoke, and would say, "Who may this be who thus speaks? a man or a god?" Then having instructed, incited, quickened, and gladdened them with religious discourse, I would vanish away. But they knew me not even when I vanished away; and would say, "Who may this be who has thus vanished away? a man or a god?"'

23. [And in the same words the Blessed One spake of how he had been used to enter into assemblies of each of the other of the eight kinds, and of how he had not been made known to them either in speaking or in vanishing away.] 'Now these, Ânanda, are the eight assemblies.'

---

24. 'Now these, Ânanda, are the eight positions of mastery [over the delusion arising from the apparent permanence of external things[1]]. What are the eight?

---

[1] Abhibhâyatanî ti abhibhavanakâra*n*âni. Ki*m* abhibhavanti? Pa*kk*anîka-dhamme pi ârammana*n*âni pi: tâni hi pa*t*ipakkha-bhâvena pa*kk*anîka-dhamme abhibhavanti puggalassa *ñ*ânuttaritâya âramma*n*âni, says Buddhaghosa. (Sum. Vil. *th*î.)

This and the next paragraph are based upon the Buddhist belief as to the long-vexed question between the Indian schools who represented more or less closely the European Idealists and Realists. When cleared of the many repetitions inserted for the benefit of the repeaters or reciters, the fundamental idea seems to be that the great necessity is to get rid of the delusion that what one sees and feels is real and permanent. Nothing is real and permanent but character.

The so-called eight Positions of Mastery are merely an expansion of the first two of the following eight Stages of Deliverance, and the whole argument is also expressed in another form in the

25. 'When a man having subjectively the idea of form sees externally forms which are finite, and pleasant or unpleasant to the sight, and having mastered them, is conscious that he knows and sees—this is the first position of mastery.

26. 'When a man having subjectively the idea of form sees externally forms which are boundless, and pleasant or unpleasant to the sight, and having mastered them, is conscious that he knows and sees—this is the second position of mastery.

27. 'When a man without the subjective idea of form sees externally forms which are finite, and pleasant or unpleasant to the sight, and having mastered them, is conscious that he knows and sees—this is the third position of mastery.

28. 'When a man without the subjective idea of form sees externally forms which are boundless, and pleasant or unpleasant to the sight, and having mastered them, is conscious that he knows and sees—this is the fourth position of mastery.

29. 'When a man without the subjective idea of form sees externally forms that are blue in colour, blue in appearance, and reflecting blue,—just, for

---

passage on the nine successive 'Cessations,' of which an abstract will be found in Childers, sub voce nirodha.

The two lists have been translated and commented upon by Burnouf (Lotus de la Bonne Loi, pp. 543, 824–832), who took the texts from the Mahânidâna Sutta and the Sangîti Sutta respectively. The former has been reprinted in Grimblot's Sept Suttas Pâlis, where the passage will be found at pp. 261, 262. I regret that in my interpretation I have been compelled to differ so greatly from Burnouf. Though I have devoted much care and time to the subject, I do not suppose that I have understood it better than he did. We cannot hope to get to the bottom of what these old Buddhists thought about matter and mind from such curt lists as these.

instance, as the Ummâ flower is blue in colour, blue in appearance, and reflecting blue; or, again, as that fine muslin of Benares which, on whichever side you look at it, is blue in colour, blue in appearance, and reflecting blue,—when a man without the subjective idea of form sees externally forms which, just in that way, are blue, blue in colour, blue in appearance, and reflecting blue, and having mastered them, is conscious that he knows and sees—that is the fifth position of mastery.'

30–32. [The sixth, seventh, and eighth positions of mastery are explained in words identical with those used to explain the fifth; save that yellow, red, and white are respectively substituted throughout for blue; and the Ka*n*ikâra flower, the Bandhu-*g*îvaka flower, and the morning star are respectively substituted for the Ummâ flower, as the first of the two objects given as examples.]

---

33. 'Now these stages of deliverance, Ânanda [from the hindrance to thought arising from the sensations and ideas due to external forms[1]], are eight in number. Which are the eight?

34. 'A man possessed with the idea of form sees forms—this is the first stage of deliverance.

35. 'Without the subjective idea of form, he sees forms externally—this is the second stage of deliverance.

---

[1] These are the A*tth*a Vimokkhâ. Buddhaghosa has no comment upon them; merely saying, 'The passage on the Vimokkhas is easy to understand'—which is tantalizing. The last five Vimokkhas occur again below, in Chap. VI, §§ 11–13, where it is clear that they are used to express the progress through deep meditation, into absent-mindedness, abstraction, and being sunk in thought, until finally the thinker falls into actual trance.

36. 'With the thought "it is well," he becomes intent (upon what he sees)—this is the third stage of deliverance.

37. 'By passing quite beyond all idea of form, by putting an end to all idea of resistance, by paying no attention to the idea of distinction, he, thinking "it is all infinite space," reaches (mentally) and remains in the state of mind in which the idea of the infinity of space is the only idea that is present—this is the fourth stage of deliverance.

38. 'By passing quite beyond all idea of space being the infinite basis, he, thinking "it is all infinite reason," reaches (mentally) and remains in the state of mind to which the infinity of reason is alone present—this is the fifth stage of deliverance.

39. 'By passing quite beyond the mere consciousness of the infinity of reason, he, thinking "nothing at all exists," reaches (mentally) and remains in the state of mind to which nothing at all is specially present—this is the sixth stage of deliverance.

40. 'By passing quite beyond all idea of nothingness he reaches (mentally) and remains in the state of mind to which neither ideas nor the absence of ideas are specially present—this is the seventh stage of deliverance.

41. 'By passing quite beyond the state of "neither ideas nor the absence of ideas" he reaches (mentally) and remains in the state of mind in which both sensations and ideas have ceased to be—this is the eighth stage of deliverance.

42. 'Now these, Ânanda, are the eight stages of deliverance.

---

43. 'On one occasion, Ânanda, I was resting under the shepherd's Nigrodha tree on the bank of the

river Nerañgarâ immediately after having reached the great enlightenment. Then Mâra, the Evil One, came, Ânanda, to the place where I was, and standing beside me he addressed me in the words: "Pass away now, Lord, from existence! Let the Blessed One now die! Now is the time for the Blessed One to pass away!"

44. 'And when he had thus spoken, Ânanda, I addressed Mâra, the Evil One, and said: "I shall not die, O Evil One! until not only the brethren and sisters of the order, but also the lay-disciples of either sex shall have become true hearers, wise and well-trained, ready and learned, versed in the Scriptures, fulfilling all the greater and the lesser duties, correct in life, walking according to the precepts—until they, having thus themselves learned the doctrine, shall be able to tell others of it, preach it, make it known, establish it, open it, minutely explain it and make it clear—until they, when others start vain doctrine, shall be able by the truth to vanquish and refute it, and so to spread the wonder-working truth abroad!

45. '"I shall not die until this pure religion of mine shall have become successful, prosperous, wide-spread, and popular in all its full extent—until, in a word, it shall have been well proclaimed among men!"

46. 'And now again to-day, Ânanda, at the *K*âpâla *K*etiya, Mâra, the Evil One, came to the place where I was, and standing beside me addressed me [in the same words].

47. 'And when he had thus spoken, Ânanda, I answered him and said: "Make thyself happy, the final extinction of the Tathâgata shall take place

before long. At the end of three months from this time the Tathâgata will die!"

48. 'Thus, Ânanda, the Tathâgata has now to-day at the *K*âpâla *K*etiya consciously and deliberately rejected the rest of his allotted term of life.'

49. And when he had thus spoken the venerable Ânanda addressed the Blessed One, and said: 'Vouchsafe, Lord, to remain during the kalpa! live on through the kalpa, O Blessed One! for the good and the happiness of the great multitudes, out of pity for the world, for the good and the gain and the weal of gods and men!'

50. 'Enough now, Ânanda, beseech not the Tathâgata!' was the reply. 'The time for making such request is past.'

51. And again, the second time, the venerable Ânanda besought the Blessed One [in the same words. And he received from the Blessed One the same reply].

52. And again, the third time, the venerable Ânanda besought the Blessed One [in the same words].

53. 'Hast thou faith, Ânanda, in the wisdom of the Tathâgata?'

'Even so, Lord!'

'Now why, then, Ânanda, dost thou trouble the Tathâgata even until the third time?'

54. 'From his own mouth have I heard from the Blessed One, from his own mouth have I received this saying, "Whosoever has thought out, Ânanda, and developed, practised, accumulated, and ascended to the very heights of the four paths to saintship, and so mastered them as to be able to use them as

a means of (mental) advancement, and as a basis for edification—he, should he desire it, could remain in the same birth for a kalpa, or for that portion of a kalpa which has yet to run." Now the Tathâgata has thought out and thoroughly practised them [in all respects as just now fully described], and might, should he desire it, remain alive for a kalpa, or for that portion of a kalpa which has yet to run.'

55. 'Hast thou faith, Ânanda?'

'Even so, Lord!'

'Then, O Ânanda, thine is the fault, thine is the offence—in that when a suggestion so evident and a hint so clear were thus given thee by the Tathâgata, thou wast yet incapable of comprehending them, and thou besoughtest not the Tathâgata, saying, "Vouchsafe, Lord, to remain during the kalpa. Live on, O Blessed One! through the kalpa for the good and the happiness of the great multitudes, out of pity for the world, for the good and the gain and the weal of gods and men." If thou shouldst then have so besought the Tathâgata, the Tathâgata might have rejected the appeal even to the second time, but the third time he would have granted it. Thine, therefore, O Ânanda, is the fault, thine is the offence!'

56. 'On one occasion, Ânanda, I was dwelling at Râgagaha, on the hill called the Vulture's Peak. Now there, Ânanda, I spoke to thee, and said: "How pleasant a spot, Ânanda, is Râgagaha; how pleasant is this Vulture's Peak. Whosoever has thought out, Ânanda, and developed, practised, accumulated, and ascended to the very heights of the four paths to saintship, and so mastered them as to be able to use them as a means of (mental) advancement, and as a basis for edification—he, should he

desire it, could remain in the same birth for a kalpa, or for that portion of a kalpa which has yet to run. But even when a suggestion so evident and a hint so clear were thus given thee by the Tathâgata, thou wast yet incapable of comprehending them, and thou besoughtest not the Tathâgata, saying, 'Vouchsafe, Lord, to remain during the kalpa. Live on, O Blessed One! through the kalpa for the good and the happiness of the great multitudes, out of pity for the world, for the good and the gain and the weal of gods and men.' If thou shouldst then have so besought the Tathâgata, the Tathâgata might have rejected the appeal even to the second time, but the third time he would have granted it. Thine, therefore, O Ânanda, is the fault, thine is the offence!"

57. 'On one occasion, Ânanda, I was dwelling at that same Râ*g*agaha in the Banyan Grove—on one occasion at that same Râ*g*agaha at the Robbers' Cliff—on one occasion at that same Râ*g*agaha in the Sattapa*nn*i cave on the slope of Mount Vebhâra—on one occasion at that same Râ*g*agaha at the Black Rock on the slope of Mount Isigili—on one occasion at that same Râ*g*agaha in the Sîtavana Grove in the mountain cave Sappaso*nd*ika — on one occasion at that same Râ*g*agaha in the Tapoda Grove—on one occasion at that same Râ*g*agaha in the Bambu Grove in the Squirrels' Feeding Ground—on one occasion at that same Râ*g*agaha in *G*îvaka's Mango Grove—on one occasion at that same Râ*g*agaha in the Deer Forest at Maddaku*kkh*i.'

58. 'Now there too, Ânanda, I spoke to thee, and said: "How pleasant, Ânanda, is Râ*g*agaha; how pleasant the Vulture's Peak; how pleasant the

Banyan tree of Gotama; how pleasant the Robbers' Cliff; how pleasant the Sattapa*nn*i cave on the slope of Mount Vebhâra; how pleasant the Black Rock on the slope of Mount Isigili; how pleasant the mountain cave Sappaso*nd*ika in the Sîtavana Grove; how pleasant the Tapoda Grove; how pleasant the Squirrels' Feeding Ground in the Bambu Grove; how pleasant *G*îvaka's Mango Grove; how pleasant the Deer Forest at Maddaku*kkh*i!

59. '"Whosoever, Ânanda, has thought out and developed, practised, accumulated, and ascended to the very heights of the four paths to saintship, and so mastered them as to be able to use them as a means of (mental) advancement and as a basis for edification—he, should he desire it, could remain in the same birth for a kalpa, or for that portion of a kalpa which has yet to run." Now the Tathâgata has thought out and thoroughly practised them [in all respects as just now fully described], and might, should he desire it, remain alive for a kalpa, or for that portion of a kalpa which has yet to run.'

60. 'On one occasion, Ânanda, I was residing here at Vesâli at the Udena *K*etiya. And there too, Ânanda, I spoke to thee, and said: "How pleasant, Ânanda, is Vesâli; how pleasant the Udena *K*etiya. Whosoever, Ânanda, has thought out and developed, practised, accumulated, and ascended to the very heights of the four paths to saintship, and so mastered them as to be able to use them as a means of (mental) advancement and as a basis for edification—he, should he desire it, could remain in the same birth for a kalpa, or for that portion of a kalpa which has yet to run." Now the Tathâgata has thought out and thoroughly practised

them [in all respects as just now fully described], and might, should he desire it, remain alive for a kalpa, or for that portion of a kalpa which has yet to run.'

61. 'On one occasion, Ânanda, I was dwelling here at Vesâli at the Gotamaka *K*etiya—on one occasion here at Vesâli at the Sattamba *K*etiya—on one occasion here at Vesâli at the Bahuputta *K*etiya—on one occasion here at Vesâli at the Sârandada *K*etiya [and on each occasion I spoke to thee, Ânanda, in the same words].

62. 'And now to-day, Ânanda, at the *K*âpâla *K*etiya, I spoke to thee, and said: "How pleasant, Ânanda, is Vesâli; how pleasant the Udena *K*etiya; how pleasant the Gotamaka *K*etiya; how pleasant the Sattamba *K*etiya; how pleasant the Bahuputta *K*etiya; how pleasant the Sârandada *K*etiya. Whosoever, Ânanda, has thought out and developed, practised, accumulated, and ascended to the very heights of the four paths to saintship, and so mastered them as to be able to use them as a means of (mental) advancement, and as a basis for edification—he, should he desire it, could remain in the same birth for a kalpa, or for that portion of a kalpa which has yet to run. Now the Tathâgata has thought and thoroughly practised them [in all respects as just now fully described], and might, should he desire it, remain alive for a kalpa, or for that portion of a kalpa which has yet to run."

---

63. 'But now, Ânanda, have I not formerly[1] de-

[1] That pa*t*iga*kk*' eva means 'formerly, already' is clear from Mahâ Vagga I, 7, 1; X, 2, 3, though its derivation would seem to render the meaning 'frequently, recurringly' more natural. The

clared to you that it is in the very nature of all things, near and dear unto us, that we must divide ourselves from them, leave them, sever ourselves from them? How then, Ânanda, can this be possible—whereas anything whatever born, brought into being, and organised, contains within itself the inherent necessity of dissolution—how then can this be possible that such a being should not be dissolved? No such condition can exist! And this mortal being, Ânanda, has been relinquished, cast away, renounced, rejected, and abandoned by the Tathâgata. The remaining sum of life has been surrendered by him. Verily, the word has gone forth from the Tathâgata, saying, "The final extinction of the Tathâgata shall take place before long. At the end of three months from this time the Tathâgata will die!" That the Tathâgata for the sake of living should repent him again of that saying—this can no wise be[1]!'

---

64. 'Come, Ânanda, let us go to the Kû*t*âgâra Hall, to the Mahâvana.'

'Even so, Lord!' said the venerable Ânanda, in assent, to the Blessed One.

Then the Blessed One proceeded, with Ânanda

---

phrase occurs pretty often. Trenckner (milinda-pañha*m*, p. 422) proposes a correction into pa*t*ika*kk*' eva. Palu*gg*îti just below is noteworthy as an unusual contraction of palu*gg*e iti.

[1] I do not understand the connection of ideas between this paragraph and the idea repeated with such tedious iteration in the preceding paragraphs. The two seem to be in marked contrast, if not in absolute contradiction. Perhaps we have here the older tradition; and certainly the latter utterance of the two is more in accordance with the general impression of the character, and with the other sayings, of Gotama as handed down in the Pâli Pi*t*akas.

with him, to the Mahâvana to the Kû*t*âgâra Hall: and when he had arrived there he addressed the venerable Ânanda, and said:

'Go now, Ânanda, and assemble in the Service Hall such of the brethren as reside in the neighbourhood of Vesâli.'

'Even so, Lord,' said the venerable Ânanda, in assent, to the Blessed One. And when he had assembled in the Service Hall such of the brethren as resided in the neighbourhood of Vesâli, he went to the Blessed One and saluted him and stood beside him. And standing beside him, he addressed the Blessed One, and said:

'Lord! the assembly of the brethren has met together. Let the Blessed One do even as seemeth to him fit.'

65. Then the Blessed One proceeded to the Service Hall, and sat down there on the mat spread out for him. And when he was seated the Blessed One addressed the brethren, and said:

'Therefore, O brethren—ye to whom the truths I have perceived have been made known by me—having thoroughly made yourselves masters of them, practise them, meditate upon them, and spread them abroad; in order that pure religion may last long and be perpetuated, in order that it may continue to be for the good and happiness of the great multitudes, out of pity for the world, to the good and the gain and the weal of gods and men!

'Which then, O brethren, are the truths which, when I had perceived, I made known to you, which, when you have mastered it behoves you to practise, meditate upon, and spread abroad, in order that pure religion may last long and be perpetuated, in order that it may continue to be for the good and the happiness of the great multitudes, out of pity for the world, to the good and the gain and the weal of gods and men?'

They are these:

The four earnest meditations.
The fourfold great struggle against sin.
The four roads to saintship.
The five moral powers.
The five organs of spiritual sense.
The seven kinds of wisdom, and
The noble eightfold path.

These, O brethren, are the truths which, when I had perceived, I made known to you, which, when you have mastered it behoves you to practise, meditate upon, and spread abroad, in order that pure religion may last long and be perpetuated, in order that it may continue to be for the good and the happiness of the great multitudes, out of pity for the world, to the good and the gain and the weal of gods and men!

---

66. And the Blessed One exhorted the brethren, and said:

'Behold now, O brethren, I exhort you, saying, "All component things must grow old. Work out your salvation with diligence. The final extinction of the Tathâgata will take place before long. At the end of three months from this time the Tathâgata will die!"

'My age is now full ripe, my life draws to its close:
I leave you, I depart, relying on myself alone!
Be earnest then, O brethren! holy, full of thought!

Be steadfast in resolve! Keep watch o'er your
own hearts!
Who wearies not, but holds fast to this truth
and law[1],
Shall cross this sea of life, shall make an end of
grief.'

End of the Third Portion for Recitation[2].

---

[1] Dhamma and vinaya. The Buddhist religion, as just summarised, and the regulations of the order.

[2] It is of great interest to notice what are the points upon which Gotama, in this last address to his disciples, and at the solemn time when death was so near at hand, is reported to have lain such emphatic stress. Unfortunately we have only a fragment of the address, and, as it would seem from its commencement, only the closing fragment. This, however, is in the form of a summary, consisting of an enumeration of certain aggregates, the details of which must have been as familiar to the early Buddhists as the details of similar numerical terms—such as the ten commandments, the twelve tribes, the seven deadly sins, the four gospels, and so on—afterwards were to the Christians. This summary of the Buddha's last address may fairly be taken as a summary of Buddhism, which thus appears to be simply a system of earnest self-culture and self-control.

The following are the details of the aggregate technical terms used in the above summary, but it will be understood that the English equivalents used give rather a general than an exact representation of the ideas expressed by the Pâli ones. To attempt more would demand a treatise rather than a note, and it has given me peculiar pleasure to learn, as these sheets are passing through the press, that my friend Dr. Morris intends to devote a book to the treatment of these seven 'Jewels of the Law,' as the *K*ulla Vagga calls them (IX, 1, 4), which form, when united, the bright diadem of Nirvâ*n*a.

The four Earnest Meditations (*k*attâro Satipa*tth*ânâ) are—

1. Meditation on the body.
2. Meditation on the sensations.
3. Meditation on the ideas.
4. Meditation on reason and character.

The fourfold Great Struggle against sin is divided into *k*attâro Samappadhânâ, which are—

1. The struggle to prevent sinfulness arising.
2. The struggle to put away sinful states which have arisen.
3. The struggle to produce goodness not previously existing.
4. The struggle to increase goodness when it does exist.

The four Roads to Saintship are four means by which Iddhî (see above, § 3, note) is to be acquired. They are the *K*attâro Iddhipâdâ:

1. The will to acquire it united to earnest meditation and the struggle against sin.

2. The necessary exertion united to earnest meditation and the struggle against sin.

3. The necessary preparation of the heart united to earnest meditation and the struggle against sin.

4. Investigation united to earnest meditation and the struggle against sin.

The five moral powers (pañ*k*a Balâni) are said to be the same as the next class, called organs (Indriyâni). It is no doubt most remarkable that, in a summary like this, two classes out of seven should be absolutely identical except in name. The difference of name is altogether too unimportant to account, by itself, for the distinction made. Either the currently accepted explanation of one of the two aggregate terms must be incorrect, or we must look for some explanation of the repetition other than the mere desire to record the double title. Is it impossible that the one class was split into two to bring the number of the classes up to the sacred number seven, corresponding to the seven Ratanas of a *K*akkavatti?

The details of both classes are—

1. Faith. 2. Energy. 3. Thought. 4. Contemplation. 5. Wisdom.

The seven kinds of Wisdom (satta Bog*g*h*a*ngâ) are—

1. Energy. 2. Thought. 3. Contemplation. 4. Investigation (of scripture). 5. Joy. 6. Repose. 7. Serenity.

The Noble Eightfold Path (ariyo a*tth*angiko Maggo) forms the subject of the Dhamma-*k*akka-ppavattana-sutta, translated in this volume, and consists of—

1. Right views. 2. High aims. 3. Right speech. 4. Upright conduct. 5. A harmless livelihood. 6. Perseverance in well-doing. 7. Intellectual activity. 8. Earnest thought.

CHAPTER IV.

1. Now the Blessed One early in the morning robed himself, and taking his bowl, entered Vesâli for alms: and when he had passed through Vesâli, and had eaten his meal and was returning from his alms-seeking he gazed at Vesâli with an elephant look[1] and addressed the venerable Ânanda, and said: 'This will be the last time, Ânanda, that the Tathâgata will behold Vesâli. Come, Ânanda, let us go on to Bha*nd*a-gâma.'

'Even so, Lord!' said the venerable Ânanda, in assent, to the Blessed One.

And the Blessed One proceeded with a great company of the brethren to Bha*nd*a-gâma; and there the Blessed One stayed in the village itself.

2. There the Blessed One addressed the brethren, and said: 'It is through not understanding and grasping four truths[2], O brethren, that we have had to run so long, to wander so long in this weary path of transmigration—both you and I.'

'And what are these four? The noble conduct of life, the noble earnestness in meditation, the noble kind of wisdom, and the noble salvation of freedom. But when noble conduct is realised and known, when noble meditation is realised and known, when noble wisdom is realised and known, when noble

[1] Nâgapalokita*m* Vesâliya*m* apaloketvâ. The Buddhas were accustomed, says Buddhaghosa, on looking backwards to turn the whole body round as an elephant does; because the bones in their neck were firmly fixed, more so than those of ordinary men!

[2] Or Conditions (Dhammâ). They must, of course, be carefully distinguished from the better known Four Noble Truths (Sa*kk*âni) above, Chap. II, § 2.

freedom is realised and known—then is the craving for existence rooted out, that which leads to renewed existence is destroyed, and there is no more birth.'

3. Thus spake the Blessed One; and when the Happy One had thus spoken, then again the teacher said[1]:

'Righteousness, earnest thought, wisdom, and freedom sublime—
These are the truths realised by Gotama, far-renowned.
Knowing them, he, the knower, proclaimed the truth to the brethren.
The master with eye divine, the quencher of griefs, must die!'

---

4. There too, while staying at Bha*nd*a-gâma, the Blessed One held that comprehensive religious discourse with the brethren on the nature of upright conduct, and of earnest contemplation, and of intelligence. 'Great is the fruit, great the advantage of earnest contemplation when set round with upright conduct. Great is the fruit, great the advantage of intellect when set round with earnest contemplation.

[1] This is merely a stock phrase for introducing verses which repeat the idea of the preceding phrase (see above, paragraph 32). It is an instructive sign of the state of mind in which such records are put together, that these verses could be ascribed to Gotama himself without any feeling of the incongruity involved. The last word means, completely gone out; and here refers to the extinction of kilesa and ta*n*hâ, which will bring about, inevitably, the extinction of being. Compare the passage quoted by Burnouf in Lotus de la Bonne Loi, p. 376. Probably the whole stanza formerly stood in some other connection, where the word parinibbuto had its more usual sense. See Buddhaghosa's note on IV, 23.

The mind set round with intelligence is freed from the great evils—that is to say, from sensuality, from individuality, from delusion, and from ignorance.'

---

5. Now when the Blessed One had remained at Bha*nd*a-gâma as long as he desired, he addressed the venerable Ânanda, and said: 'Come, Ânanda, let us go on to Hatthi-gâma.'

'Even so, Lord!' said Ânanda, in assent, to the Blessed One.

Then the Blessed One proceeded with a great company of the brethren to Hatthi-gâma.

6. [And in similar words it is then related how the Blessed One went on to Amba-gâma, to *G*ambu-gâma, and to Bhoga-nagara.]

---

7. Now there at Bhoga-nagara the Blessed One stayed at the Ânanda *K*etiya.

There the Blessed One addressed the brethren, and said: 'I will teach you, O brethren, these four Great References[1]. Listen thereto, and give good heed, and I will speak.'

'Even so, Lord!' said the brethren, in assent[2], to

---

[1] The meaning of mahâpadesa is not quite clear. Perhaps it should be rendered true authorities. I have followed Buddhaghosa in taking apadesa as the last part of the compound. He says, mahâpadesâ ti mahâ-okâse mahâ-apadese vâ. Buddhâdayo mahante mahante apadisitvâ vuttâni mahâkâra*n*âni ti attho, 'the causes (authorities) alleged when referring to Buddha and other great men.'

[2] I ought perhaps to have explained why I have ventured to differ from Childers in the rendering of the common word pa*t*i-su*n*âti. The root *s*ru seems to have meant 'to sound' before it meant 'to hear;' and, whether this be so or not, pa*t*i-su*n*âti means not simply 'to consent,' but 'to answer (assentingly).' It

the Blessed One, and the Blessed One spoke as follows:

8. 'In the first place, brethren, a brother may say thus: "From the mouth of the Blessed One himself have I heard, from his own mouth have I received it. This is the truth, this the law, this the teaching of the Master." The word spoken, brethren, by that brother should neither be received with praise nor treated with scorn. Without praise and without scorn every word and syllable should be carefully understood, and then put beside the scripture and compared with the rules of the order[1]. If when so compared they do not harmonise with the scripture, and do not fit in with the rules of the order, then you may come to the conclusion, "Verily, this is not the word of the Blessed One, and has been wrongly grasped by that brother?" Therefore, brethren, you should reject it. But if they harmonise with the scripture and fit in with the rules of the order, then you may come to the conclusion, "Verily, this is the word of the Blessed One, and has been well grasped by that brother." This, brethren, you should receive as the first Great Reference.

9. 'Again, brethren, a brother may say thus: "In such and such a dwelling-place there is a company of the brethren with their elders and leaders. From the mouth of that company have I heard,

has been pointed out to me that answer was formerly 'andswerian,' where swerian is probably not unrelated to the root svar, 'to sound.'

[1] Sutte otâretabbâni vinaye sandassetabbâni, where one would expect to find the word Pi*t*aka if it had been in use when this passage was first written or composed.

face to face have I received it. This is the truth, this the law, this the teaching of the Master." The word spoken, brethren, by that brother should neither be received with praise nor treated with scorn. Without praise and without scorn every word and syllable should be carefully understood, and then put beside the scripture and compared with the rules of the order. If when so compared they do not harmonise with the scripture, and do not fit in with the rules of the order, then you may come to the conclusion, "Verily, this is not the word of the Blessed One, and has been wrongly grasped by that company of the brethren." Therefore, brethren, you should reject it. But if they harmonise with the scripture and fit in with the rules of the order, then you may come to the conclusion, "Verily, this is the word of the Blessed One, and has been well grasped by that company of the brethren." This, brethren, you should receive as the second Great Reference.

10. 'Again, brethren, a brother may say thus: "In such and such a dwelling-place there are dwelling many elders of the order, deeply read, holding the faith as handed down by tradition, versed in the truths, versed in the regulations of the order, versed in the summaries of the doctrines and the law. From the mouth of those elders have I heard, from their mouth have I received it. This is the truth, this the law, this the teaching of the Master." The word spoken, brethren, by that brother should neither be received with praise nor treated with scorn. Without praise and without scorn every word and syllable should be carefully understood, and then put beside the scripture and

compared with the rules of the order. If when so compared they do not harmonise with the scripture, and do not fit in with the rules of the order, then you may come to the conclusion, "Verily, this is not the word of the Blessed One, and has been wrongly grasped by those elders." Therefore, brethren, you should reject it. But if they harmonise with the scripture and fit in with the rules of the order, then you may come to the conclusion, "Verily, this is the word of the Blessed One, and has been well grasped by those elders." This, brethren, you should receive as the third Great Reference.

11. 'Again, brethren, a brother may say, "In such and such a dwelling-place there is there living a brother, deeply read, holding the faith as handed down by tradition, versed in the truths, versed in the regulations of the order, versed in the summaries of the doctrines and the law. From the mouth of that elder have I heard, from his mouth have I received it. This is the truth, this the law, this the teaching of the Master." The word spoken, brethren, by that brother should neither be received with praise nor treated with scorn. Without praise and without scorn every word and syllable should be carefully understood, and then put beside the scripture and compared with the rules of the order. If when so compared they do not harmonise with the scripture, and do not fit in with the rules of the order, then you may come to the conclusion, "Verily, this is not the word of the Blessed One, and has been wrongly grasped by that brother." Therefore, brethren, you should reject it. But if they harmonise with the scripture

and fit in with the rules of the order, then you may come to the conclusion, "Verily, this is the word of the Blessed One, and has been well grasped by that brother." This, brethren, you should receive as the fourth Great Reference.'

'These, brethren, are the Four Great References.'

---

12. There, too, the Blessed One held that comprehensive religious talk with the brethren on the nature of upright conduct, and of earnest contemplation, and of intelligence. 'Great is the fruit, great the advantage of earnest contemplation when set round with upright conduct. Great is the fruit, great the advantage of intellect when set round with earnest contemplation. The mind set round with intelligence is freed from the great evils—that is to say, from sensuality, from individuality, from delusion, and from ignorance.'

---

13. Now when the Blessed One had remained as long as he desired at Bhoga-gâma, he addressed the venerable Ânanda, and said: 'Come, Ânanda, let us go on to Pâvâ.'

'Even so, Lord!' said the venerable Ânanda, in assent, to the Blessed One. And the Blessed One proceeded with a great company of the brethren to Pâvâ.

And there at Pâvâ the Blessed One stayed at the Mango Grove of *K*unda, who was by family a smith.

---

14. Now *K*unda, the worker in metals, heard that the Blessed One had come to Pâvâ, and was staying there in his Mango Grove.

And *K*unda, the worker in metals, went to the place where the Blessed One was, and saluting him took his seat respectfully on one side. And when he was thus seated, the Blessed One instructed, aroused, incited, and gladdened him with religious discourse.

15. Then he, instructed, aroused, incited, and gladdened by the religious discourse, addressed the Blessed One, and said: 'May the Blessed One do me the honour of taking his meal, together with the brethren, at my house to-morrow.'

And the Blessed One signified, by silence, his consent.

16. Then seeing that the Blessed One had consented, *K*unda, the worker in metals, rose from his seat and bowed down before the Blessed One, and keeping him on his right hand as he past him, departed thence.

17. Now at the end of the night, *K*unda, the worker in metals, made ready in his dwelling-place sweet rice and cakes, and a quantity of dried boar's flesh. And he announced the hour to the Blessed One, saying, 'The hour, Lord, has come, and the meal is ready.'

18. And the Blessed One robed himself early in the morning, and taking his bowl, went with the brethren to the dwelling-place of *K*unda, the worker in metals. When he had come thither he seated himself on the seat prepared for him. And when he was seated he addressed *K*unda, the worker in metals, and said: 'As to the dried boar's flesh you have made ready, serve me with it, *K*unda; and as to the other food, the sweet rice and cakes, serve the brethren with it.'

'Even so, Lord!' said *K*unda, the worker in metals, in assent, to the Blessed One. And the dried boar's flesh he had made ready he served to the Blessed One; whilst the other food, the sweet rice and cakes, he served to the members of the order.

19. Now the Blessed One addressed *K*unda, the worker in metals, and said: 'Whatever dried boar's flesh, *K*unda, is left over to thee, that bury in a hole. I see no one, *K*unda, on earth nor in Mâra's heaven, nor in Brahma's heaven, no one among Sama*n*as and Brâhma*n*as, among gods and men, by whom, when he has eaten it, that food can be assimilated, save by the Tathâgata.'

'Even so, Lord!' said *K*unda, the worker in metals, in assent, to the Blessed One. And whatever dried boar's flesh remained over, that he buried in a hole.

20. And he went to the place where the Blessed One was; and when he had come there, took his seat respectfully on one side. And when he was seated, the Blessed One instructed and aroused and incited and gladdened *K*unda, the worker in metals, with religious discourse. And the Blessed One then rose from his seat and departed thence.

21. Now when the Blessed One had eaten the food prepared by *K*unda, the worker in metal, there fell upon him a dire sickness, the disease of dysentery, and sharp pain came upon him, even unto death. But the Blessed One, mindful and self-possessed, bore it without complaint.

22. And the Blessed One addressed the venerable Ânanda, and said: 'Come, Ânanda, let us go on to Kusinârâ.'

'Even so, Lord!' said the venerable Ânanda, in assent, to the Blessed One.

---

23. When he had eaten *K*unda's food,
The copper-smith's—thus have I heard—
He bore with fortitude the pain,
The sharp pain even unto death!

And from the dried flesh of the boar, as soon as he had eaten it,
There fell upon the teacher sickness dire,
Then after nature was relieved the Blessed One announced and said:
'I now am going on to Kusinârâ [1].'

---

24. Now the Blessed One went aside from the path to the foot of a certain tree; and when he had come there he addressed the venerable Ânanda, and said: 'Fold, I pray you, Ânanda, the robe; and spread it out for me. I am weary, Ânanda, and must rest awhile!'

'Even so, Lord!' said the venerable Ânanda, in assent, to the Blessed One, and spread out the robe folded fourfold.

25. And the Blessed One seated himself on the seat prepared for him; and when he was seated, he addressed the venerable Ânanda, and said: 'Fetch me, I pray you, Ânanda, some water. I am thirsty, Ânanda, and would drink.'

26. When he had thus spoken, the venerable Ânanda said to the Blessed One: 'But just now,

---

[1] 'It should be understood,' says Buddhaghosa, 'that these are verses by the Theras who held the council.' And he repeats this at §§ 52, 56.

Lord, about five hundred carts have gone over. That water stirred up by the wheels has become shallow and flows fouled and turbid. This river Kakutthâ, Lord, not far off, is clear and pleasant, cool and transparent, easy to get down into, and delightful. There the Blessed One may both drink the water, and cool his limbs[1].'

27. Again the second time the Blessed One addressed the venerable Ânanda, and said: 'Fetch me, I pray you, Ânanda, some water. I am thirsty, Ânanda, and would drink.'

28. And again the second time the venerable Ânanda said to the Blessed One: 'But just now, Lord, about five hundred carts have gone over. That water stirred up by the wheels has become shallow and flows fouled and turbid. This river Kakutthâ, Lord, not far off, is clear and pleasant, cool and transparent, easy to get down into, and delightful. There the Blessed One may both drink the water, and cool his limbs.'

29. Again the third time the Blessed One addressed the venerable Ânanda, and said: 'Fetch me, I pray you, Ânanda, some water. I am thirsty, Ânanda, and would drink.'

30. 'Even so, Lord!' said the venerable Ânanda, in assent, to the Blessed One; and taking a bowl he went down to the streamlet. And lo! the streamlet which, stirred up by the wheels, was but just now become shallow, and was flowing fouled and turbid, had begun, when the venerable Ânanda came up to it, to flow clear and bright and free from all turbidity.

[1] A*kkh*odikâ ti pasannodikâ: sâtodikâ ti madhurodhikâ: sîtodikâ ti tanu-sîtala-salilâ: setakâ ti nikkaddamâ: supatitthâ ti sundara-titthâ. (S.V. *thri.*) Comp. IV, 56.

31. Then Ânanda thought: 'How wonderful, how marvellous is the great might and power of the Tathâgata! For this streamlet which, stirred up by the wheels, was but just now become shallow and flowing foul and turbid, now, as I come up to it, is flowing clear and bright and free from all turbidity.'

32. And taking water in the bowl he returned towards the Blessed One; and when he had come where the Blessed One was he said to him: 'How wonderful, how marvellous is the great might and power of the Tathâgata! For this streamlet which, stirred up by the wheels, was but just now become shallow and flowing foul and turbid, now, as I come up to it, is flowing clear and bright and free from all turbidity. Let the Blessed One drink the water! Let the Happy One drink the water!'

Then the Blessed One drank of the water.

---

33. Now at that time a man named Pukkusa[1], a young Mallian, a disciple of Â*l*âra Kâlâma's, was passing along the high road from Kusinârâ to Pâvâ.

34. And Pukkusa, the young Mallian, saw the Blessed One seated at the foot of a tree. On seeing him, he went up to the place where the Blessed One was, and when he had come there he saluted the Blessed One, and took his rest respectfully on one side. And when he was seated

[1] The Pukkusa caste was one of the lower castes of *S*ûdras. Compare Assâlâyana Sutta (Pischel), pp. 13, 35; Burnouf's 'Introduction,' &c., pp. 144, 208; Lalita Vistara XXI, 17. But Buddhaghosa says Pukkusa must here be simply a name, as the Mallas were of the Khattiya caste. He adds that this Pukkusa was the owner of the five hundred carts that had just passed by; and that Â*l*âra Kâlâma was called Â*l*âra because he was Dîgha-piṅgalo, Kâlâma being his family name.

Pukkusa, the young Mallian, said to the Blessed One: 'How wonderful a thing is it, Lord! and how marvellous, that those who have gone forth out of the world should pass their time in a state of mind so calm!'

35. 'Formerly, Lord, Â*l*âra Kâlâma was once walking along the high road; and leaving the road he sat himself down under a certain tree to rest during the heat of the day. Now, Lord, five hundred carts passed by one after the other, each close to Â*l*âra Kâlâma. And a certain man, who was following close behind that caravan of carts, went up to the place where Â*l*âra Kâlâma was, and when he was come there he spake as follows to Â*l*âra Kâlâma:

'"But, Lord, did you see those five hundred carts go by?"

'"No, indeed, sir, I saw them not."

'"But, Lord, did you hear the sound of them?"

'"No, indeed, sir, I heard not their sound."

'"But, Lord, were you then asleep?"

'"No, sir, I was not asleep."

'"But, Lord, were you then conscious."

'"Yes, I was conscious, sir."

'"So that you, Lord, though you were both conscious and awake, neither saw, nor heard the sound of five hundred carts passing by, one after the other, and each close to you. Why, Lord, even your robe was sprinkled over with the dust of them!"

'"It is even so, sir."

36. 'Then thought that man: "How wonderful a thing is it, and how marvellous, that those who have gone forth out of the world should pass their time in a state of mind so calm! So much so that a man though being both conscious and awake,

neither sees, nor hears the sound of five hundred carts passing by, one after the other, and each close to him."

'And after giving utterance to his deep faith in Â*l*âra Kâlâma, he departed thence.'

37. 'Now what think you, Pukkusa, which is the more difficult thing either to do or to meet with—that a man being conscious and awake should neither see, nor hear the sound of five hundred carts passing by, one after the other, close to him,—or that a man, being conscious and awake, should neither see, nor hear the sound thereof when the falling rain goes on beating and splashing, and the lightnings are flashing forth, and the thunderbolts are crashing?'

38. 'What in comparison, Lord, can these five hundred carts do, or six or seven or eight or nine or ten hundred, yea, even hundreds and thousands of carts. That certainly is more difficult, both to do and to meet with, that a man being conscious and awake should neither see, nor hear the sound thereof when the falling rain goes on beating and splashing, and the lightnings are flashing forth, and the thunderbolts are crashing.'

39. 'Now on one occasion, Pukkusa, I was dwelling at Âtumâ, and was at the Threshing-floor[1]. And at that time the falling rain begun to beat and to splash, and the lightnings to flash forth, and the thunderbolts to crash; and two peasants, brothers, and four oxen were killed. Then, Pukkusa, a great multitude of people went forth from Âtumâ, and went up to the place where the two peasants, brothers, and the four oxen, lay killed.

[1] Bhusâgâre ti kha*l*u-sâlâya*m*. (S.V. *thri.*)

40. 'Now at that time, Pukkusa, I had gone forth from the Threshing-floor, and was walking up and down thinking at the entrance to the Threshing-floor. And a certain man came, Pukkusa, out of that great multitude of people, up to the place where I was; and when he came up he saluted me, and took his place respectfully on one side.

41. 'And as he stood there, Pukkusa, I said to the man:

'"Why then, sir, is this great multitude of people assembled together?"

'"But just now, the falling rain began to beat and to splash, and the lightnings to flash forth, and the thunderbolts to crash; and two peasants, brothers, were killed, and four oxen. Therefore is this great multitude of people gathered together. But where, Lord, were you?"

'"I, sir, have been here all the while."

'"But, Lord, did you see it?"

'"I, sir, saw nothing."

'"But, Lord, did you hear it?"

'"I, sir, heard nothing."

'"Were you then, Lord, asleep?"

'"I, sir, was not asleep."

'"Were you then conscious, Lord?"

'"Even so, sir."

'"So that you, Lord, being conscious and awake, neither saw, nor heard the sound thereof when the falling rain went on beating and splashing, and the lightnings were flashing forth, and the thunderbolts were crashing."

'"That is so, sir."

42. 'Then, Pukkusa, the thought occurred to that man:

'"How wonderful a thing is it, and marvellous, that those who have gone forth out of the world should pass their time in a state of mind so calm!— so that a man being conscious and awake neither sees nor hears the sound thereof when the falling rain is beating and splashing, and the lightnings are flashing forth, and the thunderbolts are crashing." And after giving utterance to his deep faith in me, he departed from me with the customary demonstrations of respect.'

43. And when he had thus spoken Pukkusa, the young Mallian, addressed the Blessed One in these words: 'Now I, Lord, as to the faith that I had in Â*l*âra Kâlâma, that I winnow away as in a mighty wind, and wash it away as in a swiftly running stream. Most excellent, Lord, are the words of thy mouth, most excellent! Just as if a man were to set up that which is thrown down, or were to reveal that which is hidden away, or were to point out the right road to him who has gone astray, or were to bring a lamp into the darkness, so that those who have eyes can see external forms—just even so, Lord, has the truth been made known to me, in many a figure, by the Blessed One. And I, even I, betake myself, Lord, to the Blessed One as my refuge, to the Truth, and to the Brotherhood. May the Blessed One accept me as a disciple, as a true believer, from this day forth, as long as life endures[1]!'

[1] This is a stock phrase constituting the final answer of a hitherto unconverted man at the end of one of those argumentative dialogues by which Gotama overcame opposition or expounded the truth. After a discussion of exalted themes it fits in very appropriately; here and elsewhere it is incongruous and strained. See below, V, 50.

44. Now Pukkusa, the young Mallian, addressed a certain man, and said: 'Fetch me, I pray you, my good man, a pair of robes of cloth of gold, burnished and ready for wear.'

'So be it, sir!' said that man, in assent, to Pukkusa, the young Mallian; and he brought a pair of robes of cloth of gold, burnished and ready for wear.

45. And the Mallian Pukkusa presented the pair of robes of cloth of gold, burnished and ready for wear, to the Blessed One, saying, 'Lord, this pair of robes of burnished cloth of gold is ready for wear. May the Blessed One show me favour and accept it at my hands!'

'In that case, Pukkusa, robe me in one, and Ânanda in one.'

'Even so, Lord!' said Pukkusa, in assent, to the Blessed One; and in one he robed the Blessed One, and in one, Ânanda.

46. Then the Blessed One instructed and aroused and incited and gladdened Pukkusa, the young Mallian, with religious discourse. And Pukkusa, the young Mallian, when he had been instructed and aroused and incited and gladdened by the Blessed One with religious discourse, arose from his seat, and bowed down before the Blessed One; and keeping him on his right hand as he past him, departed thence.

---

47. Now not long after the Mallian Pukkusa had gone, the venerable Ânanda placed that pair of robes of cloth of gold, burnished and ready for wear, on the body of the Blessed One, and when it was so

placed on the body of the Blessed One it appeared to have lost its splendour[1]!

48. And the venerable Ânanda said to the Blessed One: 'How wonderful a thing is it, Lord, and how marvellous, that the colour of the skin of the Blessed One should be so clear, so exceeding bright! For when I placed even this pair of robes of burnished cloth of gold and ready for wear on the body of the Blessed One, lo! it seemed as if it had lost its splendour!'

49. 'It is even so, Ânanda. Ânanda, there are two occasions on which the colour of the skin of a Tathâgata becomes clear and exceeding bright. What are the two?'

50. 'On the night, Ânanda, on which a Tathâgata attains to the supreme and perfect insight, and on the night in which he passes finally away in that utter passing away which leaves nothing whatever to remain—on these two occasions the colour of the skin of the Tathâgata becomes clear and exceeding bright.

51. 'And now this day, Ânanda, at the third watch of the night, in the Upavattana of Kusinârâ, in the Sâla Grove of the Mallians, between the twin Sâla

---

[1] The commentator says, Bhagavato kâyam upanâmitan ti nivâsana-pârûpana-vasena alliyâpita*m*: Bhagavâ pi tato eka*m* nivâsesi eka*m* pârûpi. Vîta*kk*ika*m* (MS. *kkh*) viyâ ti yathâ (MS. tathâ) vîta*kk*iko aṅgâro antanten' eva *g*otîti bahi pan' assa pabhâ n' atthi, evam bahi pa*kkh*inna- (MS. pa*kkh*i*nn*a-) pabhâ hutvâ khâyatî ti. My MS. of the text reads vitâsika*m* (as did Yâtrâmulle's MS. here, and one MS. of Fausböll's at *G*âtaka I, 153, 154). There the word is used of embers in which food is cooked, 'without flame,'='glowing, smoldering.' Vita*kkh*ikâ, 'an eruption on the skin,' belongs to the root *k*ar*k*.

trees, the utter passing away of the Tathâgata will take place. Come, Ânanda! let us go on to the river Kakutthâ.'

'Even so, Lord!' said the venerable Ânanda, in assent, to the Blessed One.

52. The pair of robes of cloth of gold,
All burnished, Pukkusa had brought,
Clad on with them the Master then
Shone forth in colour like to gold[1]!

---

53. Now the Blessed One with a great company of the brethren went on to the river Kakutthâ; and when he had come there, he went down into the water, and bathed, and drank. And coming up out again on the other side he went on to the Mango Grove.

54. And when he was come there he addressed the venerable *K*undaka, and said: 'Fold, I pray you, *K*undaka, a robe in four and spread it out. I am weary, *K*undaka, and would lie down.'

'Even so, Lord!' said the venerable *K*undaka, in assent, to the Blessed One. And he folded a robe in four, and spread it out.

---

[1] We have here the commencement of the legend which afterwards grew into an account of an actual 'transfiguration' of the Buddha. It is very curious that it should have taken place soon after the Buddha had announced to Ânanda his approaching death, and that in the Buddhist Sutta it should be connected so closely with that event; for a similar remark applies also to the Transfiguration mentioned in the Gospels. The Mâlâlaṅkâra-vatthu, for instance, says, 'His body appeared shining like a flame. Ânanda was exceedingly surprised. Nothing of this kind had, as yet, happened. "Your exterior appearance," said he to Budha, "is all at once white, shining, and beautiful above all expression." "What you say, O Ânanda, is perfectly true. There are two occasions [&c., much as above]. The shining light emanating from my body is a certain forerunner of this great event [his Parinibbâna]."'

55. And the Blessed One laid himself down on his right side, with one foot resting on the other; and calm and self-possessed, he meditated on the idea of rising up again in due time. And the venerable *K*undaka seated himself there in front of the Blessed One.

56. The Buddha to Kakutthâ's river came,
Whose clear and pleasant waters limpid flow,
He plunged beneath the stream wearied and worn,
The Buddha without equal in the world!
When he had bathed and drunk, the teacher then
Crossed o'er, the brethren thronging round his steps;
The Blessed Master, preaching the while the truth,
The Mighty Sage came to the Mango Grove.
There spake he to the brother *K*undaka:
'Spread me the fourfold robe out as a couch.'
Cheered by the Holy One, he quickly spread
The fourfold robe in order on the ground.
The Master laid him down, wearied and worn;
And there, before him, *K*unda took his seat.

---

57. And the Blessed One addressed the venerable Ânanda, and said: 'Now it may happen, Ânanda, that some one should stir up remorse in *K*unda the smith, by saying, "This is evil to thee, *K*unda, and loss to thee in that when the Tathâgata had eaten his last meal from thy provision, then he died." Any such remorse, Ânanda, in *K*unda the smith should be checked by saying, "This is good to thee, *K*unda, and gain to thee, in that when

the Tathâgata had eaten his last meal from thy provision, then he died. From the very mouth of the Blessed One, *K*unda, have I heard, from his own mouth have I received this saying, 'These two offerings of food are of equal fruit, and of equal profit, and of much greater fruit and much greater profit than any other — and which are the two? The offering of food which, when a Tathâgata has eaten, he attains to supreme and perfect insight; and the offering of food which, when a Tathâgata has eaten, he passes away by that utter passing away in which nothing whatever remains behind— these two offerings of food are of equal fruit and of equal profit, and of much greater fruit and much greater profit than any others. There has been laid up by *K*unda the smith a karma redounding to length of life, redounding to good birth, redounding to good fortune, redounding to good fame, redounding to the inheritance of heaven, and of sovereign power.'" In this way, Ânanda, should be checked any remorse in *K*unda the smith.'

58. Then the Blessed One perceiving how the matter stood, uttered, even at that time, this hymn of exultation:

'To him who gives shall virtue be increased;
In him who curbs himself, no anger can arise;
The righteous man casts off all sinfulness,
And by the rooting out of lust, and bitterness,
And all delusion, doth to Nirvâ*n*a reach!'

End of the Fourth Portion for Recitation, containing the Episode of Â*l*âra.

CHAPTER V.

1. Now the Blessed One addressed the venerable Ânanda, and said: 'Come, Ânanda, let us go on to the Sâla Grove of the Mallas, the Upavattana of Kusinârâ, on the further side of the river Hiranyavatî.'

'Even so, Lord!' said the venerable Ânanda, in assent, to the Blessed One.

2. And the Blessed One proceeded with a great company of the brethren to the Sâla Grove of the Mallas, the Upavattana of Kusinârâ, on the further side of the river Hiranyavatî: and when he had come there he addressed the venerable Ânanda, and said:

3. 'Spread over for me, I pray you, Ânanda, the couch with its head to the north, between the twin Sâla trees[1]. I am weary, Ânanda, and would lie down.'

'Even so, Lord!' said the venerable Ânanda, in assent, to the Blessed One. And he spread a

[1] According to the commentator 'tradition says that there was a row of Sâla trees at the head (sîsa) of that couch (mañ*k*a), and another at its foot, one young Sâla tree being close to its head, and another close to its foot. The twin Sâla trees were so called because the two trees were equally grown in respect of the roots, trunks, branches, and leaves. There was a couch there in the park for the special use of the (periodically elected) râ*g*a of the Mallas, and it was this couch which the Blessed One asked Ânanda to make ready.' There is no further explanation of the term uttara-sîsaka*m*, which may have been the name for a slab of wood or stone reserved on great occasions for the use of the leaders of the neighbouring republic, but available at other times for passers by.

covering over the couch with its head to the north, between the twin Sâla trees. And the Blessed One laid himself down on his right side, with one leg resting on the other; and he was mindful and self-possessed.

---

4. Now at that time the twin Sâla trees were all one mass of bloom with flowers out of season[1]; and all over the body of the Tathâgata these dropped and sprinkled and scattered themselves, out of reverence for the successor of the Buddhas of old. And heavenly Mandârava flowers, too, and heavenly sandal-wood powder came falling from the sky, and all over the body of the Tathâgata they descended and sprinkled and scattered themselves, out of reverence for the successor of the Buddhas of old. And heavenly music was sounded in the sky, out of reverence for the successor of the Buddhas of old. And heavenly songs came wafted from the skies, out of reverence for the successor of the Buddhas of old!

5. Then the Blessed One addressed the venerable Ânanda, and said: 'The twin Sâla trees are all one mass of bloom with flowers out of season; all over the body of the Tathâgata these drop and sprinkle and scatter themselves, out of reverence for the successor of the Buddhas of old. And heavenly Mandârava flowers, too, and heavenly sandal-wood powder come falling from the sky, and all over the body of the Tathâgata they descend and sprinkle and scatter themselves, out of rever-

[1] Sabbaphâliphullâ ti sabbe samantato pupphitâ mûlato pa*tth*âya yâva aggâ eka*kkh*annâ ahesu*m*. (S.V. *thl*u.) Compare ekaphâliphulla*m* vana*m* at *G*âtaka I, 52.

ence for the successor of the Buddhas of old. And heavenly music sounds in the sky, out of reverence for the successor of the Buddhas of old. And heavenly songs come wafted from the skies, out of reverence for the successor of the Buddhas of old!'

6. 'Now it is not thus, Ânanda, that the Tathâgata is rightly honoured, reverenced, venerated, held sacred or revered. But the brother or the sister, the devout man or the devout woman, who continually fulfils all the greater and the lesser duties, who is correct in life, walking according to the precepts—it is he who rightly honours, reverences, venerates, holds sacred, and reveres the Tathâgata with the worthiest homage. Therefore, O Ânanda, be ye constant in the fulfilment of the greater and of the lesser duties, and be ye correct in life, walking according to the precepts; and thus, Ânanda, should it be taught.'

---

7. Now at that time the venerable Upâva*n*a was standing in front of the Blessed One, fanning him. And the Blessed One was not pleased with Upâva*n*a, and he said to him: 'Stand aside, O brother, stand not in front of me!'

8. Then this thought sprung up in the mind of the venerable Ânanda: 'The venerable Upâva*n*a has long been in close personal attendance and service on the Blessed One. And now, at the last moment, the Blessed One is not pleased with Upâva*n*a, and has said to him, "Stand aside, O brother, stand not in front of me!" What may be the cause and what the reason that the Blessed One is not pleased with Upâva*n*a, and speaks thus with him?'

9. And the venerable Ânanda said to the Blessed One: 'The venerable Upâva*n*a has long

been in close personal attendance and service on the Blessed One. And now, at the last moment, the Blessed One is not pleased with Upâva*n*a, and has said to him, "Stand aside, O brother, stand not in front of me!" What may be the cause and what the reason that the Blessed One is not pleased with Upâva*n*a, and speaks thus with him?'

10. 'In great numbers, Ânanda, are the gods of the ten world-systems assembled together to behold the Tathâgata. For twelve leagues, Ânanda, around the Sâla Grove of the Mallas, the Upavattana of Kusinârâ, there is no spot in size even as the pricking of the point of the tip of a hair which is not pervaded by powerful spirits[1]. And the spirits, Ânanda, are murmuring, and say, "From afar have we come to behold the Tathâgata. Few and far between are the Tathâgatas, the Arahat Buddhas who appear in the world: and now to-day, in the last watch of the night, the death of a Tathâgata will take place; and this eminent brother stands in

[1] Buddhaghosa explains that even twenty to sixty angels or gods (devatâyo) could stand âragga-ko*t*i-nittûdana- (MS. nittaddana-) matte pi, 'on a point pricked by the extreme point of a gimlet,' without inconveniencing one another (a*ññ*am a*ññ*am avyâbâdhenti). It is most curious to find this exact analogy to the notorious discussion as to how many angels could stand on the point of a needle in a commentary written at just that period of Buddhist history which corresponds to the Middle Ages of Christendom. The passage in the text does not really imply or suggest any such doctrine, though the whole episode is so absurd that the author of the text could not have hesitated to say so, had such an idea been the common belief of the early Buddhists. With these sections should be compared the similar sections in Chapter VI, of which these are perhaps merely an echo.

There is no comment on nittûdana, but there can be little doubt that Childers's conjectural reading is correct.

front of the Tathâgata, concealing him, and in his last hour we are prevented from beholding the Tathâgata;" thus, Ânanda, do the spirits murmur.'

11. 'But of what kind of spirits is the Blessed One thinking?'

12. 'There are spirits, Ânanda, in the sky, but of worldly mind, who dishevel their hair and weep, who stretch forth their arms and weep, who fall prostrate on the ground, and roll to and fro in anguish at the thought: "Too soon will the Blessed One die! Too soon will the Happy One pass away! Full soon will the Light of the world vanish away[1]!"'

13. 'There are spirits, too, Ânanda, on the earth, and of worldly mind, who tear their hair and weep, who stretch forth their arms and weep, who fall prostrate on the ground, and roll to and fro in anguish at the thought: "Too soon will the Blessed One die! Too soon will the Happy One pass away! Full soon will the Eye of the world disappear from sight!"

14. 'But the spirits who are free from passion bear it, calm and self-possessed, mindful of the saying which begins, "Impermanent indeed are all component things. How then is it possible [whereas anything whatever, when born, brought into being, and

[1] *K*akkum loke antaradhâyissati, on which there is no comment. It is literally, 'the Eye in the world will vanish away,' where Eye is of course used figuratively of that by the aid of which spiritual truths can be perceived, corresponding exactly to the similar use in Europe of the word Light. The Master is often called *K*akkhumâ, 'He with the Eye,' 'He of the spiritual Eye' (see, for instance, the last verses in this Sutta), and here by a bold figure of speech he is called the Eye itself, which was shortly about to vanish away from the world, the means of spiritual insight which was no longer to be available for the common use of all men. But this is, it will be noticed, only the lament of the foolish and ignorant.

organised, contains within itself the inherent necessity of dissolution—how then is it possible that such a being should not be dissolved? No such condition can exist!"][1]

15. 'In times past, Lord, the brethren, when they had spent the rainy season in different districts, used to come to see the Tathâgata, and we used to receive those very reverend brethren to audience, and to wait upon the Blessed One. But, Lord, after the end of the Blessed One, we shall not be able to receive those very reverend brethren to audience, and to wait upon the Blessed One.'

---

16. 'There are these four places, Ânanda, which the believing man should visit with feelings of reverence and awe. Which are the four?

17. 'The place, Ânanda, at which the believing man can say, "Here the Tathâgata was born!" is a spot to be visited with feelings of reverence and awe.

18. 'The place, Ânanda, at which the believing man can say, "Here the Tathâgata attained to the supreme and perfect insight!" is a spot to be visited with feelings of reverence and awe.

19. 'The place, Ânanda, at which the believing man can say, "Here was the kingdom of righteousness set on foot by the Tathâgata!" is a spot to be visited with feelings of reverence and awe.

20. 'The place, Ânanda, at which the believing man can say, "Here the Tathâgata passed finally away in that utter passing away which leaves nothing whatever to remain behind!" is a spot to be visited with feelings of reverence and awe.

---

[1] The words in brackets have been inserted from par. III, 63 above. See par. VI, 39 below.

21. 'And there will come, Ânanda, to such spots, believers, brethren and sisters of the order, or devout men and devout women, and will say, "Here was the Tathâgata born!" or, "Here did the Tathâgata attain to the supreme and perfect insight!" or, "Here was the kingdom of righteousness set on foot by the Tathâgata!" or, "Here the Tathâgata passed away in that utter passing away which leaves nothing whatever to remain behind!"

22. 'And they, Ânanda, who shall die while they, with believing heart, are journeying on such pilgrimage, shall be reborn after death, when the body shall dissolve, in the happy realms of heaven.'

---

23. 'How are we to conduct ourselves, Lord, with regard to womankind?'

'Don't see them, Ânanda.'

'But if we should see them, what are we to do?'

'Abstain from speech, Ânanda.'

'But if they should speak to us, Lord, what are we to do?'

'Keep wide awake, Ânanda.'

---

24. 'What are we to do, Lord, with the remains of the Tathâgata?'

'Hinder not yourselves, Ânanda, by honouring the remains of the Tathâgata. Be zealous, I beseech you, Ânanda, in your own behalf! Devote yourselves to your own good! Be earnest, be zealous, be intent on your own good! There are wise men, Ânanda, among the nobles, among the Brâhmans, among the heads of houses, who are firm believers in the Tathâgata; and they will do due honour to the remains of the Tathâgata.'

25. [1] 'What should be done, Lord, with the remains of the Tathâgata?'

'As men treat the remains of a king of kings, so, Ânanda, should they treat the remains of a Tathâgata.'

'And how, Lord, do they treat the remains of a king of kings [2]?'

26. 'They wrap the body of a king of kings, Ânanda, in a new cloth. When that is done they wrap it in carded cotton wool [3]. When that is done they wrap it in a new cloth,—and so on till they have wrapped the body in five hundred successive layers of both kinds. Then they place the body in an oil vessel of iron [4], and cover that close up with another

[1] This conversation occurs also below (VI, 33), and the older tradition probably had it only in that connection.

[2] King of kings is an inadequate rendering of *K*akkavatti Râ*g*â. It is a king whose power no other king can dispute, who is the acknowledged overlord in India. The idea can scarcely have existed before *K*andragupta, the first *K*akravarti, had raised himself to power. This passage, therefore, is a guide to the date at which the Mahâ-parinibbâna Sutta assumed its present form.

[3] Vihatena kappâsenâ ti supho*t*itena kappâsena: Kâsika-vattha*m* hi sukhumattâ tela*m* na ga*n*hati, tasmâ vihatena kappâsenâ ti âha. 'As Benâres cloth, by reason of its fineness of texture, does not take the oil, he therefore says, "with vihata cotton wool," that is, with cotton wool that has been well forced asunder.' That pho*t*ita is here the participle of the causal verb, and not of the simple verb, follows of necessity from its being used as an explanation of vihata, 'torn to pieces.' The technical use of the word, as applied to cotton wool, has only been found in this passage. It usually means 'torn with grief.'

[4] Ayasâya tela-do*n*iyâ, where one would expect âyasâya, but my MS. of the Dîgha Nikâya confirms twice over here, and twice again below, § VI, 33, 35, the reading given by Childers. Buddhaghosa says, Âyasan ti suva*nn*a*m*, suva*nn*amhi idha âyasan ti adhippeto, but here again we should expect the second time to find ayo or ayasa*m*. The meaning of the word is also not

oil vessel of iron[1]. They then build a funeral pile of all kinds of perfumes, and burn the body of the king of kings. And then at the four cross roads they erect a dâgaba[2] to the king of kings. This, Ânanda, is the way in which they treat the remains of a king of kings.

'And as they treat the remains of a king of kings, so, Ânanda, should they treat the remains of the Tathâgata. At the four cross roads a dâgaba should be erected to the Tathâgata. And whosoever shall there place garlands or perfumes or paint, or make salutation there, or become in its presence calm in heart—that shall long be to them for a profit and a joy.'

---

27. 'These men, Ânanda, worthy of a dâgaba[2], are four in number. Which are the four?

'A Tathâgata, or Arahat-Buddha, is worthy of a dâgaba. A Pa*kk*eka-Buddha is worthy of a dâgaba[3].

---

quite clear. It no doubt was originally used for bronze, and only later for iron also, and at last exclusively of iron. As ka*m*sa is already a common word for bronze in very early Buddhist Pâli texts, I think âyasa or ayasa must here mean 'of iron.' When Buddhaghosa says it is here a name for gold, we can only conclude that iron had become, in his time, a metal which he might fairly consider too base for the purpose proposed.

[1] Buddhaghosa has no note on pa*t*iku*gg*etvâ; but from its use at *G*âtaka I, 50, 29: 69, 23, it must, I think, have this meaning. I am not certain to what root it ought to be referred. I should mention that pakkhipati seems to me never to mean in Pâli, 'to hurl forth into, to throw forth,' but always 'to place (slowly and carefully) into.'

[2] A solid mound or tumulus, in the midst of which the bones and ashes are to be placed. The dome of St. Paul's as seen from the Thames Embankment gives a very good idea of one of the later Buddhist dâgabas. The Pâli word here and below is Thûpa.

[3] A Pa*kk*eka-Buddha, who has attained to the supreme and perfect insight; but dies without proclaiming the truth to the world.

A true hearer of the Tathâgata is worthy of a dâgaba. A king of kings is worthy of a ḍâgaba.

28. 'And on account of what circumstance, Ânanda, is a Tathâgata, an Arahat-Buddha, worthy of a dâgaba?

'At the thought, Ânanda, "This is the dâgaba of that Blessed One, of that Arahat-Buddha," the hearts of many shall be made calm and happy; and since they there had calmed and satisfied their hearts they will be reborn after death, when the body has dissolved, in the happy realms of heaven. It is on account of this circumstance, Ânanda, that a Tathâgata, an Arahat-Buddha, is worthy of a dâgaba.'

29. 'And on account of what circumstance, Ânanda, is a Pa*kk*eka-Buddha worthy of a dâgaba?

'At the thought, Ânanda, "This is the dâgaba of that Blessed One, of that Pa*kk*eka-Buddha," the hearts of many shall be made calm and happy; and since they there had calmed and satisfied their hearts they will be reborn after death, when the body has dissolved, in the happy realms of heaven. It is on account of this circumstance, Ânanda, that a Pa*kk*eka-Buddha is worthy of a dâgaba.

30. 'And on account of what circumstance, Ânanda, is a true hearer of the Blessed One, the Arahat-Buddha, worthy of a dâgaba?

'At the thought, Ânanda, "This is the dâgaba of that true hearer of the Blessed Arahat-Buddha," the hearts of many shall be made calm and happy; and since they there had calmed and satisfied their hearts they will be reborn after death, when the body has dissolved, in the happy realms of heaven. It is on account of this circumstance, Ânanda, that a true hearer of the Blessed One, the Arahat-Buddha, is worthy of a dâgaba.

31. 'And on account of what circumstance, Ânanda, is a king of kings worthy of a dâgaba?

'At the thought, Ânanda, "This is the dâgaba of that righteous king who ruled in righteousness," the hearts of many shall be made calm and happy; and since they there had calmed and satisfied their hearts they will be reborn after death, when the body has dissolved, in the happy realms of heaven. It is on account of this circumstance, Ânanda, that a king of kings is worthy of a dâgaba.

'These four, Ânanda, are the persons worthy of a dâgaba.'

---

32. 'Now the venerable Ânanda went into the Vihâra, and stood leaning against the lintel of the door[1], and weeping at the thought: "Alas! I remain still but a learner, one who has yet to work out his own perfection[2]. And the Master is about to pass away from me—he who is so kind!"'

33. Now the Blessed One called the brethren, and said: 'Where, then, brethren, is Ânanda?'

The venerable Ânanda, Lord, has gone into the

---

[1] Kapisîsa*m*. Buddhaghosa says, Kapisîsakan ti dvâra-bâha-ko*t*iya*m* *th*itam aggala-rukkha*m*, 'a piece of wood fixed as a bolt at the top of the door posts.' The Sanskrit lexicographers give kapi-*s*îrsha in the sense of 'coping of a wall.' Compare Pâtimokkha, Pâ*k*ittiya, No. 19.

The expression that Ânanda went 'into the Vihâra' at the end of a conversation represented as having taken place in the Sâla Grove, would seem to point to the fact that this episode originally stood in some other connection. Buddhaghosa attempts to explain away the discrepancy by saying that Vihâra here means Ma*nd*ala.

[2] Ânanda had entered the Noble Path, but had not yet reached the end of it. He had not attained to Nirvâ*n*a.

Vihâra, and stands leaning against the lintel of the door, and weeping at the thought: 'Alas! I remain still but a learner, one who has yet to work out his own perfection. And the Master is about to pass away from me—he who is so kind!'

34. And the Blessed One called a certain brother, and said: 'Go now, brother, and call Ânanda in my name, and say, "Brother Ânanda, the Master calls for thee."'

'Even so, Lord!' said that brother, in assent, to the Blessed One. And he went up to the place where the Blessed One was; and when he had come there, he said to the venerable Ânanda: 'Brother Ânanda, the Master calls for thee.'

'Very well, brother,' said the venerable Ânanda, in assent, to that brother. And he went up to the place where the Blessed One was, and when he had come there, he bowed down before the Blessed One, and took his seat respectfully on one side.

35. Then the Blessed One said to the venerable Ânanda, as he sat there by his side: 'Enough, Ânanda! Do not let yourself be troubled; do not weep! Have I not already, on former occasions, told you that it is in the very nature of all things most near and dear unto us that we must divide ourselves from them, leave them, sever ourselves from them? How, then, Ânanda, can this be possible—whereas anything whatever born, brought into being, and organised, contains within itself the inherent necessity of dissolution—how, then, can this be possible, that such a being should not be dissolved? No such condition can exist! For a long time, Ânanda, have you been very near to me by acts of love, kind and good, that never varies, and is beyond all

measure. For a long time, Ânanda, have you been very near to me by words of love, kind and good, that never varies, and is beyond all measure. For a long time, Ânanda, have you been very near to me by thoughts of love, kind and good, that never varies[1], and is beyond all measure. You have done well, Ânanda! Be earnest in effort, and you too shall soon be free from the great evils—from sensuality, from individuality, from delusion, and from ignorance[2]!'

---

36. [3] Then the Blessed One addressed the brethren, and said: 'Whosoever, brethren, have been Arahat-Buddhas through the long ages of the past, there were servitors just as devoted to those Blessed Ones as Ânanda has been to me. And whosoever, brethren, shall be Arahat-Buddhas in the long ages of the future, there shall be servitors just as devoted to those Blessed Ones as Ânanda has been to me.

37. 'He is a wise man, brethren,—is Ânanda.

---

[1] Advayena, which Buddhaghosa explains as not being that kind of love which is now one thing and now another, or which varies in the presence or the absence of the object loved. When the Buddha is called in the Amara Kosha I, 1, 1, 9, advayavâdin, that must mean in a similar way, 'One whose teaching does not vary.'

[2] Literally, thou shalt become an Anâsava, that is, one who is free from the four Âsavas, all which are explained above in § I, 12, from which I have taken the details suggested to a Buddhist by the word used. The state of mind to which an Anâsava has reached is precisely the same, though looked at from a different point of view, as the state of mind expressed by the better known word Nirvâ*n*a.

[3] What follows is repeated in the Satipatthâ*n*a Vagga of the Sa*m*yutta Nikâya; but in regard to Sâriputta (Upatissa) and Moggallâna, and reading sâvaka-yuga*m* for upa*tth*âko.

He knows when it is the right time for him to come and visit the Tathâgata, and when it is the right time for the brethren and sisters of the order, for devout men and devout women, for a king, or for a king's ministers, for other teachers or their disciples, to come and visit the Tathâgata.

38. 'Brethren, there are these four wonderful and marvellous qualities in Ânanda. Which are the four?

'If, brethren, a number of the brethren of the order should come to visit Ânanda, they are filled with joy on beholding him; and if Ânanda should then preach the truth to them, they are filled with joy at the discourse; while the company of brethren is ill at ease, brethren, when Ânanda is silent.

'If, brethren, a number of the sisters of the order, or of devout men, or of devout women, should come to visit Ânanda, they are filled with joy on beholding him; and if Ânanda should then preach the truth to them, they are filled with joy at the discourse; while the company of sisters is ill at ease, brethren, when Ânanda is silent.

39. 'Brethren, there are these four wonderful and marvellous qualities in a king of kings. What are the four?

'If, brethren, a number of nobles, or Brahman, or heads of houses, or Sama*n*as should come to visit a king of kings, they are filled with joy on beholding him; and if the king of kings should then speak, they are filled with joy at what is said; while they are ill at ease, brethren, when the king of kings is silent.

40. 'Just so, brethren, are the four wonderful and marvellous qualities in Ânanda.

'If, brethren, a number of the brethren of the

order, or of the sisters of the order, or of devout men, or of devout women, should come to visit Ânanda, they are filled with joy on beholding him; and if Ânanda should then preach the truth to them, they are filled with joy at the discourse; while the company of brethren is ill at ease, brethren, when Ânanda is silent.

'Now these, brethren, are the four wonderful and marvellous qualities that are in Ânanda.'

---

41. When he had thus spoken[1], the venerable Ânanda said to the Blessed One:

'Let not the Blessed One die in this little wattel and daub town, in this town in the midst of the jungle, in this branch township[2]. For, Lord, there are other great cities, such as *K*ampâ, Râ*g*agaha, Sâvatthi, Sâketa, Kosambi, and Benâres. Let the Blessed One die in one of them. There there are many wealthy nobles and Brâhmans and heads of houses, believers in the Tathâgata, who will pay due honour to the remains of the Tathâgata[3].'

---

[1] From here down to the end of section 44 is found also, nearly word for word, in the beginning of the Mahâ-Sudassana Sutta, translated below; compare also Mahâ-Sudassana *G*âtaka, No. 95.

[2] Ku*dd*a-nagarake ti pa*t*irûpake sambâdhe khuddaka-nagare: U*gg*aṅgala-nagarake ti visama-nagarake. (S.V.fol. *th*au.) Ku*dd*a, if this explanation be right, seems to be merely an old and unusual form for kshudra, and the Burmese correction into khudda to be unnecessary: but I venture to think it is more likely to be=ku*d*ya, and to mean a wall built of mud and sticks, or what is called in India, of wattel and daub. When Buddhaghosa explains u*gg*aṅgala as 'lawless,' he is expressing his view that a town in the jungle is likely to be a heathen, pagan sort of place.

[3] With reference to Childers's note in his Dictionary on mahâ-sâlâ, with which every one must entirely agree, Buddhaghosa's

42. 'Say not so, Ânanda! Say not so, Ânanda, that this is but a small wattel and daub town, a town in the midst of the jungle, a branch township. Long ago, Ânanda, there was a king, by name Mahâ-Sudassana, a king of kings, a righteous man who ruled in righteousness, Lord of the four quarters of the earth, conqueror, the protector of his people, possessor of the seven royal treasures. This Kusinârâ, Ânanda, was the royal city of king Mahâ-Sudassana, under the name of Kusâvatî, and on the east and on the west it was twelve leagues in length, and on the north and on the south it was seven leagues in breadth.

43. 'That royal city Kusâvatî, Ânanda, was mighty, and prosperous, and full of people, crowded with men, and provided with all things for food[1]. Just, Ânanda, as the royal city of the gods, Â*l*akamandâ by name, is mighty, prosperous, and full of people, crowded with the gods, and provided with all kinds of food, so, Ânanda, was the royal city Kusâvatî mighty and prosperous, full of people, crowded with men, and provided with all kinds of food.

44. 'Both by day and by night, Ânanda, the royal city Kusâvatî resounded with the ten cries; that is to say, the noise of elephants, and the noise of horses, and the noise of chariots; the sounds of the

explanation of the word will be interesting as a proof (if proof be needed) that the Ceylon scholars are not always trustworthy. He says, Khattiya-mahâsâlâ ti khattiya-mahâsârâ sârapattâ mahâ-khattiyâ. Eso nayo sabbattha.

[1] The first three of these adjectives are applied at *G*âtaka I, 29 (v. 212) to the religion of the Buddhas; and I think the right reading there must be phîta*m*, in accordance with the corrections in two MSS. as noted by Mr. Fausböll, and not pîta*m* as he has preferred to read. The whole set of epithets is often used of cities.

drum, of the tabor, and of the lute; the sound of singing, and the sounds of the cymbal and of the gong; and lastly, with the cry, "Eat, drink, and be merry[1]!"

---

45. 'Go now, Ânanda, and enter into Kusinârâ, and inform the Mallas of Kusinârâ, saying, "This day, O Vâse*tth*as, in the last watch of the night, the final passing away of the Tathâgata will take place. Be favourable herein, O Vâse*tth*as, be favourable. Give no occasion to reproach yourselves hereafter, saying, 'In our own village did the death of our Tathâgata take place, and we took not the opportunity of visiting the Tathâgata in his last hours.'"'

'Even so, Lord,' said the venerable Ânanda, in assent, to the Blessed One; and he robed himself, and taking his bowl[2], entered into Kusinârâ attended by another member of the order.

---

[1] This enumeration is found also at *G*âtaka, p. 3, only that the conch shell is added there—wrongly, for that makes the number of cries eleven. The Mahâ-Sudassana Sutta has in the corresponding passage, like the Burmese MS. noted here by Childers, conch instead of cymbal. My MS. reads cymbal here.

[2] Nivâsetvâ patta-*k*îvara*m* âdâya atta-dutiyo. Buddhaghosa has, naturally enough, no comment on this oft-recurring phrase. It cannot be meant that he put on only his under-garments, and carried his upper robe with him; for then his shoulders would have been bare; and it is quite against the rules to go into a village without all the robes having been put carefully on (Pâtimokkha, Sekhiya 1–3). I do not even understand how Ânanda, with due regard to the rules of the brotherhood (see Pâtimokkha, Nisaggiya 21–29), could have had a spare robe then with him. And patta-*k*îvara*m* can scarcely mean simply 'bowl-robe,' referring to the length of cotton cloth in which the bowl was carried over the shoulder ('Buddhist Birth Stories,' p. 71). 'With both his under-garments on, he entered Kusinârâ duly bowled and robed' may be impossible English, but it probably correctly catches the

46. Now at that time the Mallas of Kusinârâ were assembled in the council hall on some public affair[1].

And the venerable Ânanda went to the council hall of the Mallas of Kusinârâ; and when he had arrived there, he informed them, saying, 'This day, O Vâse*tth*as, in the last watch of the night, the final passing away of the Tathâgata will take place. Be favourable herein, O Vâse*tth*as, be favourable. Give no occasion to reproach yourselves hereafter, saying, "In our own village did the death of our Tathâgata take place, and we took not the opportunity of visiting the Tathâgata in his last hours."'

47. And when they had heard this saying of the venerable Ânanda, the Mallas with their young men and maidens and their wives were grieved, and sad, and afflicted at heart. And some of them wept, dishevelling their hair, and stretched forth their arms and wept, fell prostrate on the ground, and rolled to and fro in anguish at the thought: 'Too soon will the Blessed One die! Too soon will the Happy One pass away! Full soon will the Light of the world vanish away!'

---

48. Then the Mallas, with their young men and

idea involved, though of course one (at least) of the under-cloths had been put on long before. See p. 122. A Thera never goes about in public alone, he is always accompanied by a Sâma*n*era.

[1] Kena*k*id eva kara*n*îyena. Professor Pischel, in his edition of the Assalâyana Sutta (p. 1), prints this expression kena*k*i devakara*n*îyena, and translates it (p. 28), 'for some religious purposes.' It seems to me that he has been misled by the commentary, which really presupposes the more correct division adopted by Childers.

maidens and their wives, being grieved and sad and afflicted at heart, went to the Sâla Grove of the Mallas, to the Upavattana, and to the place where the venerable Ânanda was.

49. Then the venerable Ânanda thought: 'If I allow the Mallas of Kusinârâ, one by one, to pay their respects to the Blessed One, the whole of the Mallas of Kusinârâ will not have been presented to the Blessed One until this night brightens up into the dawn. Let me, now, cause the Mallas of Kusinârâ to stand in groups, each family in a group, and so present them to the Blessed One, saying, "Lord! a Malla of such and such a name, with his children, his wives, his retinue, and his friends, humbly bows down at the feet of the Blessed One."'

50. And the venerable Ânanda caused the Mallas of Kusinârâ to stand in groups, each family in a group, and so presented them to the Blessed One, and said: 'Lord! a Malla of such and such a name, with his children, his wives, his retinue, and his friends, humbly bows down at the feet of the Blessed One.'

51. And after this manner the venerable Ânanda presented all the Mallas of Kusinârâ to the Blessed One in the first watch of the night.

---

52. Now at that time a mendicant named Subhadda, who was not a believer, was dwelling at Kusinârâ. And the mendicant Subhadda heard the news: 'This very day, they say, in the third watch of the night, will take place the final passing away of the Sama*n*a Gotama.'

53. Then thought the mendicant Subhadda: 'This have I heard from fellow mendicants of mine, old and well stricken in years, teachers and

disciples, when they said: "Sometimes and full seldom do Tathâgatas appear in the world, the Arahat Buddhas." Yet this day, in the last watch of the night, the final passing away of the Samana Gotama will take place. Now a certain feeling of uncertainty has sprung up in my mind; and this faith have I in the Samana Gotama, that he, methinks, is able so to present the truth that I may get rid of this feeling of uncertainty.'

54. Then the mendicant Subhadda went to the Sâla Grove of the Mallas, to the Upavattana of Kusinârâ, to the place where the venerable Ânanda was.

55. And when he had come there he said to the venerable Ânanda: 'Thus have I heard from fellow mendicants of mine, old and well stricken in years, teachers and disciples, when they said: "Sometimes and full seldom do Tathâgatas appear in the world, the Arahat Buddhas." Yet this day, in the last watch of the night, the final passing away of the Samana Gotama will take place. Now a certain feeling of uncertainty has sprung up in my mind; and this faith have I in the Samana Gotama, that he, methinks, is able so to present the truth that I may get rid of this feeling of uncertainty. O that I, even I, Ânanda, might be allowed to see the Samana Gotama!'

56. And when he had thus spoken the venerable Ânanda said to the mendicant Subhadda: 'Enough! friend Subhadda. Trouble not the Tathâgata. The Blessed One is weary.'

57. And again the mendicant Subhadda [made the same request in the same words, and received the same reply]; and the third time the mendicant Subhadda [made the same request in the same words, and received the same reply].

58. Now the Blessed One overheard this conversation of the venerable Ânanda with the mendicant Subhadda. And the Blessed One called the venerable Ânanda, and said: 'It is enough, Ânanda! Do not keep out Subhadda. Subhadda, Ânanda, may be allowed to see the Tathâgata. Whatever Subhadda may ask of me, he will ask from a desire for knowledge, and not to annoy me. And whatever I may say in answer to his questions, that he will quickly understand.'

59. Then the venerable Ânanda said to Subhadda, the mendicant: 'Enter in, friend Subhadda; for the Blessed One gives you leave.'

60. Then Subhadda, the mendicant, went in to the place where the Blessed One was, and saluted him courteously, and after exchanging with him the compliments of esteem and of civility, he took his seat on one side. And when he was thus seated, Subhadda, the mendicant, said to the Blessed One: 'The Brâhmans by saintliness of life[1], Gotama, who

[1] Samana-brâhmanâ, which compound may possibly mean Samanas and Brâhmans as it has usually been rendered, but I think not necessarily. Not one of those here specified were Brâhmans by caste, as is apparent from the Sumangala Vilâsinî on the Sâmañña Phala Sutta, p. 114. Compare the use of Kshatriya-brâhmano, 'a soldier priest,' a Kshatriya who offered sacrifice; and of Brâhmano, absolutely, as an epithet of an Arahat. In the use of the word samana there seems to me to be a hopeless confusion between, a complete mingling of the meanings of, the two roots sram and sam (which, in Pâli, would both become sam). It connotes both asceticism and inward peace, and might best be rendered 'devotee,' were it not for the intellectual inferiority implied by that word in our language. A Samana Brâhman should therefore mean a man of any caste, who by his saintliness of life, by his renunciation of the world, and by his reputation as a religious thinker, had acquired the position of a quasi Brâhman, and

are heads of companies of disciples and students, teachers of students, well known, renowned, founders of schools of doctrine, esteemed as good men by the multitude—to wit, Pûra*n*a Kassapa, Makkhali of the cattle-pen, A*g*ita of the garment of hair, Ka*kk*âyana of the Pakudha tree, Sañ*g*aya the son of the Belat*th*i slave-girl, and Nigan*th*a of the Nâtha clan—have they all, according to their own assertion, thoroughly understood things? or have they not? or are there some of them who have understood, and some who have not[1]?'

61. 'Enough, Subhadda! Let this matter rest whether they, according to their own assertion, have thoroughly understood things, or whether they have not, or whether some of them have understood and some have not! The truth, Ânanda, will I teach you. Listen well to that, and give ear attentively, and I will speak.'

'Even so, Lord!' said the mendicant Subhadda, in assent, to the Blessed One.

62. And the Blessed One spake: 'In whatsoever doctrine and discipline, Subhadda, the noble eightfold path is not found, neither in it is there found a man of true saintliness of the first or of the second or of the third or of the fourth degree[2].

---

was looked up to by the people in the same way as that in which they looked up to a Brâhman by caste. Compare further my 'Buddhist Birth Stories,' vol. i. p. 260; and also Mr. Beal's remarks in the Indian Antiquary for May, 1880; and Professor Max Müller's note on Dhammapada, verse 265.

[1] Buddhaghosa has an exegetical note on abbha*ññ*amsu, but passes over those celebrated Six Teachers in silence. The little that is thus far known of them will be discussed in another place.

[2] This refers to the four divisions of the Noble Eightfold Path. See above, chap. II, § 8, where their characters are described. The

And in whatsoever doctrine and discipline, Subhadda, the noble eightfold path is found, is found the man of true saintliness of the first and the second and the third and the fourth degree. Now in this doctrine and discipline, Subhadda, is found the noble eightfold path, and in it alone, Subhadda, is the man of true saintliness. Void are the systems of other teachers—void of true saints. And in this one, Subhadda, may the brethren live the Life that's Right, so that the world be not bereft of Arahats[1].

---

word translated 'man of true saintliness,' or 'true saint,' is in the text Sama*n*o, on which see the note on page 105. I am at a loss how to render the word adequately here.

[1] Arahats are those who have reached Nirvâ*n*a, the 'supreme goal,' the 'highest fruit' of the Noble Eightfold Path. To live 'the Life that's Right' (sammâ) is to live in the Noble Path, each of the eight divisions of which is to be sammâ, round, right and perfect, normal and complete. To live right (sammâ) is therefore to have—1. Right views, free from superstition. 2. Right aims, high and worthy of the intelligent and earnest man. 3. Right speech, kindly, open, truthful. 4. Right conduct, in all concerns of life. 5. Right livelihood, bringing hurt or danger to no living thing. 6. Right perseverance, in all the other seven. 7. Right mindfulness, the watchful, active mind. 8. Right contemplation, earnest thought on the deep mysteries of life. In each of these the word right is sammâ, and the whole paragraph being on the Noble Path, the allusion is certainly to this central doctrine of the Buddhist Dhamma.

Buddhaghosa says that that bhikkhu sammâ viharati, who, having himself entered the Noble Path, leads his brother into it, and this is, no doubt, good Buddhism. But it is a practical application of the text, a theological exegesis, and not a philological explanation. Even so it seems to lay the stress too much on 'bereft,' and too little on 'Arahats.'

In the last words of the prose we seem to have a reminiscence of what were once verses, which may have run—

Su*ññ*â pavâdâ sama*n*ehi a*ññ*e;

'But twenty-nine was I when I renounced
The world, Subhadda, seeking after good.
For fifty years and one year more, Subhadda,
Since I went out, a pilgrim have I been
Through the wide realms of virtue and of truth,
And outside these no really "saint" can be[1]!

'Yea, not of the first, nor of the second, nor of the third, nor of the fourth degree. Void are the systems of other teachers—void of true saints. But in this one, Subhadda, may the brethren live the perfect life, that the world be not bereft of those who have reached the highest fruit.'

63. And when he had thus spoken, Subhadda, the mendicant, said to the Blessed One: 'Most excellent, Lord, are the words of thy mouth, most excellent! Just as if a man were to set up that which is thrown down, or were to reveal that which is hidden away, or were to point out the right road to him who has gone astray, or were to bring a lamp into the darkness, so that those who have eyes can see external forms;—just even so, Lord, has the truth been made known to me, in many a figure, by the Blessed One. And I, even I, betake myself, Lord, to the Blessed One as my refuge, to the truth, and to the order. May the Blessed One accept me as a disciple, as a true believer, from this day forth, as long as life endures!'

Ime *k*a sammâ vihareyyu bhikkhû,
Asu*ññ*o loko 'rahatehi assa.

[1] I have followed, though with some doubt, Childers's punctuation. Buddhaghosa refers padesa-vattî to sama*n*o; and ito, not to padesa, but to magga, understood; and it is quite possible that this is the correct explanation. On samâdhikâni see the comment at *G*âtaka II, 383.

64. 'Whosoever, Subhadda, that has formerly been a follower of another doctrine and then desires to be received into the higher or the lower grade in this doctrine and discipline, he remains on probation for the space of four months; and at the end of the four months, the brethren, exalted in spirit, receive him into the lower or into the higher grade of the order. Nevertheless in this case I acknowledge the difference in persons.'

65. 'If, Lord, whosoever that has formerly been a follower of another doctrine and then desires to be received into the higher or the lower grade in this doctrine and discipline,—if, in that case, such a person remains on probation for the space of four months; and at the end of the four months, the brethren, exalted in spirit, receive him into the lower or into the higher grade of the order—I too, then, will remain on probation for the space of four months; and at the end of the four months let the brethren, exalted in spirit, receive me into the lower or into the higher grade of the order!'

66. But the Blessed One called the venerable Ânanda, and said: 'As it is, Ânanda, receive Subhadda into the order!'

'Even so, Lord!' said the venerable Ânanda, in assent, to the Blessed One.

67. And Subhadda, the mendicant, said to the venerable Ânanda: 'Great is your gain, friend Ânanda, great is your good fortune, friend Ânanda, that you all have been sprinkled with the sprinkling of discipleship in this brotherhood at the hands of the Master himself!'

68. So Subhadda, the mendicant, was received

into the higher grade of the order under the Blessed One; and from immediately after his ordination the venerable Subhadda remained alone and separate, earnest, zealous, and resolved. And e'er long he attained to that supreme goal of the higher life[1] for the sake of which men go out from all and every household gain and comfort to become houseless wanderers—yea, that supreme goal did he, by himself, and while yet in this visible world, bring himself to the knowledge of, and continue to realise, and to see face to face! And he became conscious that birth was at an end, that the higher life had been fulfilled, that all that should be done had been accomplished, and that after this present life there would be no beyond!

69. So the venerable Subhadda became yet another among the Arahats; and he was the last disciple whom the Blessed One himself converted[2].

End of the Hira*ññ*avatiya portion, being the Fifth Portion for Recitation.

---

[1] That is, Nirvâ*n*a. Compare Ma*n*gala Sutta V, 11, and the Dhammapada, verses 180, 354, and above Chap. I, § 7.

[2] Buddhaghosa says that the last five words in the text (the last twelve words in my translation) were added by the Theras who held the Council. On Subhadda's ordination he has the following interesting note: 'The Thero (that is, Ânanda), they say, took him on one side, poured water over his head from a water vessel, made him repeat the formula of meditation on the impermanency of the body (Ta*k*a-pa*ñk*aka-kamma*tth*âna*m*; see my "Buddhist Birth Stories," p. 161), shaved off his hair and beard, clad him in the yellow robes, made him repeat the "Three Refuges," and led him back to the Blessed One. The Blessed One himself admitted him then into the higher rank of the brotherhood, and pointed out to him a subject for meditation (kamma*tth*âna*m*; see "Buddhist

Birth Stories," p. 147). He accepted this, and walking up and down in a quiet part of the grove, he thought and meditated upon it, till overcoming the Evil Spirit, he had acquired Arahatship, and with it the discriminating knowledge of all the Scriptures (Pa*t*i-sambhidâ). Then, returning, he came and took his seat beside the Blessed One.'

According to this, no set ceremony for ordination (Sangha-kamma*m*), as laid down in the Vinaya, took place; and it is otherwise probable that no such ceremony was usual in the earliest days of Buddhism.

Chapter VI.

1. Now the Blessed One addressed the venerable Ânanda, and said: 'It may be, Ânanda, that in some of you the thought may arise, "The word of the Master is ended, we have no teacher more!" But it is not thus, Ânanda, that you should regard it. The truths and the rules of the order which I have set forth and laid down for you all, let them, after I am gone, be the Teacher to you.'

---

2. 'Ânanda! when I am gone address not one another in the way in which the brethren have heretofore addressed each other—with the epithet, that is, of "Âvuso" (Friend). A younger brother may be addressed by an elder with his name, or his family name, or the title "Friend." But an elder should be addressed by a younger brother as "Lord" or as "Venerable Sir."'

---

3. 'When I am gone, Ânanda, let the order, if it should so wish, abolish all the lesser and minor precepts[1].'

---

4. 'When I am gone, Ânanda, let the higher penalty be imposed on brother *Kh*anna.'

'But what, Lord, is the higher penalty?'

---

[1] In *K*ulla Vagga XI, 1, 9, 10, is related how the brotherhood formally considered the permission thus accorded to them, and resolved to adhere to all the precepts as laid down in the Buddha's lifetime. In his comment on this passage Buddhaghosa incidentally refers to a conversation on the subject between Nâgasena and Milinda Râ*g*a, but makes no mention of the work known as Milinda Pa*ñ*ha. Compare Trenckner's edition of that work, p. 142.

'Let *Kh*anna say whatever he may like, Ânanda, the brethren should neither speak to him, nor exhort him, nor admonish him[1].'

---

5. Then the Blessed One addressed the brethren, and said: 'It may be, brethren, that there may be doubt or misgiving in the mind of some brother as to the Buddha, or the truth, or the path, or the way. Enquire, brethren, freely. Do not have to reproach yourselves afterwards with the thought, "Our teacher was face to face with us, and we could not bring ourselves to enquire of the Blessed One when we were face to face with him."'

And when he had thus spoken the brethren were silent.

6. And again the second and the third time the Blessed One addressed the brethren, and said: 'It may be, brethren, that there may be doubt or misgiving in the mind of some brother as to the Buddha, or the truth, or the path, or the way. Enquire, brethren, freely. Do not have to reproach yourselves afterwards with the thought, "Our teacher was face to face with us, and we could not bring ourselves to enquire of the Blessed One when we were face to face with him."'

And even the third time the brethren were silent.

---

[1] Compare *K*ulla Vagga I, 25–31: IV, 14, 1: XI, 1, 12–14. *Kh*anna is represented as an obstinate, perverse man; so destitute of the proper 'esprit de corps' that he dared to take part with the sisterhood, and against the brotherhood, in a dispute which had arisen between them. But after the social penalty here referred to had been duly imposed upon him, even his proud and independent spirit was tamed; he became humble: his eyes were opened; and he, also, attained to the 'supreme goal' of the Buddhist faith.

7. Then the Blessed One addressed the brethren, and said: 'It may be, brethren, that you put no questions out of reverence for the teacher. Let one friend communicate to another.'

And when he had thus spoken the brethren were silent.

8. And the venerable Ânanda said to the Blessed One: 'How wonderful a thing is it, Lord, and how marvellous! Verily, I believe that in this whole assembly of the brethren there is not one brother who has any doubt or misgiving as to the Buddha, or the truth, or the path, or the way!'

9. 'It is out of the fulness of faith that thou hast spoken, Ânanda! But, Ânanda, the Tathâgata knows for certain that in this whole assembly of the brethren there is not one brother who has any doubt or misgiving as to the Buddha, or the truth, or the path, or the way! For even the most backward, Ânanda, of all these five hundred brethren has become converted, and is no longer liable to be born in a state of suffering, and is assured of final salvation[1].'

---

10. Then the Blessed One addressed the brethren, and said: 'Behold now, brethren, I exhort you, saying, "Decay is inherent in all component things! Work out your salvation with diligence!"'

This was the last word of the Tathâgata!

---

11. Then the Blessed One entered into the first

[1] Compare above, Chap. II, § 7. By 'the most backward,' according to Buddhaghosa, the Blessed One referred to Ânanda, and he said this to encourage him.

stage of deep meditation[1]. And rising out of the first stage he passed into the second. And rising out of the second he passed into the third. And rising out of the third stage he passed into the fourth. And rising out of the fourth stage of deep meditation he entered into the state of mind to which the infinity of space is alone present[2]. And passing out of the mere consciousness of the infinity of space he entered into the state of mind to which the infinity of thought is alone present. And passing out of the mere consciousness of the infinity of thought he entered into a state of mind to which nothing at all was specially present. And passing out of the consciousness of no special object he fell into a state between consciousness and unconsciousness. And passing out of the state between consciousness and unconsciousness he fell into a state in which the consciousness both of sensations and of ideas had wholly passed away.

12. Then the venerable Ânanda said to the venerable Anuruddha: 'O my Lord, O Anuruddha, the Blessed One is dead!'

'Nay! brother Ânanda, the Blessed One is not dead. He has entered into that state in which both sensations and ideas have ceased to be!'

13. Then the Blessed One passing out of the state in which both sensations and ideas have ceased to be, entered into the state between consciousness and unconsciousness. And passing out of the state between consciousness and unconsciousness he entered into the state of mind to

---

[1] *Gh*âna, the full text and an explanation of which will be found in the translator's 'Buddhism,' pp. 174–176.

[2] Compare above, Chap. III, §§ 37–42.

which nothing at all is specially present. And passing out of the consciousness of no special object he entered into the state of mind to which the infinity of thought is alone present. And passing out of the mere consciousness of the infinity of thought he entered into the state of mind to which the infinity of space is alone present. And passing out of the mere consciousness of the infinity of space he entered into the fourth stage of deep meditation. And passing out of the fourth stage he entered into the third. And passing out of the third stage he entered into the second. And passing out of the second he entered into the first. And passing out of the first stage of deep meditation he entered into the second. And passing out of the second stage he entered into the third. And passing out of the third stage he entered into the fourth stage of deep meditation. And passing out of the last stage of deep meditation he immediately expired.

---

14. When the Blessed One died there arose, at the moment of his passing out of existence, a mighty earthquake, terrible and awe-inspiring: and the thunders of heaven burst forth.

15. When the Blessed One died, Brahmâ Sahampati, at the moment of his passing away from existence, uttered this stanza:

'They all, all beings that have life, shall lay
Aside their complex form—that aggregation
Of mental and material qualities,
That gives them, or in heaven or on earth,
Their fleeting individuality!
E'en as the teacher—being such a one,

Unequalled among all the men that are,
Successor of the prophets of old time,
Mighty by wisdom, and in insight clear—
Hath died[1]!'

16. When the Blessed One died, Sakka, the king of the gods, at the moment of his passing away from existence, uttered this stanza:

'They're transient all, each being's parts and powers,
Growth is their nature, and decay.
They are produced, they are dissolved again:
And then is best, when they have sunk to rest[2]!'

---

[1] Brahmâ, the first cause, the highest result of Indian theological speculation, the one God of the Indian Pantheists, is represented as using expressions full of deep allusions to the most characteristic Buddhist doctrines. The Samussaya is the result of the temporary collocation of the 'aggregations' (khandhâ) of mental and material qualities which give to each being (bhûto, that is, man, animal, god, ghost, fairy, or what not) its outward and visible shape, its individuality. Loka is here not the world in our sense, but the 'locality' in the Buddhist universe which such an individual occupies until it is dissolved. (Comp. Chap. II, §§ 14, 34.) Brahmâ appears therefore as a veritable Vibhaggavâdî.

[2] On this celebrated verse see below the Introduction to Mahâ-Sudassana Sutta. It must be the original of the first verse in the Chinese work, Fa Kheu Pi Hu (Beal, Dhammapada, p. 32), though it is there so changed that every clause has lost its point.

'Whatever exists is without endurance.
And hence the terms "flourishing" and "decaying."
A man is born, and then he dies.
Oh, the happiness of escaping from this condition!'

The very meaning which is here the most essential connotation of saṅkhârâ is lost in the phrase 'whatever exists.' By a misapprehension of the, no doubt, difficult word Dhamma, which, however, never means 'term,' the second clause has lost its point. And by a grammatical blunder the third clause in the Chinese confines the doctrine, erroneously, to man. In a Chinese tale, called

17. When the Blessed One died, the venerable Anuruddha, at the moment of his passing away from existence, uttered these stanzas:

'When he who from all craving want was free,
Who to Nirvâ*n*a's tranquil state had reached,
When the great sage finished his span of life,
No gasping struggle vexed that steadfast heart!

All resolute, and with unshaken mind,
He calmly triumphed o'er the pain of death.
E'en as a bright flame dies away, so was
His last deliverance from the bonds of life[1]!'

18. When the Blessed One died, the venerable Ânanda, at the moment of his passing away from existence, uttered this stanza:

'Then was there terror!
Then stood the hair on end!
When he endowed with every grace—
The supreme Buddha—died[2]!'

Ngan shih niu, translated by Mr. Beal, in the Indian Antiquary for May, 1880, the following verses occur; and they are possibly another reflection of this stanza:

'All things that exist are transitory.
They must of necessity perish and disappear;
Though joined together, there must be separation;
Where there is life there must be death.'

[1] *K*etaso Vimokho. Kena*k*i dhammena anâvara*n*a-vimokho sabbaso apa*ññ*atti-bhâvûpagamo, says Buddhaghosa; that is, 'the deliverance which is free from the restraint of each and every mental quality completely vanishing away' (dhammâ being here = sa*ññ*â and vedanâ and sańkhârâ; see 'Buddhism,' pp. 91, 92). See also below, p. 153.

[2] In these four stanzas we seem to have the way in which the death of the Buddha would be regarded, as the early Buddhist thought, by four representative persons—the exalted God of the theologians; the Jupiter of the multitude (allowing in the case of

19[1]. When the Blessed One died, of those of the brethren who were not yet free from the passions, some stretched out their arms and wept, and some fell headlong on the ground, rolling to and fro in anguish at the thought: 'Too soon has the Blessed One died! Too soon has the Happy One passed away from existence! Too soon has the Light gone out in the world!'

But those of the brethren who were free from the passions (the Arahats) bore their grief collected and composed at the thought: 'Impermanent are all component things! How is it possible that [they should not be dissolved]?'

20. Then the venerable Anuruddha exhorted the brethren, and said: 'Enough, my brethren! Weep not, neither lament! Has not the Blessed One formerly declared this to us, that it is in the very nature of all things near and dear unto us, that we must divide ourselves from them, leave them, sever ourselves from them? How then, brethren, can this be possible—that whereas anything whatever born, brought into being, and organised, contains within itself the inherent necessity of dissolution—how then can this be possible that such a being should not be dissolved? No such condition can exist! Even the spirits, brethren, will reproach us[2].

---

each of these for the change in character resulting from their conversion to Buddhism); the holy, thoughtful Arahat; and the loving, childlike disciple.

[1] Nearly=V, 11–14; and below, VI, 39.

[2] U*ggh*âyanti. I have followed the reading of my own MS., which is confirmed by the Sumangala Vilâsinî and the Mâlâlaṅkâra-vatthu. Vi*ggh*âyanti, which Childers reads, would be questionable Buddhism. The spirits do not become extinct; that is, not as a general rule, as would be implied by the absolute state-

'But of what kind of spirits is the Lord, the venerable Anuruddha, thinking?'

21. 'There are spirits, brother Ânanda, in the sky, but of worldly mind, who dishevel their hair and weep, and stretch forth their arms and weep, fall prostrate on the ground, and roll to and fro in anguish at the thought: "Too soon has the

---

ment, 'Even the spirits, brethren, become extinct.' It is no doubt true that all spirits, from the lowest to the highest, from the most insignificant fairy to the God of theological speculation, are regarded as temporary. But when they cease to exist as gods or spirits (devatâ), they do not go out, they are not extinguished (vigghâyanti); they continue to exist in some other form. And though that other form would, from the European point of view, be a different being, as there would be no continuity of consciousness, no passage of a 'soul' from the one to the other; it would, from the Buddhist point of view, be the same being, as it would be the resultant effect of the same Karma. There would follow on the death of a devatâ, not extinction, but a transmutation of force, a transmigration of character, a passing on, an inheritance of Karma. Only in the exceedingly rare case of an anâgâmin, of which an instance will be found above, Chap. II, § 7, could it be said that a spirit becomes extinct.

The expression 'of worldly mind,' here and above in V, 11, is in Pâli pathavi-saññiniyo, an ambiguous phrase which has only been found in this connection. Buddhaghosa says merely, 'because they made (mâpetvâ) an earth in heaven.' This gloss again may be taken either in a figurative or in a literal sense; but, if not impossible, it is at least unlikely that the good commentator means calmly to state that the angels created a floor in the skies—for the greater convenience of tumbling! The word seems to me also to be opposed to vîtarâgâ, 'free from passion,' and I have therefore taken it in a spiritual sense. There is a third possibility, viz. that it is used in an intellectual sense, 'having the idea of the world present to their mind;' and this would be in accordance with the more usual use of saññî. But how easily, especially in Buddhism, the intellectual merges into the religious may be seen from such a phrase as marana-saññino, used at Mahâvamsa 33 of the bhikkhus. Compare also above, III, 14.

Blessed One died! Too soon has the Happy One passed away! Too soon has the Light gone out in the world!"'

'There are spirits, too, Ânanda, on the earth, and of worldly mind, who tear their hair and weep, and stretch forth their arms and weep, fall prostrate on the ground, and roll to and fro in anguish at the thought: "Too soon has the Blessed one died! Too soon has the Happy One passed away! Too soon has the Light gone out in the world!"

'But the spirits who are free from passion bear it, calm and self-possessed, mindful of the saying which begins, "Impermanent indeed are all component things. How then is it possible [that such a being should not be dissolved]?"'

---

22. Now the venerable Anuruddha and the venerable Ânanda spent the rest of that night in religious discourse. Then the venerable Anuruddha said to the venerable Ânanda: 'Go now, brother Ânanda, into Kusinârâ and inform the Mallas of Kusinârâ, saying, 'The Blessed One, O Vâse*tth*as, is dead: do, then, whatever seemeth to you fit!'

'Even so, Lord!' said the venerable Ânanda, in assent, to the venerable Anuruddha. And having robed himself early in the morning, he took his bowl, and went into Kusinârâ with one of the brethren as an attendant.

23. Now at that time the Mallas of Kusinârâ were assembled in the council hall concerning that very matter.

And the venerable Ânanda went to the council hall of the Mallas of Kusinârâ; and when he had arrived there, he informed them, saying, 'The

Blessed One, O Vâse*tth*as, is dead; do, then, whatever seemeth to you fit!'

24. And when they had heard this saying of the venerable Ânanda, the Mallas, with their young men and their maidens and their wives, were grieved, and sad, and afflicted at heart. And some of them wept, dishevelling their hair, and some stretched forth their arms and wept, and some fell prostrate on the ground, and some reeled to and fro in anguish at the thought: 'Too soon has the Blessed One died! Too soon has the Happy One passed away! Too soon has the Light gone out in the world!'

---

25. Then the Mallas of Kusinârâ gave orders to their attendants, saying, 'Gather together perfumes and garlands, and all the music in Kusinârâ!'

26. And the Mallas of Kusinârâ took the perfumes and garlands, and all the musical instruments, and five hundred suits of apparel, and went to the Upavattana, to the Sâla Grove of the Mallas, where the body of the Blessed One lay. There they past the day in paying honour, reverence, respect, and homage to the remains of the Blessed One with dancing, and hymns, and music, and with garlands and perfumes; and in making canopies of their garments, and preparing decoration wreaths to hang thereon[1].

[1] The dress of the Mallas consisted probably of mere lengths of muslin or cotton cloth; and a suit of apparel consisted of two or, at the outside, of three of these—one to wrap round the loins, one to throw over the shoulders, and one to use as a turban. To make a canopy on occasions of state they would join such pieces together; to make the canopy into a tent they would simply add walls of the same material; and the only decoration, as simple as it

27. Then the Mallas of Kusinârâ thought:

'It is much too late to burn the body of the Blessed One to-day. Let us now perform the cremation to-morrow.' And in paying honour, reverence, respect, and homage to the remains of the Blessed One with dancing, and hymns, and music, and with garlands and perfumes; and in making canopies of their garments, and preparing decoration wreaths to hang thereon, they past the second day too, and then the third day, and the fourth, and the fifth, and the sixth day also.

---

28. Then on the seventh day the Mallas of Kusinârâ thought:

'Let us carry the body of the Blessed One, by the south and outside, to a spot on the south, and outside of the city,—paying it honour, and reverence, and respect, and homage, with dance and song and music, with garlands and perfumes,—and there, to the south of the city, let us perform the cremation ceremony!'

29. And thereupon eight chieftains among the Mallas bathed their heads, and clad themselves in new garments with the intention of bearing the body of the Blessed One. But, behold, they could not lift it up!

30. Then the Mallas of Kusinârâ said to the venerable Anuruddha: 'What, Lord, can be the reason, what can be the cause that eight chieftains of the Mallas who have bathed their heads, and clad themselves in new garments with the intention

---

is beautiful, would be wreaths of flowers, or single lotuses, hanging from the roof, or stretched along the sides.

of bearing the body of the Blessed One, are unable to lift it up?'

'It is because you, O Vâse*tth*as, have one purpose, and the spirits have another purpose.'

31. 'But what, Lord, is the purpose of the spirits?'

'Your purpose, O Vâse*tth*as, is this, Let us carry the body of the Blessed One, by the south and outside, to a spot on the south, and outside of the city,—paying it honour, and reverence, and respect, and homage, with dance and song and music, with garlands and perfumes,—and there, to the south of the city, let us perform the cremation ceremony. But the purpose of the spirits, Vâse*tth*as, is this, Let us carry the body of the Blessed One by the north to the north of the city, and entering the city by the north gate, let us bring it through the midst of the city into the midst thereof. And going out again by the eastern gate,—paying honour, and reverence, and respect, and homage to the body of the Blessed One, with heavenly dance, and song, and music, and garlands, and perfumes,—let us carry it to the shrine of the Mallas called Maku*t*a-bandhana, to the east of the city, and there let us perform the cremation ceremony.'

'Even according to the purpose of the spirits, so, Lord, let it be!'

32. Then immediately all Kusinârâ down even to the dust bins and rubbish heaps became strewn knee-deep with Mandârava flowers from heaven! and while both the spirits from the skies, and the Mallas of Kusinârâ upon earth, paid honour, and reverence, and respect, and homage to the body of the Blessed One, with dance and song and music, with garlands and with perfumes, they carried the

body by the north to the north of the city; and entering the city by the north gate they carried it through the midst of the city into the midst thereof; and going out again by the eastern gate they carried it to the shrine of the Mallas, called Maku*t*a-bandhana; and there, to the east of the city, they laid down the body of the Blessed One[1].

---

33. [2] Then the Mallas of Kusinârâ said to the venerable Ânanda: 'What should be done, Lord, with the remains of the Tathâgata?'

'As men treat the remains of a king of kings, so, Vâse*tth*as, should they treat the remains of a Tathâgata.'

'And how, Lord, do they treat the remains of a king of kings?'

'They wrap the body of a king of kings, Vâse*tth*as, in a new cloth. When that is done they wrap it in cotton wool. When that is done they wrap it in a new cloth,—and so on till they have wrapped the body in five hundred successive layers of both kinds. Then they place the body in an oil vessel of iron, and cover that close up with another oil vessel of iron. They then build a funeral pile of all kinds of perfumes, and burn the body of the king of kings. And then at the four cross roads they erect a dâgaba to the king of kings. This, Vâse*tth*as, is the way in which they treat the remains of a king of kings.

'And as they treat the remains of a king of kings, so, Vâse*tth*as, should they treat the remains of the

---

[1] The point of this interesting legend is that the inhabitants of an Indian village of that time would have considered it a desecration or pollution to bring a dead body into or through their village.

[2] Compare Chap. V, §§ 25–30.

Tathâgata. At the four cross roads a dâgaba should be erected to the Tathâgata. And whosoever shall there place garlands or perfumes or paint, or make salutation there, or become in its presence calm in heart—that shall long be to them for a profit and a joy.'

34. Therefore the Mallas gave orders to their attendants, saying, 'Gather together all the carded cotton wool of the Mallas!'

35. Then the Mallas of Kusinârâ wrapped the body of the Blessed One in a new cloth. And when that was done, they wrapped it in cotton wool. And when that was done, they wrapped it in a new cloth, —and so on till they had wrapped the body of the Blessed One in five hundred layers of both kinds. And then they placed the body in an oil vessel of iron, and covered that close up with another oil vessel of iron. And then they built a funeral pile of all kinds of perfumes, and upon it they placed the body of the Blessed One.

---

36. Now at that time the venerable Mahâ Kassapa was journeying along the high road from Pâvâ to Kusinârâ with a great company of the brethren, with about five hundred of the brethren. And the venerable Mahâ Kassapa left the high road, and sat himself down at the foot of a certain tree.

37. Just at that time a certain naked ascetic who had picked up a Mandârava flower in Kusinârâ was coming along the high road to Pâvâ.

38. And the venerable Mahâ Kassapa saw the naked ascetic coming in the distance; and when he had seen him he said to the naked ascetic:

'O friend! surely thou knowest our Master?'

'Yea, friend! I know him. This day the Sama*n*a Gotama has been dead a week! That is how I obtained this Mandârava flower.'

39. And immediately of those of the brethren who were not yet free from the passions, some stretched out their arms and wept, and some fell headlong on the ground, and some reeled to and fro in anguish at the thought: 'Too soon has the Blessed One died! Too soon has the Happy One passed away from existence! Too soon has the Light gone out in the world!'

But those of the brethren who were free from the passions (the Arahats) bore their grief collected and composed at the thought: 'Impermanent are all component things! How is it possible that they should not be dissolved?'

---

40. Now at that time a brother named Subhadda, who had been received into the order in his old age, was seated there in their company[1].

And Subhadda the old addressed the brethren, and said: 'Enough, brethren! Weep not, neither lament! We are well rid of the great Sama*n*a. We used to be annoyed by being told, "This beseems you, this beseems you not." But now we shall be able to do whatever we like; and what we do not like, that we shall not have to do!'

---

[1] At p. xxvi of the Introduction to his edition of the Mahâ Vagga, Dr. Oldenberg identifies this Subhadda with Subhadda the last convert, mentioned above in Chap. V, §§ 52–68. They are different persons; the last convert being represented as a young man of high character, incapable of the conduct here ascribed to this Subhadda. The last convert was a Brâhman, traditionally supposed to be younger brother to A*ññ*a Konda*ññ*a, the first convert; this Subhadda had been a barber in the village Âtumâ.

41. But the venerable Mahâ Kassapa addressed the brethren, and said: 'Enough, my brethren! Weep not, neither lament! Has not the Blessed One formerly declared this to us, that it is in the very nature of all things, near and dear unto us, that we must divide ourselves from them, leave them, sever ourselves from them? How then, brethren, can this be possible—that whereas anything whatever born, brought into being, and organised contains within itself the inherent necessity of dissolution—how then can this be possible that such a being should not be dissolved? No such condition can exist!'

---

42. Now just at that time four chieftains of the Mallas had bathed their heads and clad themselves in new garments with the intention of setting on fire the funeral pile of the Blessed One. But, behold, they were unable to set it alight!

43. Then the Mallas of Kusinârâ said to the venerable Anuruddha: 'What, Lord, can be the reason, and what the cause, that four chieftains of the Mallas who have bathed their heads, and clad themselves in new garments, with the intention of setting on fire the funeral pile of the Blessed One, are unable to set it on fire?'

'It is because you, O Vâse*tth*as, have one purpose, and the spirits have another purpose.'

44. 'But what, Lord, is the purpose of the spirits?'

'The purpose of the spirits, O Vâse*tth*as, is this: That venerable brother Mahâ Kassapa is now journeying along the high road from Pâvâ to Kusinârâ with a great company of the brethren, with five hundred of the brethren. The funeral pile of the Blessed One shall not catch fire, until the venerable Mahâ Kassapa shall have been able reverently to salute the sacred feet of the Blessed One.'

'Even according to the purpose of the spirits, so, Lord, let it be!'

---

45. Then the venerable Mahâ Kassapa went on to Maku*t*a-bandhana of Kusinârâ, to the shrine of the Mallas, to the place where the funeral pile of the Blessed One was. And when he had come up to it, he arranged his robe on one shoulder; and bowing down with clasped hands he thrice walked reverently round the pile; and then, uncovering the feet, he bowed down in reverence at the feet of the Blessed One.

46. And those five hundred brethren arranged their robes on one shoulder; and bowing down with clasped hands, they thrice walked reverently round the pile, and then bowed down in reverence at the feet of the Blessed One.

47. And when the homage of the venerable Mahâ Kassapa and of those five hundred brethren was ended, the funeral pile of the Blessed One caught fire of itself[1].

---

[1] It is possible that we have here the survival of some ancient custom. Spence Hardy appropriately refers to a ceremony among Jews (of what place or time is not mentioned) in the following terms: 'Just before a Jew is taken out of the house to be buried, the relatives and acquaintances of the departed stand round the coffin; when the feet are uncovered; and each in rotation lays hold of the great toes, and begs pardon for any offence given to the deceased, and requests a favourable mention of them in the next world.' (Manual of Buddhism, p. 348.)

The Buddhist bhikkhus in Siam and the great majority of those in Ceylon (the adherents of the Siyam-samâgama) always keep one shoulder uncovered. It is evident that the bhikkhus

48. Now as the body of the Blessed One burned itself away, from the skin and the integument, and the flesh, and the nerves, and the fluid of the joints, neither soot nor ash was seen: and only the bones remained behind.

Just as one sees no soot or ash when glue or oil is burned; so, as the body of the Blessed One burned itself away, from the skin and the integument, and the flesh, and the nerves, and the fluid of the joints, neither soot nor ash was seen: and only the bones remained behind. And of those five hundred pieces of raiment the very innermost and outermost were both consumed.

49. And when the body of the Blessed One had been burnt up, there came down streams of water from the sky and extinguished the funeral pile of the Blessed One; and there burst forth streams of water from the storehouse of the waters (beneath the earth), and extinguished the funeral pile of the Blessed One. The Mallas of Kusinârâ also brought water scented with all kinds of perfumes, and extinguished the funeral pile of the Blessed One[1].

---

in Burma, and those in Ceylon who belong to the Amara-pura-samâgama, are more in accordance with ancient custom in wearing the robe ordinarily over both shoulders.

[1] There is something very quaint in the way in which the faithful Mallas are here represented as bringing coals to Newcastle. The 'storehouse of the waters' is in Pâli udaka-sâla, on which Buddhaghosa has two theories: first, that the Sâla trees around shed down a miraculous rain from their trunks and branches and leaves; and next, that the waters burst up from the earth and became as it were a diadem of crystal round the pyre. On the belief that water thus burst up miraculously through the earth, see 'Buddhist Birth Stories,' pp. 64, 67. If the reading be correct it is scarcely possible that sâla can here have anything to do with Sâla trees; but the other interpretation is open to the objections

50. Then the Mallas of Kusinârâ surrounded the bones of the Blessed One in their council hall with a lattice work of spears, and with a rampart of bows; and there for seven days they paid honour and reverence and respect and homage to them with dance and song and music, and with garlands and perfumes.

---

51. Now the king of Magadha, A*g*âtasattu, the son of the queen of the Videha clan, heard the news that the Blessed One had died at Kusinârâ.

Then the king of Magadha, A*g*âtasattu, the son of the queen of the Videha clan, sent a messenger to the Mallas, saying, 'The Blessed One belonged to the soldier caste, and I too am of the soldier caste. I am worthy to receive a portion of the relics of the Blessed One. Over the remains of the Blessed One will I put up a sacred cairn, and in their honour will I celebrate a feast[1]!'

52. And the Li*kkh*avis of Vesâli heard the news that the Blessed One had died at Kusinârâ. And the Li*kkh*avis of Vesâli sent a messenger to the Mallas, saying, 'The Blessed One belonged to the soldier caste, and we too are of the soldier caste. We are worthy to receive a portion of the relics of the Blessed One. Over the remains of the Blessed One will we put up a sacred cairn, and in their honour will we celebrate a feast!'

53. And the Sâkiyas of Kapila-vatthu heard the

that sâla means an open hall rather than a storehouse, and that the belief in a 'storehouse of water' has not, as yet, been found elsewhere.

[1] The commentator gives a long account of A*g*âtasattu's proceedings on this occasion.

news that the Blessed One had died at Kusinârâ. And the Sâkiyas of Kapila-vatthu sent a messenger to the Mallas, saying, 'The Blessed One was the pride of our race. We are worthy to receive a portion of the relics of the Blessed One. Over the remains of the Blessed One will we put up a sacred cairn, and in their honour will we celebrate a feast!'

54. And the Bulis of Allakappa heard the news that the Blessed One had died at Kusinârâ. And the Bulis of Allakappa sent a messenger to the Mallas, saying, 'The Blessed One belonged to the soldier caste, and we too are of the soldier caste. We are worthy to receive a portion of the relics of the Blessed One. Over the remains of the Blessed One will we put up a sacred cairn, and in their honour will we celebrate a feast!'

55. And the Koliyas of Râmagâma heard the news that the Blessed One had died at Kusinârâ. And the Koliyas of Râmagâma sent a messenger to the Mallas, saying, 'The Blessed One belonged to the soldier caste, and we too are of the soldier caste. We are worthy to receive a portion of the relics of the Blessed One. Over the remains of the Blessed One will we put up a sacred cairn, and in their honour will we celebrate a feast!'

56. And the Brâhman of Ve*th*adîpa heard the news that the Blessed One had died at Kusinârâ. And the Brâhman of Ve*th*adîpa sent a messenger to the Mallas, saying, 'The Blessed One belonged to the soldier caste, and I am a Brâhman. I am worthy to receive a portion of the relics of the Blessed One. Over the remains of the Blessed One will I put up a sacred cairn, and in their honour will I celebrate a feast!'

57. And the Mallas of Pâvâ heard the news that the Blessed One had died at Kusinârâ.

Then the Mallas of Pâvâ sent a messenger to the Mallas, saying, 'The Blessed One belonged to the soldier caste, and we too are of the soldier caste. We are worthy to receive a portion of the relics of the Blessed One. Over the remains of the Blessed One will we put up a sacred cairn, and in their honour will we celebrate a feast!'

---

58. When they heard these things the Mallas of Kusinârâ spoke to the assembled brethren, saying, 'The Blessed One died in our village domain. We will not give away any part of the remains of the Blessed One!'

59. When they had thus spoken, Dona the Brâhman addressed the assembled brethren, and said:

'Hear, reverend sirs, one single word from me.
Forbearance was our Buddha wont to teach.
Unseemly is it that over the division
Of the remains of him who was the best of beings
Strife should arise, and wounds, and war!
Let us all, sirs, with one accord unite
In friendly harmony to make eight portions.
Wide spread let Thûpas rise in every land
That in the Enlightened One mankind may trust!'

60. 'Do thou then, O Brâhman, thyself divide the remains of the Blessed One equally into eight parts, with fair division[1].'

'Be it so, sir!' said Dona, in assent, to the assem-

---

[1] Here again the commentator expands and adds to the comparatively simple version of the text.

bled brethren. And he divided the remains of the Blessed One equally into eight parts, with fair division. And he said to them: 'Give me, sirs, this vessel, and I will set up over it a sacred cairn, and in its honour will I establish a feast.'

And they gave the vessel to Do*n*a the Brâhman.

---

61. And the Moriyas of Pipphalivana heard the news that the Blessed One had died at Kusinârâ.

Then the Moriyas of Pipphalivana sent a messenger to the Mallas, saying, 'The Blessed One belonged to the soldier caste, and we too are of the soldier caste. We are worthy to receive a portion of the relics of the Blessed One. Over the remains of the Blessed One will we put up a sacred cairn, and in their honour will we celebrate a feast!'

And when they heard the answer, saying, 'There is no portion of the remains of the Blessed One left over. The remains of the Blessed One are all distributed,' then they took away the embers.

---

62. Then the king of Magadha, A*g*âtasattu, the son of the queen of the Videha clan, made a mound in Râ*g*agaha over the remains of the Blessed One, and held a feast.

And the Li*kkh*avis of Vesâli made a mound in Vesâli over the remains of the Blessed One, and held a feast.

And the Bulis of Allakappa made a mound in Allakappa over the remains of the Blessed One, and held a feast.

And the Koliyas of Râmagâma made a mound in Râmagâma over the remains of the Blessed One, and held a feast.

And Ve*th*adîpaka the Brâhman made a mound in Ve*th*adîpa over the remains of the Blessed One, and held a feast.

And the Mallas of Pâvâ made a mound in Pâvâ over the remains of the Blessed One, and held a feast.

And the Mallas of Kusinârâ made a mound in Kusinârâ over the remains of the Blessed One, and held a feast.

And Do*n*a the Brâhman made a mound over the vessel in which the body had been burnt, and held a feast.

And the Moriyas of Pipphalivana made a mound over the embers, and held a feast.

Thus were there eight mounds [Thûpas] for the remains, and one for the vessel, and one for the embers. This was how it used to be[1].

[63. Eight measures of relics there were of him of the far-seeing eye,
Of the best of the best of men. In India seven are worshipped,
And one measure in Râmagâma, by the kings of the serpent race.
One tooth, too, is honoured in heaven, and one in Gandhâra's city,
One in the Kâlinga realm, and one more by the Nâga race.

---

[1] Here closes Buddhaghosa's long and edifying commentary. He has no note on the following verses, which he says were added by Theras in Ceylon. The additional verse found in the Phayre MS. was in the same way probably added in Burma.

Through their glory the bountiful earth is made
 bright with offerings painless—
For with such are the Great Teacher's relics best
 honoured by those who are honoured,
By gods and by Nâgas and kings, yea, thus by
 the noblest of monarchs—
Bow down with clasped hands!
Hard, hard is a Buddha to meet with through
 hundreds of ages!]

End of the Book of the Great Decease.

DHAMMA*K*AKKAPPAVAT-
TANA-SUTTA.

INTRODUCTION

TO THE

FOUNDATION OF THE KINGDOM OF RIGHTEOUSNESS.

THIS translation is made from a transcript of the text as found in the very beautiful Ceylon MS. on silver plates, now in the British Museum[1]. The letters, which are perfectly formed, are cut into the silver; and the MS. has this peculiarity, that every sentence is repeated with a slight change in the collocation of the words. Thus the first sentence is given as follows:—

Eva*m* me suta*m*. Eka*m* samaya*m* Bhagavâ Bârâ*n*asiya*m* viharati Isipatane Migadâye. Me eva*m* suta*m*. Eka*m* samaya*m* Bhagavâ Bârâ*n*asiya*m* Isipatane Migadâye viharati.

As this repetition is merely carried out for the further security of the text it has not been followed in the translation.

This text belongs to the Aṅguttara Nikâya. M. Léon Feer has lithographed the Sa*m*yutta treatment in his 'Textes tirés du Kandjour[2],' together with the text of the corresponding passage in the Lalita Vistara, and the Tibetan translation from that poem. The Sanskrit text, so far as it runs parallel with our Sutta, will also be found in Rajendra Lal Mitra's edition of the Lalita Vistara (p. 540 and foll.) and the Tibetan text, with a French translation, in M. Foucaux's 'rGya Cher Rol Pa.' Dr. Oldenberg has just published the Vinaya treatment contained in the Mahâ Vagga I, 6. It is the same word for word as our Sutta (except § 1, which is of course not found there). The Sa*m*yutta expands the idea of the portion numbered below §§ 9-20, having also similar paragraphs in reference to the bhikkhus themselves. The

---

[1] MS. Egerton, 794; bought from a bookseller named Rodel in 1839.

[2] Livraison, No. X.

Lalita Vistara differs a good deal in minor details, but is substantially the same as regards the Noble Truths, and the eight divisions of the Noble Path.

A translation of this Sutta, found among Mr. Gogerly's papers after his death, was published in the Journal of the Ceylon Asiatic Society for 1865: and the Journal Asiatique for 1870 contained a translation and full analysis by M. Léon Feer.

It would be difficult to estimate too highly the historical value of this Sutta. There can be no reasonable doubt that the very ancient tradition accepted by all Buddhists as to the substance of the discourse is correct, and that we really have in it a summary of the words in which the great Indian thinker and reformer for the first time successfully promulgated his new ideas. And it presents to us in a few short and pithy sentences the very essence of that remarkable system which has had so profound an influence on the religious history of so large a portion of the human race.

The name given to it by the early Buddhists—the setting in motion onwards of the royal chariot-wheel of the supreme dominion of the Dhamma—means, as I have shown elsewhere[1], not 'the turning of the wheel of the law,' as it has been usually rendered; but 'the inauguration, or foundation, of the Kingdom of Righteousness.'

Is it possible that the praying wheels of Thibet have led to the misapprehension and mistranslation now so common? But who would explain a passage in the New Testament by a superstition current, say, in Spain in the twelfth century? And so when Mr. Da Cuñha thinks that the Dhamma is symbolised by the wheel, because 'Gotama ignored the beginning, and was uncertain as to the end[2],' he seems to me to be following a vicious method of interpreting such figures of speech. It cannot be disputed that the term 'wheel' might have implied such an idea as he puts into it. But if we want to know what it did imply, we must be guided wholly by the previous use of the word at the

---

[1] 'Buddhism,' p. 45. [2] 'Memoir on the Tooth Relic,' &c., p. 15.

time when it was first used in a figurative sense: and that previous use allows only of the interpretation given above. Perhaps, however, Mr. Da Cuñha is only copying (not very exactly) Mr. Alabaster, who has said, 'Buddha, as I have tried to show in other parts of this book, did not attempt to teach the beginning of existence, but assumed it as a rolling circle of causes or effects. This was his circle or wheel of the law[1].'

Mr. Alabaster therefore calls his very useful book on Siamese Buddhism, 'The Wheel of the Law;'—an expression which he on the first page of his preface takes to be about equivalent to Buddhism. But his theory of the meaning of the term seems to be based upon a misunderstanding of a passage in the Siamese 'Life of Buddha,' which he there translates. At page 78 he renders his text, 'The Holy Wheel which the Law taught is plenteous in twelve ways,' and he explains this on p. 169 as referring to the twelve Nidânas, the chain of causes and effects. But the passage in the Siamese text is evidently a reminiscence of the 'twelvefold manner' spoken of in the same connection in our Sutta (§ 21), and does not refer to the Nidânas at all.

A better comment on the word is the legend of the Treasure of the Wheel, which will be found below in the 'Book of the Great King of Glory[2],' a passage which shows that this figure belonged to that circle of poetical imagery which the early Buddhists so often borrowed from the previous poets of Vedic literature to aid them in their attempts to describe the most important events in the life of their revered Teacher. And, like the day of Pentecost by the early Christians, this Inauguration of the Kingdom of Righteousness was rightly regarded by them as a turning-point in the history of their faith. We find this even in the closing sections of our Sutta; and in later times the poets of every Buddhist clime have vied one with another in endeavouring to express their sense of the importance of the occasion.

'The evening was like a lovely maiden; the stars

[1] 'Wheel of the Law,' p. 288.

[2] Chap. I, §§ 10–20.

were the pearls upon her neck; the dark clouds her braided hair; the deepening space her flowing robe. As a crown she had the heavens where the angels dwell; these three worlds were as her body; her eyes were the white lotus flowers which open to the rising moon; and her voice was as it were the humming of the bees. To do homage to the Buddha, and to hear the first preaching of his word, this lovely maiden came.' The angels (devas) throng to hear the discourse until the heavens are empty; and the sound of their approach is like the rain of a storm; all the worlds in which there are sentient beings are made void of life, so that the congregation assembled was in number infinite, but at the sound of the blast of the glorious trumpet of Sakka, the king of the gods, they became still as a waveless sea. And then each of the countless listeners thought that the sage was looking towards himself, and was speaking to him in his own tongue, though the language used was Mâgadhi!

It is most curious that this last figure should be so closely analogous to the language used with respect to the corresponding event in the history of the Christian church: and I do not know the exact source from which Hardy (Manual of Buddhism, p. 186) derives it. But I think it is highly improbable that there is any borrowing on the one side or on the other.

It cannot be denied that there is a real beauty of an Oriental kind in the various expressions which the Buddhists use; and that there was real ground for the enthusiasm which gave them birth. Never in the history of the world had a scheme of salvation been put forth so simple in its nature, so free from any superhuman agency, so independent of, so even antagonistic to the belief in a soul, the belief in God, and the hope for a future life. And we must not allow our estimate of the importance of the event to be influenced by our disagreement from the opinions put forth. Whether these be right or wrong, it was a turning-point in the religious history of man when a reformer, full of the most earnest moral purpose, and trained in all the intellectual culture of his time, put forth deliberately, and with a knowledge of the opposing views, the doctrine of a salvation to be found here, in this life, in an inward change of heart, to be brought about by perseverance in a mere system of self-culture and of self-control.

That system, it will be seen, is called the Noble Path, and is divided into eight sections or divisions, each of which commences with the word sammâ—a word for which we have no real equivalent in English, though it has been rendered by such terms as 'right,' 'perfect,' and 'correct.' Our word 'right,' in some of its uses, would be a sufficiently adequate translation, but it is based on a different derivation, and connotes a set of ideas not alluded to by sammâ. If used as an adjective this word—signifying literally 'going with'—means either 'general, common,' or 'corresponding, mutual,' and as an adverb, 'commonly, usually, normally,' or 'fittingly, properly, correctly;' and hence, in a secondary sense, and with allusion to both these ideas, 'round, fit, and perfect, normal and complete.' When used to characterise such widely different things as language, livelihood, and belief, the meaning of the term is by no means difficult to grasp; but it is difficult, if not impossible, to find any single English word which in each case would convey its full force without importing also some extraneous idea. From a desire to follow closely the Pâli form of expression I had first in my manual of 'Buddhism' adopted the one word 'right' throughout the translation of the text; and I have kept to this below, though I feel that that word quite fails to give the force of the preposition sam (συν-, con-), which is the essential part of the Pâli sammâ. But I think the meaning of the Buddhist ideal, of the summary which is the most essential doctrine, the very pith of Buddhism, would be better brought out by a diversified rendering in the way I afterwards attempted in an article in the Fortnightly Review (No. CLVI); or, as above (p. 107), with the authorised interpretation appended. It would then run—

1. Right Views; free from superstition or delusion.
2. Right Aims; high, and worthy of the intelligent, earnest man.
3. Right Speech; kindly, open, truthful.
4. Right Conduct; peaceful, honest, pure.
5. Right Livelihood; bringing hurt or danger to no living thing.
6. Right Effort; in self-training, and in self-control.
7. Right Mindfulness; the active, watchful mind.
8. Right Contemplation; earnest thought on the deep mysteries of life.

It is interesting to notice that Gogerly, who first rendered sammâ throughout by correct[1], afterwards adopted the other method[2]; and as these eight divisions of the perfect life are of such vital importance for a correct understanding of what Buddhism really was, I here add in parallel columns his two versions of the terms used :—

1. Correct views (of truth).	Correct doctrines.
2. Correct thoughts.	A clear perception (of their nature).
3. Correct words.	Inflexible veracity.
4. Correct conduct.	Purity of conduct.
5. Correct (mode of obtaining a) livelihood.	A sinless occupation.
6. Correct efforts.	Perseverance in duty.
7. Correct meditation.	Holy meditation.
8. Correct tranquillity.	Mental tranquillity.

The varying expressions in these two lists are intended in all cases, (except perhaps the second,) to convey the same idea. The second division (sammâ-saṅkappo) is not really open to any doubt. Saṅkappo is will, volition, determination, desire; that exertion of the will in the various affairs of life which results from the feeling that a certain result will be desirable. The only variation in the meaning is that sometimes more stress is laid upon the implied exertion of the will, sometimes more stress upon the implied desire

[1] Journal of the Ceylon Asiatic Society, 1845. [2] Ibid. 1865.

which calls it into action. 'Motive' would be somewhat too impersonal, 'volition' too metaphysical a rendering; 'aims' or 'aspirations' seems to me to best express the sense intended in this passage.

In No. 7 (sammâ-sati) sati is literally 'memory,' but is used with reference to the constantly repeated phrase 'mindful and thoughtful' (sato sampa*g*âno); and means that activity of mind and constant presence of mind which is one of the duties most frequently inculcated on the good Buddhist. Gogerly's rendering of the term should have been reserved for the last division (sammâ-samâdhi), that prolonged meditation on the deep mysteries of life, which is stated in the Great Decease[1] to be the necessary complement and accessory to intelligence and goodness. Reason and works are good in themselves, but they require to be made perfect by that samâdhi which in Buddhism corresponds to faith in Christianity.

This Buddhist ideal of the perfect life has an analogy most instructive from a historical point of view with the ideals of the last pagan thinkers in Europe before the rise of Christianity, and of the modern exponents of what has been called fervent atheism. When after many centuries of thought a pantheistic or monotheistic unity has been evolved out of the chaos of polytheism,—which is itself a modified animism or animistic polydæmonism,—there has always arisen at last a school to whom theological discussions have lost their interest, and who have sought for a new solution of the questions to which the theologies have given inconsistent answers, in a new system in which man was to work out here, on earth, his own salvation. It is their place in the progress of thought that helps us to understand how it is that there is so much in common between the Agnostic philosopher of India, the Stoics of Greece and Rome, and some of the newest schools in France, in Germany, and among ourselves.

[1] Chap. I, § 12, and often afterwards.

THE FOUNDATION
OF THE
KINGDOM OF RIGHTEOUSNESS.

DHAMMA-*K*AKKA-PPAVATTANA-SUTTA.

Reverence to the Blessed One, the Holy One, the Fully-Enlightened One.

1. Thus have I heard. The Blessed One was once staying at Benares, at the hermitage called Migadâya. And there the Blessed One addressed the company of the five Bhikkhus [1], and said:

2. 'There are two extremes, O Bhikkhus, which the man who has given up the world [2] ought not to follow—the habitual practice, on the one hand, of those things whose attraction depends upon the passions, and especially of sensuality—a low and pagan [3] way (of seeking satisfaction) unworthy, unprofitable, and fit only for the worldly-minded—

---

[1] These are the five mendicants who had waited on the Bodisat during his austerities, as described in 'Buddhist Birth Stories,' pp. 88, 89. Their names are given on p. 113 of that book; see below, the note on § 32.

[2] Pabba*g*ito, one who has gone forth, who has renounced worldly things, a 'religious.'

[3] Gamma, a word of the same derivation as, and corresponding meaning to, our word 'pagan.'

and the habitual practice, on the other hand, of asceticism (or self-mortification), which is painful, unworthy, and unprofitable.

3. 'There is a middle path, O Bhikkhus, avoiding these two extremes, discovered by the Tathâgata[1]—a path which opens the eyes, and bestows understanding, which leads to peace of mind, to the higher wisdom, to full enlightenment, to Nirvâ*n*a!

4. 'What is that middle path, O Bhikkhus, avoiding these two extremes, discovered by the Tathâgata—that path which opens the eyes, and bestows understanding, which leads to peace of mind, to the higher wisdom, to full enlightenment, to Nirvâ*n*a? Verily! it is this noble eightfold path; that is to say:

'Right views;
Right aspirations;
Right speech;
Right conduct;
Right livelihood;
Right effort;
Right mindfulness; and
Right contemplation.

'This, O Bhikkhus, is that middle path, avoiding these two extremes, discovered by the Tathâgata—that path which opens the eyes, and bestows under-

[1] The Tathâgata is an epithet of a Buddha. It is interpreted by Buddhaghosa, in the Samangala Vilâsinî, to mean that he came to earth for the same purposes, after having passed through the same training in former births, as all the supposed former Buddhas; and that, when he had so come, all his actions corresponded with theirs.

'Avoiding these two extremes' should perhaps be referred to the Tathâgata, but I prefer the above rendering.

standing, which leads to peace of mind, to the higher wisdom, to full enlightenment, to Nirvâ*n*a!

---

5. 'Now[1] this, O Bhikkhus, is the noble truth concerning suffering.

'Birth is attended with pain[2], decay is painful, disease is painful, death is painful. Union with the unpleasant is painful, painful is separation from the pleasant; and any craving that is unsatisfied, that too is painful. In brief, the five aggregates which spring from attachment (the conditions of individuality and their cause)[3] are painful.

'This then, O Bhikkhus, is the noble truth concerning suffering.

6. 'Now this, O Bhikkhus, is the noble truth concerning the origin of suffering.

'Verily, it is that thirst (or craving), causing the renewal of existence, accompanied by sensual delight, seeking satisfaction now here, now there—that is to say, the craving for the gratification of the passions, or the craving for (a future) life, or the craving for success (in this present life)[4].

---

[1] On the following 'four truths' compare Dhammapada, verse 191, and Mahâ-parinibbâna Sutta II, 2, 3, and IV, 7, 8.

[2] Or 'is painful.'

[3] Pa*ñk*' upâdânakkhandhâ. On the Khandhâ, or the material and mental aggregates which go to make up an individual, see my 'Buddhism,' Chap. III. Upâdâna, or 'grasping' is their source, and the uprooting of this upâdâna from the mind is Arahatship.

One might express the central thought of this First Noble Truth in the language of the nineteenth century by saying that pain results from existence as an individual. It is the struggle to maintain one's individuality which produces pain—a most pregnant and far-reaching suggestion. See for a fuller exposition the Fortnightly Review for December, 1879.

[4] 'The lust of the flesh, the lust of the eye, and the pride of life'

'This then, O Bhikkhus, is the noble truth concerning the origin of suffering.

7. 'Now this, O Bhikkhus, is the noble truth concerning the destruction of suffering.

'Verily, it is the destruction, in which no passion remains, of this very thirst; the laying aside of, the getting rid of, the being free from, the harbouring no longer of this thirst.

'This then, O Bhikkhus, is the noble truth concerning the destruction of suffering.

8. 'Now this, O Bhikkhus, is the noble truth concerning the way[1] which leads to the destruction of sorrow. Verily! it is this noble eightfold path[2]; that is to say:

---

correspond very exactly to the first and third of these three tanhâs. 'The lust of the flesh, the lust of life, and the pride of life,' or 'the lust of the flesh, the lust of life, and the love of this present world,' would be not inadequate renderings of all three.

The last two are in Pâli bhava-tanhâ and vibhava-tanhâ, on which Childers, on the authority of Vigesinha, says: 'The former applies to the sassata-ditthi, and means a desire for an eternity of existence; the latter applies to the ukkheda-ditthi, and means a desire for annihilation in the very first (the present) form of existence.' Sassata-ditthi may be called the 'everlasting life heresy,' and ukkheda-ditthi the 'let-us-eat-and-drink-for-to-morrow-we-die heresy.' These two heresies, thus implicitly condemned, have very close analogies to theism and materialism.

Spence Hardy says ('Manual of Buddhism,' p. 496): 'Bhawa-tanhâ signifies the pertinacious love of existence induced by the supposition that transmigatory existence is not only eternal, but felicitous and desirable. Wibhawa-tanhâ is the love of the present life, under the notion that existence will cease therewith, and that there is to be no future state.'

Vibhava in Sanskrit means, 1. development; 2. might, majesty, prosperity; and 3. property: but the technical Buddhist sense, as will be seen from the above, is something more than this.

[1] Patipadâ.

[2] Ariyo atangiko Maggo.

'Right views;
Right aspirations;
Right speech;
Right conduct;
Right livelihood;
Right effort;
Right mindfulness; and
Right contemplation.

'This then, O Bhikkhus, is the noble truth concerning the destruction of sorrow.

---

9. 'That this was the noble truth concerning sorrow, was not, O Bhikkhus, among the doctrines handed down, but there arose within me the eye (to perceive it), there arose the knowledge (of its nature), there arose the understanding (of its cause), there arose the wisdom (to guide in the path of tranquillity), there arose the light (to dispel darkness from it)[1].

10. 'And again, O Bhikkhus, that I should comprehend that this was the noble truth concerning sorrow, though it was not among the doctrines handed down, there arose within me the eye, there arose the knowledge, there arose the understanding, there arose the wisdom, there arose the light.

11. 'And again, O Bhikkhus, that I had comprehended that this was the noble truth concerning sorrow, though it was not among the doctrines handed down, there arose within me the eye, there

[1] The words in parentheses have been added by Gogerly, doubtless from some comment not accessible to me; and I have included them also, but in parentheses, as they seem to complete the ideas actually involved in the text.

arose the knowledge, there arose the understanding, there arose the wisdom, there arose the light.

12. 'That this was the noble truth concerning the origin of sorrow, though it was not among the doctrines handed down, there arose within me the eye; but there arose within me the knowledge, there arose the understanding, there arose the wisdom, there arose the light.

13. 'And again, O Bhikkhus, that I should put away the origin of sorrow, though the noble truth concerning it was not among the doctrines handed down, there arose within me the eye, there arose the knowledge, there arose the understanding, there arose the wisdom, there arose the light.

14. 'And again, O Bhikkhus, that I had fully put away the origin of sorrow, though the noble truth concerning it was not among the doctrines handed down, there arose within me the eye, there arose the knowledge, there arose the understanding, there arose the wisdom, there arose the light.

15. 'That this, O Bhikkhus, was the noble truth concerning the destruction of sorrow, though it was not among the doctrines handed down; but there arose within me the eye, there arose the knowledge, there arose the understanding, there arose the wisdom, there arose the light.

16. 'And again, O Bhikkhus, that I should fully realise the destruction of sorrow though the noble truth concerning it was not among the doctrines handed down, there arose within me the eye, there arose the knowledge, there arose the understanding, there arose the wisdom, there arose the light.

17. 'And again, O Bhikkhus, that I had fully realised the destruction of sorrow, though the noble

truth concerning it was not among the doctrines handed down, there arose within me the eye, there arose the knowledge, there arose the understanding, there arose the wisdom, there arose the light.

18. 'That this was the noble truth concerning the way which leads to the destruction of sorrow, was not, O Bhikkhus, among the doctrines handed down; but there arose within me the eye, there arose the knowledge, there arose the understanding, there arose the wisdom, there arose the light.

19. 'And again, O Bhikkhus, that I should become versed in the way which leads to the destruction of sorrow, though the noble truth concerning it was not among the doctrines handed down, there arose within me the eye, there arose the knowledge, there arose the understanding, there arose the wisdom, there arose the light.

20. 'And again, O Bhikkhus, that I had become versed in the way which leads to the destruction of sorrow, though the noble truth concerning it was not among the doctrines handed down, there arose within me the eye, there arose the knowledge, there arose the understanding, there arose the wisdom, there arose the light.

---

21. 'So long, O Bhikkhus, as my knowledge and insight were not quite clear, regarding each of these four noble truths in this triple order, in this twelvefold manner—so long was I uncertain whether I had attained to the full insight of that wisdom which is unsurpassed in the heavens or on earth, among the whole race of Sama*n*as and Brâhmans, or of gods or men.

22. 'But as soon, O Bhikkhus, as my knowledge

and insight were quite clear regarding each of these four noble truths, in this triple order, in this twelvefold manner—then did I become certain that I had attained to the full insight of that wisdom which is unsurpassed in the heavens or on earth, among the whole race of Samanas and Brâhmans, or of gods or men.

23. 'And now this knowledge and this insight has arisen within me. Immovable is the emancipation of my heart. This is my last existence. There will now be no rebirth for me!'

---

24. Thus spake the Blessed One. The company of the five Bhikkhus, glad at heart, exalted the words of the Blessed One. And when the discourse had been uttered, there arose within the venerable Kondañña the eye of truth, spotless, and without a stain, (and he saw that) whatsoever has an origin, in that is also inherent the necessity of coming to an end[1].

---

25. And when the royal chariot wheel of the truth had thus been set rolling onwards by the Blessed One, the gods of the earth gave forth a shout, saying:

'In Benâres, at the hermitage of the Migadâya, the supreme wheel of the empire of Truth has been set rolling by the Blessed One—that wheel which not by any Samana or Brâhman, not by any god,

---

[1] It is the perception of this fact which is the Dhammakakkhu, the Eye of Truth, or the Eye for Qualities as it might be rendered with reference to the meaning of Dhamma in the words that follow.

They are in Pâli yam kiñki samudaya-dhammam, sabbam tam nirodha-dhammam, literally, 'whatever has the quality of beginning, that has the quality of ceasing.'

not by any Brahma or Mâra, not by any one in the universe, can ever be turned back!'

26. And when they heard the shout of the gods of the earth, the attendant gods of the four great kings[1] (the guardian angels of the four quarters of the globe) gave forth a shout, saying:

'In Benâres, at the hermitage of the Migadâya, the supreme wheel of the empire of Truth has been set rolling by the Blessed One—that wheel which not by any Samana or Brâhman, not by any god, not by any Brahma or Mâra, not by any one in the universe, can ever be turned back!'

27. [And thus as the gods in each of the heavens heard the shout of the inhabitants of the heaven beneath, they took up the cry until the gods in the highest heaven of heavens] gave forth the shout, saying:

'In Benâres, at the hermitage of the Migadâya, the supreme wheel of the empire of Truth has been set rolling by the Blessed One—that wheel which not by any Samana or Brâhman, not by any god, not by any Brahma or Mâra, not by any one in the universe, can ever be turned back[2]!'

---

[1] Their names are given in the Mahâ Samaya Sutta in Grimblot's 'Sept Suttas Palis.'

[2] The text repeats § 26 for each of the heavens; and the gods thus enumerated are as follows, beginning with Bhummâ Devâ in § 25:

1. Bhummâ Devâ.
2. *K*atumahârâ*g*ika Devâ.
3. Yâmâ Devâ.
4. Tusitâ Devâ.
5. Nimmânaratî Devâ.
6. Paranimmitavasavattî Devâ.
7. Brahmakâyikâ Devâ.

See the Mahâ Samaya Sutta in Grimblot's 'Sept Suttas Palis,' and

28. And thus, in an instant, a second, a moment, the sound went up even to the world of Brahmâ: and this great ten-thousand-world-system quaked and trembled and was shaken violently, and an immeasurable bright light appeared in the universe, beyond even the power of the gods!

---

29. Then did the Blessed One give utterance to this exclamation of joy: 'Kondañña hath realised it. Kondañña hath realised it!' And so the venerable Kondañña acquired the name of Aññâta-Kondañña ('the Kondañña who realised')[1].

End of the Dhamma-*k*akka-ppavattana-sutta.

---

compare Professor Max Müller's note in 'Buddhaghosha's Parables,' p. xxxiii, and Hardy in the 'Manual of Buddhism,' p. 25.

[1] The Mahâ Vagga completes the narrative as follows: 'And then the venerable Aññâta-Kondoñña having seen the truth, having arrived at the truth, having known the truth, having penetrated the truth, having past beyond doubt, having laid aside uncertainty, having attained to confidence, and being dependent on no one beside himself for knowledge of the religion of the teacher, spake thus to the Blessed One:

'"May I become, O my Lord, a novice under the Blessed One, may I receive full ordination!"

'"Welcome, O brother!" said the Blessed One, "the truth has been well laid down. Practice holiness to the complete suppression of sorrow!"

'And that was the ordination of the Venerable One.'

The other four, Vappa, Bhaddiya, Mahânâma, and Assa*g*i, were converted on the following days, according to the 'Buddhist Birth Stories,' p. 113.

It is there also said that 'myriads of the angels (devas) had been converted simultaneously with Kondanya.'

TEVI*GG*A-SUTTANTA.

INTRODUCTION

TO

THE TEVI*GG*A SUTTA.

THIS is the twelfth and last Sutta in the first division of the Dîgha Nikâya, which is called the Sîlakkhandha Vaggo, because the whole of its twelve Dialogues deal, from one point of view or another, with Sîla, or Right Conduct.

There is another Sutta sometimes called by the same name, No. 21 in the Middle Fifty of the Ma*ggh*ima Nikâya: but it has nothing, except the name, in common with the present. It is called Tevi*gg*a Sutta merely because Gotama is there described by the complimentary title of Tevi*gg*a, 'Wise in the Vedas;' and its full name is the Tevi*gg*a-va*kkh*agotta-sutta[1].

I have made the present translation from a text constituted from three MSS.,—my own MS. of the Dîgha Nikâya, referred to as D; the Turnour MS. of the same in the Indian Office, referred to as T; both in Sinhalese characters: and the Phayre MS. in the same place, in Burmese characters, referred to as P.

In this book we have Right Conduct used as a sort of argumentum ad hominem for the conversion of two earnest young Brâhmans.

They ask which is the true path to a state of union (in the next birth) with God. After arguing, in a kind of Socratic dialogue, that on their own showing, on the

---

[1] It may be noted, in passing, that the substance of it recurs as the Va*kkh*a-gotta Sa*m*yutta in the Sa*m*yutta Nikâya.

basis of facts they themselves admitted, the Brâhmans could have no real knowledge of their God, Gotama maintains that union with a God whom they admitted to be pure and holy must be unattainable by men impure and sinful and self-righteous, however great their knowledge of the Vedas. And he then lays down, not without occasional beauty of language, that system of Right Conduct, which must be the only direct way to a real union with God.

One would think perhaps that such a Sutta might be adapted, without very great difficulty, for use as a missionary tract, so closely does it remind us of the argument of many a sermon on the text, 'Except your righteousness shall exceed the righteousness of the Scribes and Pharisees, ye shall in no wise enter the kingdom of heaven!' And it is true that the Tevi*gg*â—the men of special knowledge in the three Vedas—correspond exactly in most essential particulars with the Scribes and Pharisees of the New Testament. They were the official preservers by repeating, as the Scribes were by copying, the sacred books; and they were the recognised interpreters, and the sole custodians of the traditional interpretation—which too often explained away the real meaning—of those books. It follows that as the law in both cases was included in the sacred books, it was they who, in both cases, were the real lawgivers, and practically the only lawyers. And as almost all learning was confined to, or in close connection with the sacred books, the Tevi*gg*â were the chief Pa*nd*its, as the Scribes were the 'Doctors of the Law.' Like the Pharisees, too, the Brâhmans laid claim to peculiar sanctity; and many of them in the pride of their education, their birth, and their wealth, looked down with self-righteous scorn on the masses of the people. And while, on the other hand, the Brâhmans further resembled the Scribes and Pharisees in that many of them were justly deserving of the respect in which they were held; it is only the undeserving who, in both cases, are intended to be condemned.

But whatever interpretation of the 'kingdom of heaven'

the reader may adopt, it must be very different from anything the Sutta can mean by 'a state of union with Brahmâ.' It is not easy to say what opinion is really imputed to the young Brâhmans before their conversion. It is probably meant that they were seeking a way by which their Self should become identified, after death, with Brahman; a way by which they could escape from the immortality of transmigration, from existence altogether as separate individuals[1]. And in holding out a hope of union with Brahmâ as a result of the practice of universal love[2], the Buddha is most probably intended to mean 'a union with Brahmâ' in the Buddhist sense—that is to say, a temporary companionship as a separate being with the Buddhist Brahmâ, to be enjoyed by a new individual not consciously identical with its predecessor. It is just possible that the argumentum ad hominem should be extended to this part of the Sutta; and that the statement in III, 1 should be taken to mean, 'This (universal love) is the only way to that kind of union with your own Brahmâ which you desire.' But such a yielding to heretical opinion at the close of his own exposition of the truth would scarcely be imputed to a Buddha.

Just as during the time of the early Christians, in the way which Archbishop Trench has so instructively pointed out, it was not men only who received a new birth and a new baptism, but old words and terms of common use were also infused with a new spirit; so the Indian reformer, while clothing his new system in the current phraseology, infused a different and in many cases a higher meaning into the old expressions.

Thus, for instance, Tevi*gg*a (Sanskrit Traividya) meant either knowledge of the Three Vedas, or as an adjective, a Brâhman possessed of that knowledge; and then, as a noun of multitude, such an assembly of those Brâhmans

[1] Compare Professor Max Müller's Preface to the Sacred Books of the East, vol. i. p. xxx.

[2] See Chapter III, §§ 1, 2.

as is described in the first sections of our Sutta. As there were many Brâhmans who had not that knowledge, the word naturally came to imply a person worthy of the respect due to special learning, and was used as a complimentary title, not very different from our Doctor. It is preserved as an epithet of Arahats in the Buddhist writings, but as meaning one possessed of the knowledge of a fundamental threefold doctrine of Buddhism, the doctrine of the impermanency, the inherent pain, and the absence of any abiding principle (any Self) in the confections or component things[1]. That is to say, the knowledge of the Vedas was replaced by a knowledge of the real character of the deceptive and evanescent phenomena by which we are encircled, and of which we form a part.

So also with regard to Brahmâ. The name was retained, but the idea was entirely changed. The course of religious belief had passed among the Indian section of the Âryan tribes through the usual stages of animism and polytheism to a kind of pantheism peculiar to India, in which Brahman was held to be a first cause, the highest self, emotionless, infinite, absolute. As the Buddhist system was constructed without any use of the previous idea of a separate soul, or self, or ghost, or spirit, supposed to exist inside the human body, this woven chain of previous speculation had as little importance for it as theological discussions have for positivism. But Buddhism fell into what to the positivist would be the unpardonable sin—perhaps inevitable at the time and place of its youth—of continuing to express a belief in the external spirits, big and little, of the then Hindu pantheon.

They were preserved very much in the previous order of precedence, and were all—except Mâra, the Evil One, and his personal following, and a few others—supposed to be passably good Buddhists. They were not feared any more; they were patronized as a kind of fairies, usually beneficent,

[1] See *K*ulla Vagga VI, 6, 2, = *G*âtaka, vol. i. p. 217; Mahâva*m*sa, p. 79; Dîpava*m*sa XV, 80 (where the Arahats are women); and on 'confections' below, in the Introduction to the 'Book of the Great King of Glory.'

though always more or less foolish and ignorant. They were of course not worshipped any more, for they were much less worthy of reverence than any wise and good man. And they were not eternal,—all of them, even the very best or highest, being liable, like all things and all other creatures, to dissolution. If they had behaved well they were then reborn under happy outward conditions, and might even look forward to being some day born as men, so that they could attain to the supreme goal of the Buddhist faith, to that bliss which passeth not away,—the Nirvâ*n*a of a perfect life in Arahatship.

The duty of a Buddhist who had entered the Noble Path towards these light and airy shapes—for to such vain things had the great gods fallen—was the same as his duty towards every fellow creature; pity for his ignorance, sympathy with his weakness, equanimity (the absence of fear or malice, or the sense of any differing or opposing interest), and the constant feeling of a deep and lasting love, all pervading, grown great, and beyond measure.

No exception was made in the case of Brahmâ. He, like every other creature that had life, was evanescent, was bound by the chain of existence, the result of ignorance, and could only find salvation by walking along the Noble Eightfold Path. It must be remembered that the Brahmâ of modern times, the God of the ardent theism of some of the best of the later Hindus, had not then come into existence: that conception was one effect of the influence of Mohammadan and Christian thought upon Hindu minds. And it would be useless to conjecture how the Buddhist theory might have been modified by contact with that ideal.

While regarded however as essentially of the same class as all other external spirits, Brahmâ was still regarded as a superior spirit, as a very devout Buddhist, and as a kind of king among the angels. The Brahmâ of this world system, who was living in Gotama's time, and who is living now, acquired his present exalted position from his virtue in a previous birth as a Bhikkhu named Sahaka in the time when Kassapa Buddha's religion flourished upon earth[1]. According to the author of the *G*âtaka commentary, he assisted at the future Buddha's birth[2]; and twice afterwards he rendered service to the Bodisat just before the great conflict with Mâra[3]. And when after the victory the Blessed One hesitated whether it would be of any use to tell to others the truth he had found, it was Brahmâ who appeared and besought him to proclaim the truth[4]. Brahmâ Sahampati was the first to give utterance to the universal sorrow which followed on the death of the Buddha[5]; and at a critical period in the later history of the Buddhist church he is represented to have descended from heaven, and to have appeared to the Thera Sâ*ll*a, to confirm his wavering faith[6].

These instances will show the high character ascribed to the Brahmâ of the world system in which we live; and in each of the infinite world systems which are scattered through space there is supposed to be a like finite, temporary, virtuous Brahmâ sitting as king over the most exalted of the angel hosts.

It must be evident that it follows, without the possibility of question, that the early Buddhists cannot with any accuracy be described as 'monotheists,' and it is much to be regretted that even cultured and scholarly writers still speak of them as such, and can suggest that the independent monotheism of the later Jews can be paralleled by a supposed monotheism among the Buddhists[7].

And even if the idea of Brahmâ were at all the same as the idea of God, a union with this Brahmâ would mean a merely temporary life as an angel in the Brahmâ heaven —such a life as is represented below to have been the result of the noble life and noble thoughts of the Great King

---

1 Teste a comment quoted by Childers, Dict. p. 227.

2 'Buddhist Birth Stories,' p. 66.

3 Ibid. pp. 92, 97.

4 Ibid. p. 111. Related already in the Mahâ Vagga I, 2; 6, 7.

5 Book of the Great Decease, Chapter VI, § 14.

6 Mahâva*m*sa, p. 17.

7 'Their (the Jews') monotheism was perhaps independently evolved; but the Buddhists at least showed a contemporary monotheism.' Mr. Huth, in 'Life &c. of Buckle,' p. 238.

of Glory. But this was not the supreme goal of the Buddhist faith; and the angel, though the same person as the king, from the Buddhist point of view (as resulting from, and carrying on, the same Karma), would be a different person from the king, according to the Christian point of view; for there is no mention of the passage of a soul from the earth to heaven, no conscious identity, no continuing memory.

We may draw, from the above, two conclusions. Firstly, that the use of a word in Sanskrit authors is but very little guide to the meaning of the corresponding word in the Pâli Buddhist scriptures whenever the word has reference to an idea of a religious character.

And, secondly, that very little reliance can be placed, without careful investigation, on a resemblance—however close at first sight—between a passage in the Pâli Pi*t*akas and a passage in the New Testament.

It is true that many passages in these two literatures can be easily shown to have a similar tendency. But when some writers on the basis of such similarities proceed to argue that there must have been some historical connection between the two, and that the New Testament, as the later, must be the borrower, I venture to think that they are wrong. There does not seem to me to be the slightest evidence of any historical connection between them; and whenever the resemblance is a real one—and it often turns out to be really least when it first seems to be greatest, and really greatest when it first seems least—it is due, not to any borrowing on the one side or on the other, but solely to the similarity of the conditions under which the two movements grew.

This does not of course apply to the later literature of the two religions; and it ought not to detract from the very great value and interest of the parallels which may be adduced from the earlier books. If we wish to understand what it was that gave such life and force to the stupendous movement which is called Buddhism, we cannot refrain from comparing it—not only in the points in which it agrees with it, but also in the points in which it differs from it—with our own faith. I trust I have not been wrong in making use occasionally of this method, though the absence of any historical connection between the New Testament and the Pâli Pi*t*akas has always seemed to me so clear, that it would be unnecessary to mention it. But when a reviewer who has been kind enough to appreciate, I am afraid too highly, what he calls my 'service in giving, for the first time, a thoroughly human, acceptable, and coherent' account of the 'life of Buddha,' and of the 'simple groundwork of his religion' has gone on to conclude that the parallels I had thus adduced are 'an unanswerable indication of the obligations of the New Testament to Buddhism,' I must ask to be allowed to enter a protest against an inference which seems to me to be against the rules of sound historical criticism.

ON KNOWLEDGE OF THE VEDAS.

TEVIGGA-SUTTA.

CHAPTER I.

1. This have I heard. At one time when the Blessed One was journeying through Kosala with a great company of the brethren, with about five hundred brethren, he came to the Brâhman village in Kosala which is called Manasâka*t*a. And there at Manasâka*t*a the Blessed One stayed in the mango grove, on the bank of the river A*k*iravatî, to the south of Manasâka*t*a [1].

2. Now at that time many very distinguished and wealthy Brâhmans were staying at Manasâka*t*a—to wit, *K*ankî the Brâhman, Târukkha the Brâhman, Pokkharasâti the Brâhman, *G*â*n*usso*n*i the Brâhman, Todeyya the Brâhman, and other very distinguished and wealthy Brâhmans [2].

---

[1] Burnouf, in a long note at 'Lotus,' &c., p. 491, already attempted to show that the river A*k*iravatî is the same as the modern Rapti, which he supposed to be a corruption of the latter part of the longer name. Hiouen Thsang mentions a river A-chi-lo-fa-ti, which is doubtless the same. It is evidently the river on which stood the town of Sâvatthi, and near to which lay the *G*etavana monastery (see 'Buddhist Birth Stories,' p. 331); and it must therefore, in accordance with Burnouf's conjecture, be the Rapti, which is the Sanskrit Irâvati. The Phayre Burmese MS. has almost always A*k*îravatî.

[2] Buddhaghosa says that

*K*anki lived at Opasâda,
Târukkha lived at I*kkh*agala,

3. Now a conversation sprung up between Vâsettha and Bhâradvâga, when they were taking exercise (after their bath) and walking up and down in thoughtful mood, as to which was the true path, and which the false[1].

4. The young Brâhman Vâsettha spake thus:

'This is the straight path, this the direct way which leads him, who acts according to it, into a state of union with Brahmâ[2]—I mean that which has been announced by the Brâhman Pokkarasâti.'

5. The young Brâhman Bhâradvâga spake thus:

Pokkharasâdi (sic MS.) lived at Ukkattha,
Gânussoni lived at Sâvatthi, and
Todeyya lived at Tudigâma.

There is some difference in the MSS. as to the spelling of these names: T. reads *K*ankî; P. T. and D. Pokkharasâti (Sanskrit Paushkarasâdi); P. *G*ânuyoni, T. *G*ânusoni, D. *G*ânusoni; P. Toreyya, and Burnouf Nodeyya (which is possibly merely a misreading). *G*ânusoni was converted by the Bhaya-bherava Sutta; and I think it very probable that the other names are also those of subsequent converts.

Buddhaghosa adds that because Manasâkata was a pleasant place the Brâhmans had built huts there on the bank of the river and fenced them in, and used to go and stay there from time to time to repeat their mantras.

[1] *G*anghâvihâram anukankamantânam anuvikarantânam. On the first word see *G*âtaka II, 272 (and comp. II, 240). *K*ankamati is to walk up and down thinking. I have added 'after their bath' from Buddhaghosa, who says that this must be understood to have taken place when, after learning by heart and repeating all day, they went down in the evening to the river-side to bathe, and then walked up and down on the sand.

[2] Brahma-sahavyatâya. The first part of the compound is masculine (see below, § 12), but the Buddhists probably included under the name, when put into the mouth of Brâhmans, all that the Brâhmans included under both Brahmâ and Brahman. The Buddhist archangel or god Brahmâ is different from both, being part of an entirely different system of thought.

'This is the straight path, this the direct way which leads him, who acts according to it, into a state of union with Brahmâ—I mean that which has been announced by the Brâhman Târukkha.'

6. But neither was the young Brâhman Vâse*tth*a able to convince the young Brâhman Bhâradvâ*g*a, nor was the young Brâhman Bhâradvâ*g*a able to convince the young Brâhman Vâse*tth*a.

7. Then the young Brâhman Vâse*tth*a said to the young Brâhman Bhâradvâ*g*a:

'That Sama*n*a Gotama, Bhâradvâ*g*a, of the Sakya clan, who left the Sakya tribe to adopt the religious life, is now staying at Manasâka*t*a, in the mango grove, on the bank of the river A*k*iravatî, to the south of Manasâka*t*a. Now regarding that venerable Gotama, such is the high reputation that has been noised abroad, that he is said to be "a fully enlightened one, blessed and worthy, abounding in wisdom and goodness, happy, with knowledge of the world, unsurpassed as a guide to erring mortals, a teacher of gods and men, a blessed Buddha[1]." Come, then, Bhâradvâ*g*a, let us go to the place where the Sama*n*a Gotama is; and when we have come there, let us ask the Sama*n*a Gotama touching this matter. What the Sama*n*a Gotama shall declare unto us, that let us bear in mind.'

'Very well, my friend!' said the young Brâhman Bhâradvâ*g*a, in assent, to the young Brâhman Vâse*tth*a.

---

8. Then the young Brâhman Vâse*tth*a and the young Brâhman Bhâradvâ*g*a went on to the place where the Blessed One was.

[1] See below, § 46.

And when they had come there, they exchanged with the Blessed One the greetings and compliments of friendship and civility, and sat down beside him.

And while they were thus seated the young Brâhman Vâse*tth*a said to the Blessed One:

'As we, Gotama, were taking exercise and walking up and down, there sprung up a conversation between us on which was the true path and which the false. I said thus:

'"This is the straight path, this the direct way which leads him, who acts according to it, into a state of union with Brahmâ—I mean that which has been announced by the Brâhman Pokkarasâti."

'Bhâradvâ*g*a said thus:

'"This is the straight path, this the direct way which leads him, who acts according to it, into a state of union with Brahmâ—I mean that which has been announced by the Brâhman Târukkha."

'Regarding this matter, Gotama, there is a strife, a dispute, a difference of opinion between us.'

---

9. 'So you say, Vâse*tth*a, that you said thus:

'"This is the straight path, this the direct way which leads him, who acts according to it, into a state of union with Brahmâ—I mean that which has been announced by the Brâhman Pokkarasâti."

'While Bhâradvâ*g*a said thus:

'"This is the straight path, this the direct way which leads him, who acts according to it, into a state of union with Brahmâ—I mean that which has been announced by the Brâhman Târukkha."

'Wherein, then, O Vâse*tth*a, is there a strife, a dispute, a difference of opinion between you[1]?'

10. 'Concerning the true path and the false, Gotama. Various Brâhmans, Gotama, teach various paths—the Addhariya Brâhmans, the Tittiriya Brâhmans, the *Kh*andoka Brâhmans, the *Kh*andava Brâhmans, the Brahma*k*ariya Brâhmans[2]. Are all those saving paths? Are they all paths which will lead him, who acts according to them, into a state of union with Brahmâ?

'Just, Gotama, as near a village or a town there are many and various paths[3], yet they all meet together in the village—just in that way are all the various paths taught by various Brâhmans—the Addhariya Brâhmans, the Tittiriya Brâhmans, the *Kh*andoka Brâhmans, the *Kh*andava Brâhmans, the Brahma*k*ariya Brâhmans. Are all these saving paths? Are they all paths which will lead him, who acts according to them, into a state of union with Brahmâ?'

11. 'Do you say that they all lead aright, Vâse*tth*a?'

'I say so, Gotama.'

'Do you really say that they all lead aright, Vâse*tth*a?'

'So I say, Gotama.'

---

[1] This is either mildly sarcastic—as much as to say, 'that is six to one, and half a dozen to the other'—or is intended to lead on Vâse*tth*a to confess still more directly the fact that the different theologians held inconsistent opinions.

[2] P. here Atthariyâ, but below Addhariyâ (Sans. Adhvaryu); D. Titittiriyâ, T. Tattiriyâ, P. apparently Titthiriyâ (Sans. Taittirîya); D. *Kh*andâva, T. P. omit (? Sans. *Kh*ândasa); all three MSS. *Kh*andoka (Sans. *Kh*andoga); P. Bavhadi*g*â here and below *K*avhadi*g*â for Brahma*k*ariyâ (? Sans. Brahma*k*ârî). See 'Lotus,' p. 493.

[3] Maggâni, which is noteworthy as a curious change of gender.

12. 'But then, Vâse*tth*a, is there a single one of the Brâhmans versed in the Three Vedas who has ever seen Brahmâ face to face?'

'No, indeed, Gotama.'

'But is there then, Vâse*tth*a, a single one of the teachers of the Brâhmans versed in the Three Vedas who has seen Brahmâ face to face?'

'No, indeed, Gotama!'

'But is there then, Vâse*tth*a, a single one of the pupils of the teachers of the Brâhmans versed in the Three Vedas who has seen Brahmâ face to face?'

'No, indeed, Gotama!'

'But is there then, Vâse*tth*a, a single one of the Brâhmans up to the seventh generation who has seen Brahmâ face to face?'

'No, indeed, Gotama!'

13. 'Well then, Vâse*tth*a, those ancient *Ri*shis of the Brâhmans versed in the Three Vedas, the authors of the verses, the utterers of the verses, whose ancient form of words so chaunted, uttered, or composed, the Brâhmans of to-day chaunt over again or repeat; intoning or reciting exactly as has been intoned or recited—to wit, A*tth*aka, Vâmaka, Vâmadeva, Vessâmitta, Yamataggi, Aṅgirasa, Bhâradvâ*g*a, Vâse*tth*a, Kassapa, and Bhagu[1]—did even they speak thus, saying: "We know it, we have seen it, where Brahmâ is, whence Brahmâ is, whither Brahmâ is?"'

'Not so, Gotama!'

14. 'Then you say, Vâse*tth*a [that not one of the Brâhmans, or of their teachers, or of their pupils, even up to the seventh generation, has ever seen Brahmâ face to face. And that even the *Ri*shis of

[1] See Mahâ Vagga VI, 35, 2.

old, the authors and utterers of the verses, of the ancient form of words which the Brâhmans of to-day so carefully intone and recite precisely as they have been handed down—even they did not pretend to know or to have seen where or whence or whither Brahmâ is][1]. So that the Brâhmans versed in the Three Vedas have forsooth said thus: "What we know not, what we have not seen, to a state of union with that we can show the way, and can say: 'This is the straight path, this is the direct way which leads him, who acts according to it, into a state of union with Brahmâ!'"

'Now what think you, Vâse*tth*a? Does it not follow, this being so, that the talk of the Brâhmans, versed though they be in the Three Vedas, is foolish talk?'

'In sooth, Gotama, that being so, it follows that the talk of the Brâhmans versed in the Three Vedas is foolish talk!'

15. 'Verily, Vâse*tth*a, that Brâhmans versed in the Three Vedas should be able to show the way to a state of union with that which they do not know, neither have seen—such a condition of things has no existence!

'Just, Vâse*tth*a, as when a string of blind men are clinging one to the other[2], neither can the foremost

---

[1] In the text §§ 12, 13 are repeated word for word.

[2] Andhave*n*î parampara*m* sa*m*sattâ. The Phayre MS. has replaced ve*n*î by pave*n*î, after the constant custom of the Burmese MSS. to improve away unusual or difficult expressions. Buddhaghosa explains andhave*n*i by andhapave*n*i, and tells a tale of a wicked wight, who meeting a company of blind men, told them of a certain village wherein plenty of good food was to be had. When they besought him for hire to lead them there, he took the money, made one blind man catch hold of his stick, the next of that one, and so on, and then led them on till they came to a wilderness. There he deserted them, and they all—still

see, nor can the middle one see, nor can the hindmost see—just even so, methinks, Vâse*tth*a, is the talk of the Brâhmans versed in the Three Vedas but blind talk: the first sees not, the middle one sees not, nor can the latest see. The talk then of these Brâhmans versed in the Three Vedas turns out to be ridiculous, mere words, a vain and empty thing!'

---

16. 'Now what think you, Vâse*tth*a? Can the Brâhmans versed in the Three Vedas—like other, ordinary, folk—see the sun and the moon as they pray to, and praise, and worship them, turning round with clasped hands towards the place whence they rise and where they set?'

'Certainly, Gotama, they [can][1].'

17. 'Now what think you, Vâse*tth*a? The Brâhmans versed in the Three Vedas, who can very well—like other, ordinary, folk—see the sun and the moon as they pray to, and praise, and worship them, turning round with clasped hands to the place whence they rise and where they set—are those Brâhmans, versed in the Three Vedas, able to point out the way to a state of union with the sun or the moon, saying: "This is the straight path, this the direct way which leads him, who acts according to it, to a state of union with the sun or the moon?"'

'Certainly not, Gotama!'

18. 'So you say, Vâse*tth*a, that the Brâhmans [are not able to point out the way to union with that

---

holding each the other, and vainly, and with tears, seeking both their guide and the path—came to a miserable end!

[1] The words of the question are repeated in the text in this and the following answers. It must be remembered, for these sections, that the sun and moon were Gods just as much as Brahmâ.

which they have seen], and you further say that [neither any one of them, nor of their pupils, nor of their predecessors even to the seventh generation has ever seen Brahmâ]. And you further say that even the *Ri*shis of old, [whose words they hold in such deep respect, did not pretend to know, or to have seen where, or whence, or whither Brahmâ is. Yet these Brâhmans versed in the Three Vedas say, forsooth, that they can point out the way to union with that which they know not, neither have seen!][1] Now what think you, Vâse*tth*a? Does it not follow that, this being so, the talk of the Brâhmans, versed though they be in the Three Vedas, is foolish talk?'

'In sooth, Gotama, that being so, it follows that the talk of the Brâhmans versed in the Three Vedas is foolish talk!'

19. 'Very good, Vâse*tth*a. Verily then, Vâse*tth*a, that Brâhmans versed in the Three Vedas should be able to show the way to a state of union with that which they do not know, neither have seen—such a condition of things has no existence.

'Just, Vâse*tth*a, as if a man should say, "How I long for, how I love the most beautiful woman in this land!"

'And people should ask him, "Well! good friend! this most beautiful woman in the land whom you thus love and long for, do you know whether that beautiful woman is a noble lady or a Brâhman woman, or of the trader class, or a *S*ûdra?"

'But when so asked he should answer "No."

'And when people should ask him, "Well! good

[1] The text repeats at length the words of §§ 12, 13, 14.

friend! this most beautiful woman in all the land, whom you so love and long for, do you know what the name of that most beautiful woman is, or what is her family name, whether she be tall or short, dark or of medium complexion, black or fair, or in what village or town or city she dwells?"

'But when so asked he should answer "No."

'And then people should say to him, "So then, good friend, whom you know not, neither have seen, her do you love and long for?"

'And then when so asked he should answer "Yes."'

'Now what think you, Vâse*tth*a? Would it not turn out, that being so, that the talk of that man was foolish talk?'

'In sooth, Gotama, it would turn out, that being so, that the talk of that man was foolish talk!'

20. 'And just even so, Vâse*tth*a, though you say that the Brâhmans [are not able to point out the way to union with that which they have seen], and you further say that [neither any one of them, nor of their pupils, nor of their predecessors even to the seventh generation has ever seen Brahmâ]. And you further say that even the *Ri*shis of old, [whose words they hold in such deep respect, did not pretend to know, or to have seen where, or whence, or whither Brahmâ is. Yet these Brâhmans versed in the Three Vedas say, forsooth, that they can point out the way to union with that which they know not, neither have seen!] Now what think you, Vâse*tth*a? Does it not follow that, this being so, the talk of the Brâhmans, versed though they be in the Three Vedas, is foolish talk?'

'In sooth, Gotama, that being so, it follows that

the talk of the Brâhmans versed in the Three Vedas is foolish talk!'

'Very good, Vâsettha. Verily then, Vâsettha, that Brâhmans versed in the Three Vedas should be able to show the way to a state of union with that which they do not know, neither have seen—such a condition of things has no existence.'

---

21. 'Just, Vâsettha, as if a man should make a staircase in the place where four roads cross, to mount up into a mansion. And people should say to him, "Well, good friend, this mansion, to mount up into which you are making this staircase, do you know whether it is in the east, or in the south, or in the west, or in the north? whether it is high or low or of medium size?'

'And when so asked he should answer "No."'

'And people should say to him, "But then, good friend, you are making a staircase to mount up into something—taking it for a mansion—which, all the while, you know not, neither have seen!"

'And when so asked he should answer "Yes."'

'Now what think you, Vâsettha? Would it not turn out, that being so, that the talk of that man was foolish talk?'

'In sooth, Gotama, it would turn out, that being so, that the talk of that man was foolish talk!'

22. 'And just even so, Vâsettha, though you say that the Brâhmans [are not able to point out the way to union with that which they have seen], and you further say that [neither any one of them, nor of their pupils, nor of their predecessors even to the seventh generation has ever seen Brahmâ]. And you further say that even the *Ri*shis of old, [whose

words they hold in such deep respect, did not pretend to know, or to have seen where, or whence, or whither Brahmâ is. Yet these Brâhmans versed in the Three Vedas say, forsooth, that they can point out the way to union with that which they know not, neither have seen!] Now what think you, Vâse*tth*a? Does it not follow that, this being so, the talk of the Brâhmans versed in the Three Vedas is foolish talk?'

'In sooth, Gotama, that being so, it follows that the talk of the Brâhmans versed in the Three Vedas is foolish talk!'

23. 'Very good, Vâse*tth*a. Verily then, Vâse*tth*a, that Brâhmans versed in the Three Vedas should be able to show the way to a state of union with that which they do not know, neither have seen—such condition of things has no existence.'

---

24. 'Again, Vâse*tth*a, if this river A*k*iravatî were full of water even to the brim, and overflowing[1]. And a man with business on the other

[1] Samatittikâ kâkapeyyâ, a stock phrase used of a river in flood time. Buddhaghosa says, Samatittikâ ti samaharitâ (sic? samâharitâ): kâkapeyyâ ti yatthakattha*k*i tîre *th*itena kâkena sakkâ pâtun ti kâkapeyyâ, which does not seem to me to solve the question as to the origin and history of these difficult terms. With respect to the right form of samatittikâ it should be noticed that the northern Buddhist spelling is samatîrthakâ (Sukhavatîvyûha, ed. Max Müller in J. R. A. S. for 1880, p. 182), and that both Childers and Oldenberg have read samatitthikâ in the Burmese MSS. of Mahâparinibbâna Sutta I, 33 = Mahâ Vagga VI, 28. Now the difference in Burmese letters between tt and tth (ဋ္ဌ and ဋ္ဋ) is so very small that the copyists frequently write one for the other; and even in good MSS. where the two are not confounded, it is sometimes difficult to tell which is really meant. When talking of rivers the mention of titthas seems so appro-

side, bound for the other side, should come up, and want to cross over. And he, standing on this bank, should invoke the further bank, and say, "Come hither, O further bank! come over to this side!"

---

priate that a copyist, and especially a Burmese copyist, would naturally read a doubtful combination as tth; so that even if all Burmese MSS. spell this word with tth (which is by no means certain), very little reliance should be placed upon the fact. On the other hand, the distinction in Sinhalese between tt and tth is very marked (ත්ත and ත්ථ), and the Sinhalese MSS. all read tt. I think therefore that Childers was right in finally adopting samatittikâ as the correct Pâli form. In the numerous words in which Buddhist Sanskrit has a form differing in a way which sets philological rules at defiance from the corresponding Pâli form, Childers thought (see Dict. p. xi, where the list of words might be greatly extended) that the Sanskrit was always derived from the Pâli, and the Sanskrit writers had merely blundered. I venture, with great diffidence, to doubt this. It seems more likely that, at least in many instances, both Pâli and Sanskrit were alike derived from a previous Prâkrit form, and that in differently interpreting a difficult word, both Sanskrit and Pâli authors made mistakes. That may be the case here; and it is almost certain that the original word had nothing to do with tîrtha. How easily this idea could be adopted we see from the fact that Childers when first editing the MSS. (in the J. R. A. S. for 1874), and when he had only Sinhalese MSS. then before him, altered their reading into samatitthikâ, and put this form into his Dictionary; though he afterwards (in the separate edition), and after noting that reading in the Phayre MS., chose the other. But what, after all, does 'having equal or level tîrthas or landing-places' mean, when spoken of a river? Comp. Samatittika*m* bhu*ñg*âmi (Mil. 213, 214); Sabbato titta*m* pokkhara*n*i*m* (*G*ât. I, 339, text tittha*m*); and Samatittiko telapatto (ibid. 393, text °iyo, but see p. 400). The root perhaps is TR*I*P.

Kâkapeyya, according to Buddhaghosa, would mean 'crow-drinkable.' Crows do not drink on the wing; and they could stand to drink either when a river actually overflowed its banks and formed shallows on the adjoining land; or when in the hot season it had formed shallows in its own bed. 'Crow-drinkable' might mean therefore just as well 'shallow' as 'overflowing.' Had the word originally anything to do with kâka after all?

N 2

'Now what think you, Vâse*tth*a? Would the further bank of the river A*k*iravatî, by reason of that man's invoking and praying and hoping and praising, come over to this side?'

'Certainly not, Gotama!'

25. 'In just the same way, Vâse*tth*a, do the Brâhmans versed in the Three Vedas—omitting the practice of those qualities which really make a man a Brâhman, and adopting the practice of those qualities which really make men not Brâhmans—say thus: "Indra we call upon, Soma we call upon, Varu*n*a we call upon, Îsâna we call upon, Pa*g*âpati we call upon, Brahmâ we call upon, Mahiddhi we call upon, Yama we call upon[1]!" Verily, Vâse*tth*a, that those Brâhmans versed in the Three Vedas, but omitting the practice of those qualities which really make a man a Brâhman, and adopting the practice of those qualities which really make men not Brâhmans—that they, by reason of their invoking and praying and hoping and praising, should, after death and when the body is dissolved, become united with Brahmâ—verily such a condition of things has no existence!'

---

26. 'Just, Vâse*tth*a, as if this river A*k*iravatî were full, even to the brim, and overflowing. And a man with business on the other side, bound for the other side, should come up, and want to cross over. And he, on this bank, were to be bound tightly, with his arms behind his back, by a strong

[1] The Sinhalese MSS. omit Mahiddhi and Yama, but repeat the verb 'we call upon' three times after Brahmâ. It is possible that the Burmese copyist has wrongly inserted them to remove the strangeness of this repetition. The comment is silent.

chain. Now what think you, Vâse*tth*a, would that man be able to get over from this bank of the river A*k*iravatî to the further bank?'

'Certainly not, Gotama!'

27. 'In the same way, Vâse*tth*a, there are five things leading to lust, which are called in the Discipline of the Noble One a "chain" and a "bond."'

'What are the five?'

'Forms perceptible to the eye; desirable, agreeable, pleasant, attractive forms, that are accompanied by lust and cause delight. Sounds of the same kind perceptible to the ear. Odours of the same kind perceptible to the nose. Tastes of the same kind perceptible to the tongue. Substances of the same kind perceptible to the body by touch. These five things predisposing to passion are called in the Discipline of the Noble One a "chain" and a "bond." And these five things predisposing to lust, Vâse*tth*a, do the Brâhmans versed in the Three Vedas cling to, they are infatuated by them, guilty of them, see not the danger of them, know not how unreliable they are, and so enjoy them.

28. 'And verily, Vâse*tth*a, that Brâhmans versed in the Three Vedas, but omitting the practice of those qualities which really make a man a Brâhman, and adopting the practice of those qualities which really make men non-Brâhmans—clinging to these five things predisposing to passion, infatuated by them, guilty of them, seeing not their danger, knowing not their unreliability, and so enjoying them—that these Brâhmans should after death, on the dissolution of the body, become united to Brahmâ—such a condition of things has no existence.'

29. 'Again, Vâse*tth*a, if this river A*k*iravatî were full of water even to the brim, and overflowing. And a man with business on the other side, bound for the other side, should come up, and want to cross over. And if he covering himself up, even to his head, were to lie down, on this bank, to sleep.

'Now what think you, Vâse*tth*a? Would that man be able to get over from this bank of the river A*k*iravatî to the further bank?'

'Certainly not, Gotama!'

30. 'And in the same way, Vâse*tth*a, there are these five hindrances, in the Discipline of the Noble One, which are called "veils[1]," and are called "hindrances[2]," and are called "obstacles[3]," and are called "entanglements[4]."

'Which are the five?'

'The hindrance of lustful desire,
The hindrance of malice,
The hindrance of sloth and idleness,
The hindrance of pride and self-righteousness,
The hindrance of doubt.

'These are the five hindrances, Vâse*tth*a, which, in the Discipline of the Noble One, are called veils, and are called hindrances, and are called obstacles, and are called entanglements.

31. 'Now with these five hindrances, Vâse*tth*a, the Brâhmans versed in the Three Vedas are veiled, hindered, obstructed, and entangled.

32. 'And verily, Vâse*tth*a, that Brâhmans versed

---

[1] Âvara*n*â. [2] Nîvara*n*â.

[3] All three MSS. onahâ. S. V. reads onaddha*m* in the text, and explains it by onahâ.

[4] All three MSS. pariyonahâ. S. V. reads pariyoddha*m* in the text, and explains it by pariyonahâ.

in the Three Vedas, but omitting the practice of those qualities which really make a man a Brâhman, and adopting the practice of those qualities which really make men non-Brâhmans—veiled, hindered, obstructed, and entangled by these Five Hindrances—that these Brâhmans should after death, on the dissolution of the body, become united to Brahmâ—such a condition of things has no existence.'

---

33. 'Now what think you, Vâse*tth*a, and what have you heard from the Brâhmans aged and well-stricken in years, when the learners and teachers are talking together? Is Brahmâ in possession of wives and wealth, or is he not[1]?'

'He is not, Gotama.'

'Is his mind full of anger, or free from anger?'

'Free from anger, Gotama.'

'Is his mind full of malice, or free from malice?'

'Free from malice, Gotama.'

'Is his mind depraved, or pure[2]?'

'It is pure, Gotama.'

'Has he self-mastery, or has he not[3]?'

'He has, Gotama.'

34. 'Now what think you, Vâse*tth*a, are the

---

[1] Sapariggaho vâ Brahmâ apariggaho vâ ti. Buddhaghosa says on Vâse*tth*a's reply, 'Kâma*kkh*andassa abhâvato itthipariggaheno apariggaho,' thus restricting the 'possession' to women, with especial reference to the first 'hindrance;' but the word in the text, though doubtless alluding to possession of women in particular, includes more. Compare, on the general idea of the passage, the English expression 'no encumbrances.'

[2] Asaṅkili*tth*a-*k*itto. That is, says Buddhaghosa, 'free from mental sloth and idleness, self-righteousness, and pride.'

[3] Vasavattî vâ avasavattî vâ. Buddhaghosa says, in explanation of the answer: 'By the absence of doubt he has his mind under control' (vase vatteti).

Brâhmans versed in the Vedas in the possession of wives and wealth, or are they not?'

'They are, Gotama.'

'Have they anger in their hearts, or have they not?'

'They have, Gotama.'

'Do they bear malice, or do they not?'

'They do, Gotama.'

'Are they pure in heart, or are they not?'

'They are not, Gotama.'

'Have they self-mastery, or have they not?'

'They have not, Gotama.'

35. 'Then you say, Vâse*tth*a, that the Brâhmans are in possession of wives and wealth, and that Brahmâ is not. Can there, then, be agreement and likeness between the Brâhmans with their wives and property, and Brahmâ, who has none of these things?'

'Certainly not, Gotama!'

36. 'Very good, Vâse*tth*a. But, verily, that these Brâhmans versed in the Vedas, who live married and wealthy should after death, when the body is dissolved, become united with Brahmâ, who has none of these things—such a condition of things has no existence.'

---

37. 'Then you say, too, Vâse*tth*a, that the Brâhmans bear anger and malice in their hearts, and are sinful and uncontrolled, whilst Brahmâ is free from anger and malice, and sinless, and has self-mastery. Now can there, then, be concord and likeness between the Brâhmans and Brahmâ?'

'Certainly not, Gotama!'

38. 'Very good, Vâse*tth*a. That these Brâhmans versed in the Vedas and yet bearing anger and malice in their hearts, sinful, and uncontrolled,

should after death, when the body is dissolved, become united to Brahmâ, who is free from anger and malice, sinless, and has self-mastery—such a condition of things has no existence.'

---

39. 'So that thus then, Vâse*tth*a, the Brâhmans, versed though they be in the Three Vedas, while they sit down (in confidence), are sinking down (in the mire)[1]; and so sinking they are arriving only at despair, thinking the while that they are crossing over into some happier land.

'Therefore is it that the threefold wisdom of the Brâhmans, wise in their Three Vedas, is called a waterless desert, their threefold wisdom is called a pathless jungle, their threefold wisdom is called destruction!'

---

40. When he had thus spoken, the young Brâhman Vâse*tth*a said to the Blessed One:

'It has been told me, Gotama, that the Sama*n*a Gotama knows the way to the state of union with Brahmâ.

41. 'What do you think, Vâse*tth*a, is not Manasâka*t*a near to this spot, not distant from this spot?'

'Just so, Gotama. Manasâka*t*a is near to, is not far from here.

42. 'Now what think you, Vâse*tth*a, suppose there were a man born in Manasâka*t*a, and people should

---

[1] Âsîditva sa*m*sîdanti. I have no doubt the commentator is right in his explanation of these figurative expressions. Confident in their knowledge of the Vedas, and in their practice of Vedic ceremonies, they neglect higher things; and so, sinking into sin and superstition, 'they are arriving only at despair, thinking the while that they are crossing over into some happier land.'

ask him, who never till that time had left Manasâka*t*a, which was the way to Manasâka*t*a. Would that man, born and brought up in Manasâka*t*a, be in any doubt or difficulty?'

'Certainly not, Gotama! And why? If the man had been born and brought up in Manasâka*t*a, every road that leads to Manasâka*t*a would be perfectly familiar to him.'

43. 'That man, Vâse*tth*a, born and brought up at Manasâka*t*a might, if he were asked the way to Manasâka*t*a, fall into doubt and difficulty, but to the Tathâgata, when asked touching the path which leads to the world of Brahmâ, there can be neither doubt nor difficulty. For Brahmâ, I know, Vâse*tth*a, and the world of Brahmâ, and the path which leadeth unto it. Yea, I know it even as one who has entered the Brahmâ world, and has been born within it!'

---

44. When he had thus spoken, Vâse*tth*a the young Brâhman said to the Blessed One:

'So has it been told me, Gotama, even that the Sama*n*a Gotama knows the way to a state of union with Brahmâ. It is well! Let the venerable Gotama be pleased to show us the way to a state of union with Brahmâ, let the venerable Gotama save the Brâhman race!'

45. 'Listen then, Vâse*tth*a, and give ear attentively, and I will speak!'

'So be it, Lord!' said the young Brâhman Vâse*tth*a, in assent, to the Blessed One.

46. Then the Blessed One spake, and said:

'[1] Know, Vâse*tth*a, that[1] (from time to time) a

[1] From here down to the end of p. 200 is a repetition word for

Tathâgata is born into the world, a fully Enlightened One, blessed and worthy, abounding in wisdom and goodness, happy, with knowledge of the world, unsurpassed as a guide to erring mortals, a teacher of gods and men, a Blessed Buddha [1]. He, by himself, thoroughly understands, and sees, as it were, face to face this universe—the world below with all its spirits, and the worlds above, of Mâra and of Brahmâ—and all creatures, Samanas and Brâhmans, gods and men, and he then makes his knowledge known to others. The truth doth he proclaim both in its letter and in its spirit, lovely in its origin, lovely in its progress, lovely in its consummation: the higher life doth he make known, in all its purity and in all its perfectness.

47. 'A householder (gahapati), or one of his children, or a man of inferior birth in any class, listens to that truth [2]. On hearing the truth he has faith in the Tathâgata, and when he has acquired that faith he thus considers with himself:

'"Full of hindrances is household life, a path defiled by passion: free as the air is the life of him who has renounced all worldly things. How difficult is it for the man who dwells at home to live the higher life in all its fulness, in all its purity, in all its bright perfection! Let me then cut off my hair and beard, let me clothe myself in the

word of Sâmañña Phala Sutta, pp. 133 and following; including the passages there parallel to those in Subha Sutta, p. 157, and in Brahma-gâla Sutta, pp. 5–16.

[1] See above, § 7.

[2] The point is, that the acceptance of this 'Doctrine and Discipline' is open to all, not of course that Brâhmans never accept it.

orange-coloured robes, and let me go forth from a household life into the homeless state!"

48. 'Then before long, forsaking his portion of wealth, be it great or be it small; forsaking his circle of relatives, be they many or be they few, he cuts off his hair and beard, he clothes himself in the orange-coloured robes, and he goes forth from the household life into the homeless state.

49. 'When he has thus become a recluse he passes a life self-restrained according to the rules of the Pâtimokkha; uprightness is his delight, and he sees danger in the least of those things he should avoid; he adopts and trains himself in the precepts; he encompasses himself with holiness in word and deed; he sustains his life by means that are quite pure; good is his conduct, guarded the door of his senses; mindful and self-possessed, he is altogether happy[1]!'

---

[1] The argument is resumed after the Three Sîlas, or Descriptions of Conduct—a text, doubtless older than the Suttas in which it occurs, setting forth the distinguishing moral characteristics of a member of the Order.

The First Sîla is an expansion of the Ten Precepts ('Buddhism,' p. 160), but omitting the fifth, against the use of intoxicating drinks. The Second Sîla is a further expansion of the first and then of the last four, and finally of the fourth Precept. The Third Sîla is directed against auguries, divinations, prophecies, astrology, quackery, ritualism, and the worship of Gods (including Brahmâ).

These Three Sîlas may perhaps have been inserted in the Sutta as a kind of counterpoise to the Three Vedas. Our Sutta really reads better without them; but they are interesting in themselves, and the third is especially valuable as evidence of ancient customs and beliefs.

Chapter II.

The Short Paragraphs on Conduct.

THE *KÛLA* SÎLA*M*[1].

1. 'Now wherein, Vâse*tth*a, is his conduct good?'

'Herein, O Vâse*tth*a, that putting away the murder of that which lives, he abstains from destroying life. The cudgel and the sword he lays aside; and, full of modesty and pity, he is compassionate and kind to all creatures that have life!

'This is the kind of goodness that he has.

2. 'Putting away the theft of that which is not his, he abstains from taking anything not given. He takes only what is given, therewith is he content, and he passes his life in honesty and in purity of heart!

'This, too, is the kind of goodness that he has.

3. 'Putting away inchastity, he lives a life of chastity and purity, averse to the low habit of sexual intercourse.

'This, too, (&c., see § II, 2.)[2]

---

[1] There is no division into actual chapters in the original, but it is convenient to arrange the following enumeration of moral precepts separately, as they occur in various suttas in the same order; and are always divided into the three divisions of Lower, Medium, and Higher Morality.

[2] The clause 'this, too, is the kind of goodness that he has' is repeated in the text after each section. The clause, which differs

4. 'Putting away lying, he abstains from speaking falsehood. He speaks truth, from the truth he never swerves; faithful and trustworthy, he injures not his fellow man by deceit.

'This, too, (&c., see § II, 2.)

5. 'Putting away slander, he abstains from calumny. What he hears here he repeats not elsewhere to raise a quarrel against the people here: what he hears elsewhere he repeats not here to raise a quarrel against the people there. Thus he lives as a binder together of those who are divided, an encourager of those who are friends, a peacemaker, a lover of peace, impassioned for peace, a speaker of words that make for peace.

'This, too, (&c., see § II, 2.)

6. 'Putting away bitterness of speech, he abstains from harsh language. Whatever word is humane, pleasant to the ear, lovely, reaching to the heart, urbane, pleasing to the people, beloved of the people—such are the words he speaks.

'This, too, (&c., see § II, 2.)

7. 'Putting away foolish talk, he abstains from vain conversation. In season he speaks; he speaks that which is; he speaks fact; he utters good doctrine; he utters good discipline; he speaks, and at the right time, that which redounds to profit, is well-grounded, is well-defined, and is full of wisdom.

'This, too, (&c., see § II, 2.)

8. 'He refrains from injuring any herb or any creature. He takes but one meal a day; abstaining

in the different suttas in which this enumeration of Buddhist morality is found, is distinct from the enumeration itself, and, like the opening reference to Vâse*tth*a, characteristic only of the particular Sutta.

from food at night time, or at the wrong time. He abstains from dancing, singing, music, and theatrical shows. He abstains from wearing, using, or adorning himself with garlands, and scents, and unguents, and he abstains from lofty couches and large beds.

'This, too, (&c., see § II, 2.)

9. 'He abstains from the getting of silver or gold. He abstains from the getting of grain uncooked. He abstains from the getting of flesh that is raw. He abstains from the getting of any woman or girl. He abstains from the getting of bondmen or bondwomen. He abstains from the getting of sheep or goats. He abstains from the getting of fowls or swine. He abstains from the getting of elephants, cattle, horses, and mares. He abstains from the getting of fields or lands.

'This, too, (&c., see § II, 2.)

10. 'He refrains from carrying out those commissions on which messengers can be sent. He refrains from buying and selling. He abstains from tricks with false weights, alloyed metals, or false measures. He abstains from bribery, cheating, fraud, and crooked ways.

'This, too, (&c., see § II, 2.)

11. 'He refrains from maiming, killing, imprisoning, highway robbery, plundering villages, or obtaining money by threats of violence.

'This, too, (&c., see § II, 2.)'

End of the Short Paragraphs on Conduct.

The Middle Paragraphs on Conduct.

THE MAGGHIMA SÎLAM.

1. 'Or whereas some Samana-Brâhmans, who live on the food provided by the faithful, continue addicted to injuring plants or vegetables: that is to say, the germs arising from roots, the germs arising from trunks of trees, the germs arising from joints, the germs arising from buds, or the germs arising from seeds. He, on the other hand, refrains from injuring such plants or animals.

'This, too, (&c., see § II, 2.)

2. 'Or whereas some Samana-Brâhmans, who live on the food provided by the faithful, continue addicted to storing up property: that is to say, meat, drink, clothes, equipages, beds, perfumes, and grain. He, on the other hand, refrains from storing up such property.

'This, too, (&c., see § II, 2.)

3. 'Or whereas some Samana-Brâhmans, who live on the food provided by the faithful, continue addicted to witnessing public spectacles: that is to say, dancing, singing, concerts, theatrical representations, recitations, instrumental music, funeral ceremonies, drummings, balls, gymnastics, tumblings, feasts in honour of the dead, combats between elephants, horses, buffaloes, bulls, goats, rams, cocks, and quails, cudgel playing, boxing, wrestling, fencing, musters, marching, and reviews of troops. He, on the other hand, refrains from such public spectacles.

'This, too, (&c., see § II, 2.)

4. 'Or whereas some Samana-Brâhmans, who live on the food provided by the faithful, continue addicted to occupying their time with games detrimental to their progress in virtue: that is to say, with a board of sixty-four squares, or of one hundred squares; tossing up; hopping over diagrams formed on the ground; removing substances from a heap without shaking the remainder; dicing; trap-ball; sketching rude figures; tossing balls; blowing trumpets; ploughing matches; tumbling; forming mimic windmills; guessing at measures; chariot races; archery; shooting marbles from the fingers; guessing other people's thoughts; and mimicking other people's acts. He, on the other hand, refrains from such games detrimental to virtue.

'This, too, (&c., see § II, 2.)

5. 'Or whereas some Samana-Brâhmans, who live on the food provided by the faithful, continue addicted to the use of elevated and ornamented couches or things to recline upon: that is to say, of large couches; ornamented beds; coverlets with long fleece; embroidered counterpanes; woollen coverlets, plain or worked with thick flowers; cotton coverlets, worked with knots, or dyed with figures of animals; fleecy carpets; carpets inwrought with gold or with silk; far-spreading carpets; rich elephant housings, trappings, or harness; rugs for chariots; skins of the tiger or antelope; and pillows or cushions ornamented with gold lace or embroidery. He, on the other hand, refrains from the use of such elevated or ornamented couches or things to recline upon.

'This, too, (&c., see § II, 2.)

6. 'Or whereas some Sama*n*a-Brâhmans, who live on the food provided by the faithful, continue addicted to the use of articles for the adornment of their persons: that is to say, unguents; fragrant oils; perfumed baths; shampooings; mirrors; antimony for the eyebrows and eyelashes; flowers; cosmetics; dentifrices; bracelets; diadems; handsome walking-sticks; tiaras; swords; umbrellas; embroidered slippers; fillets; jewelry; fans of the buffalo tail; and long white garments. He, on the other hand, refrains from the use of such articles for the adornment of the person.

'This, too, (&c., see § II, 2.)

7. 'Or whereas some Sama*n*a-Brâhmans, who live on the food provided by the faithful, continue addicted to mean talk: that is to say, tales of kings, of robbers, or of ministers of state; tales of arms, of war, of terror; conversation respecting meats, drinks, clothes, couches, garlands, perfumes, relationships, equipages, streets, villages, towns, cities, provinces, women, warriors, demigods; fortune-telling; hidden treasures in jars; ghost stories; empty tales; disasters by sea; accidents on shore; things which are, and things which are not. He, on the other hand, refrains from such mean conversation.

'This, too, (&c., see § II, 2.)

8. 'Or whereas some Sama*n*a-Brâhmans, who live on the food provided by the faithful, continue addicted to wrangling: that is to say, to saying, "You are ignorant of this doctrine and discipline, but I understand them!" "What do you know of doctrine or discipline?" "You are heterodox, but I am orthodox!" "My discourse is profitable, but yours is worthless!" "That which you should speak

first you speak last, and that which you should speak last you speak first!" "What you have long studied I have completely overturned!" "Your errors are made quite plain!" "You are disgraced!" "Go away and escape from this disputation; or if not, extricate yourself from your difficulties!" He, on the other hand, refrains from such wrangling.

'This, too, (&c., see § II, 2.)

9. 'Or whereas some Samana-Brâhmans, who live on the food provided by the faithful, continue addicted to performing the servile duties of a go-between: that is to say, between kings, ministers of state, soldiers, Brâhmans, people of property, or young men, who say, "Come here!" "Go there!" "Take this to such a place!" "Bring that here!" But he refrains from such servile duties of a messenger.

'This, too, (&c., see § II, 2.)

10. 'Or whereas some Samana-Brâhmans, who live on the food provided by the faithful, continue addicted to hypocrisy: that is to say, they speak much; they make high professions; they disparage others; and they are continually thirsting after gain. But he refrains from such hypocritical craft.

'This, too, (&c., see § II, 2.)'

End of the Middle Paragraphs on Conduct.

The Long Paragraphs on Conduct.

THE MAHÂ SÎLA*M*.

1. 'Or whereas some Sama*n*a-Brâhmans, who live on the food provided by the faithful, continue to gain a livelihood by such low arts, by such lying practices as these: that is to say, by divination from marks on the body; by auguries; by the interpretation of prognostics, of dreams, and of omens, good or bad; by divinations from the manner in which cloth and other such things have been bitten by rats; by sacrifices to the god of fire, offerings of Dabba grass, offerings with a ladle, offerings of husks, of bran, of rice, of clarified butter, of oil, and of liquids ejected from the mouth; and by bloody sacrifices; by teaching spells for preserving the body, for determining lucky sites, for protecting fields, for luck in war, against ghosts and goblins, to secure good harvests, to cure snake bites, to serve as antidotes for poison, and to cure bites of scorpions or rats; by divination, by the flight of hawks, or by the croaking of ravens; by guessing at length of life; by teaching spells to ward off wounds; and by pretended knowledge of the language of beasts.—

'He, on the other hand, refrains from seeking a livelihood by such low arts, by such lying practices.

'This, too, (&c., see § II, 2.)

2. 'Or whereas some Sama*n*a-Brâhmans, who live on the food provided by the faithful, continue to gain a livelihood by such low arts, by such lying

practices as these: that is to say, by explaining the good and bad points in jewels, sticks, garments, swords, arrows, bows, weapons of war, women, men, youths, maidens, male and female slaves, elephants, horses, bulls, oxen, goats, sheep, fowl, snipe, iguanas, long-eared creatures, turtle, and deer.—

'He, on the other hand, refrains from seeking a livelihood by such low arts, by such lying practices.

'This, too, (&c., see § II, 2.)

3. 'Or whereas some Samana-Brâhmans, who live on the food provided by the faithful, continue to gain a livelihood by such low arts and such lying practices as these: that is to say, by foretelling future events, as these:

'"There will be a sortie by the king." "There will not be a sortie by the king." "The king within the city will attack." "The king outside the city will retreat." "The king within the city will gain the victory." "The king outside the city will be defeated." "The king outside the city will be the conqueror." "The king inside the city will be vanquished." Thus prophesying to this one victory and to that one defeat.—

'He, on the other hand, refrains from seeking a livelihood by such low arts, by such lying practices.

'This, too, (&c., see § II, 2.)

4. 'Or whereas some Samana-Brâhmans, who live on the food provided by the faithful, continue to gain a livelihood by such low arts and such lying practices as these: that is to say, by predicting—

'"There will be an eclipse of the moon." "There will be an eclipse of the sun." "There will be an eclipse of a planet." "The sun and the moon will be in conjunction." "The sun and the moon will be in opposition." "The planets will be in conjunction." "The planets will be in opposition." "There will be falling meteors, and fiery coruscations in the atmosphere." "There will be earthquakes, thunderbolts, and forked lightnings." "The rising and setting of the sun, moon, or planets will be cloudy or clear." And then: "The eclipse of the moon will have such and such a result." "The eclipse of the sun will have such and such a result." "The eclipse of the moon will have such and such a result." "The sun and the moon being in conjunction will have such and such a result." "The sun and the moon being in opposition will have such and such a result." "The planets being in conjunction will have such and such a result." "The planets being in opposition will have such and such a result." "The falling meteors and fiery coruscations in the atmosphere will have such and such a result." "The earthquakes, thunderbolts, and forked lightnings will have such and such a result." "The rising and setting of the sun, moon, or planets, cloudy or clear, will have such and such a result."

'He, on the other hand, refrains from seeking a livelihood by such low arts, by such lying practices.

'This, too, (&c., see § II, 2.)

5. 'Or whereas some Sama*n*a-Brâhmans, who live on the food provided by the faithful, continue to gain a livelihood by such low arts and such lying practices as these: that is to say, by predicting—

'"There will be an abundant rainfall." "There will be a deficient rainfall." "There will be an abundant harvest." "There will be famine." "There will be tranquillity." "There will be disturbances." "The season will be sickly." "The season will be healthy."

Or by drawing deeds, making up accounts, giving pills, making verses, or arguing points of casuistry—

'He, on the other hand, refrains from seeking a livelihood by such low arts, by such lying practices.

'This, too, (&c., see § II, 2.)

6. 'Or whereas some Sama*n*a-Brâhmans, who live on the food provided by the faithful, continue to gain a livelihood by such low arts and such lying practices as these: that is to say, by giving advice touching the taking in marriage, or the giving in marriage; the forming of alliances, or the dissolution of connections; the calling in property, or the laying of it out. By teaching spells to procure prosperity, or to cause adversity to others; to remove sterility; to produce dumbness, locked-jaw, deformity, or deafness. By obtaining oracular responses by the aid of a mirror, or from a young girl, or from a god. By worshipping the sun, or by worshipping Brahmâ; by spitting fire out of their mouths, or by laying hands on people's heads—

'He, on the other hand, refrains from seeking a livelihood by such low arts, by such lying practices.

'This, too, (&c., see § II, 2.)

7. 'Or whereas some Sama*n*a-Brâhmans, who live on the food provided by the faithful, continue to gain a livelihood by such low arts and such lying practices as these: that is to say, by teaching the ritual for making vows and performing them; for blessing fields; for imparting virility and rendering impotent; for choosing the site of a house; for performing a house-warming. By teaching forms of words to be used when cleansing the mouth, when bathing, and when making offerings to the god of

fire. By prescribing medicines to produce vomiting or purging, or to remove obstructions in the higher or lower intestines, or to relieve head-ache. By preparing oils for the ear, collyriums, catholicons, antimony, and cooling drinks. By practising cautery, midwifery, or the use of root decoctions or salves—

'He, on the other hand, refrains from seeking a livelihood by such low arts, by such lying practices.

'This, too, (&c., see § II, 2.)'

End of the Long Paragraphs on Conduct.

CHAPTER III.

1. [1] 'And he lets his mind pervade one quarter of the world with thoughts of Love, and so the second, and so the third, and so the fourth. And thus the whole wide world, above, below, around, and everywhere, does he continue to pervade with heart of Love, far-reaching, grown great, and beyond measure.

2. 'Just, Vâse*tth*a, as a mighty trumpeter makes himself heard—and that without difficulty—in all the four directions; even so of all things that have shape or life, there is not one that he passes by or leaves aside, but regards them all with mind set free, and deep-felt love.

'Verily this, Vâse*tth*a, is the way to a state of union with Brahmâ.

3. 'And he lets his mind pervade one quarter of the world with thoughts of pity, sympathy, and equanimity, and so the second, and so the third, and so the fourth. And thus the whole wide world, above, below, around, and everywhere, does he continue to pervade with heart of pity, sympathy, and equanimity, far-reaching, grown great, and beyond measure.

4. 'Just, Vâse*tth*a, as a mighty trumpeter makes himself heard—and that without difficulty—in all the four directions; even so of all things that have

[1] This paragraph occurs frequently; see, inter alia, below, Mahâ-Sudassana Sutta II, 8. It will be seen from 'Buddhism,' pp. 170, 171, that these meditations play a great part in later Buddhism, and occupy very much the place that prayer takes in Christianity. A fifth, the meditation on Impurity, has been added, at what time I do not know, before the last. All five are practised in Siam (Alabaster, 'Wheel of the Law,' p. 168).

shape or life, there is not one that he passes by or leaves aside, but regards them all with mind set free, and deep-felt pity, sympathy, and equanimity.

'Verily this, Vâse*tth*a, is the way to a state of union with Brahmâ.'

---

5. 'Now what think you, Vâse*tth*a, will the Bhikkhu[1] who lives thus be in possession of women and of wealth, or will he not?'

'He will not, Gotama!'

'Will he be full of anger, or free from anger?'

'He will be free from anger, Gotama!'

'Will his mind be full of malice, or free from malice?'

'Free from malice, Gotama!'

'Will his mind be sinful, or pure?'

'It will be pure, Gotama!'

'Will he have self-mastery, or will he not?'

'Surely he will, Gotama!'

6. 'Then you say, Vâse*tth*a, that the Bhikkhu is free from household cares, and that Brahmâ is free from household cares. Is there then agreement and likeness between the Bhikkhu and Brahmâ?'

'There is, Gotama!'

7. 'Very good, Vâse*tth*a. Then in sooth, Vâse*tth*a, that the Bhikkhu who is free from household cares should after death, when the body is dissolved, become united with Brahmâ, who is the same—such a condition of things is every way possible!

8. 'And so you say, Vâse*tth*a, that the Bhikkhu is free from anger, and free from malice, pure in mind, and master of himself; and that Brahmâ is

[1] Or 'Member of our Order.' See the note on Mahâparinibbâna Sutta I, 6.

free from anger, and free from malice, pure in mind, and master of himself. Then in sooth, Vâse*ttha*, that the Bhikkhu who is free from anger, free from malice, pure in mind, and master of himself should after death, when the body is dissolved, become united with Brahmâ, who is the same—such a condition of things is every way possible!'

---

9. When he had thus spoken, the young Brâhmans Vâse*ttha* and Bhâradvâ*g*a addressed the Blessed One, and said:

'Most excellent, Lord, are the words of thy mouth, most excellent! Just as if a man were to set up that which is thrown down, or were to reveal that which is hidden away, or were to point out the right road to him who has gone astray, or were to bring a lamp into the darkness, so that those who have eyes can see external forms;—just even so, Lord, has the truth been made known to us, in many a figure, by the Blessed One. And we, even we, betake ourselves, Lord, to the Blessed One as our refuge, to the Truth, and to the Brotherhood. May the Blessed One accept us as disciples, as true believers, from this day forth, as long as life endures!'

End of the Tevi*gg*a Suttanta.

ÂKAṄKHEYYA-SUTTA.

INTRODUCTION

TO THE

ÂKAṄKHEYYA SUTTA.

JUST as the Tevi*gg*a Sutta is an argumentum ad hominem to the man wise in the Vedas, and seeking through that knowledge for union with the Deity, urging him to adopt rather the Buddhist method of a life of righteousness here on earth; so the present Sutta is a similar argument addressed to the seeker after the various things specified in its different sections. If he should desire any of these things then let him live the life of uprightness as set out in the opening section, and cultivate the intelligent earnestness and spiritual insight described in the refrain.

The two combined amount, as would naturally be expected, to the Nirvâ*n*a of a perfect life in Arahatship—the supreme goal not only of every good Buddhist, but of every good Buddhist argument. As applied in the earlier sections it is only a re-statement of a familiar doctrine; as applied in the later sections it has the additional interest of showing us the answer of early Buddhism to the mystics, as the Tevi*gg*a shows us its answer to the theologians. And in the answer we find the details of some curious beliefs which existed in India when Buddhism arose, and which in after times, and especially in the northern church, had so disastrous an effect upon it.

With regard to the reality of these mystical powers our Sutta gives an uncertain sound; leaving, however, an impression rather in its favour. The argument is equally good either way, but the author of the Sutta is so engrossed with Arahatship that he does not stay to say whether he regards the belief in the powers referred to as a delusion or not. I have no doubt that he really believed in their theoretical possibility, which is elsewhere also in the Pâli Piṭakas accepted or implied; though the practical effect of the belief has greatly varied among Buddhists in different times and countries. In the southern church, which adhered more closely to the simple doctrines of early Buddhism, these beliefs have been relegated to the region of legend and fairy tale; in the northern church there have been found, from time to time, believers who attached to them a practical importance. There is a useful analogy between the expressions used in 1 Samuel xxviii, and those in the latter part of our Suttas; and between the general position of witchcraft in the history of Christianity, and of these beliefs in the history of Buddhism; but it would take too long to carry out the comparison and contrast in detail here, and with due regard to the necessary limitations under which the comparison should be made. The analogy only reaches to their history, and to their relative importance in the religious systems with which they were connected; the two sets of belief themselves are fundamentally different, the Indian beliefs being much more nearly allied to modern spiritualism and mesmerism.

We have a curious instance of the way in which such legends grow in a parallel passage of the earlier and later lives of Gotama as accepted by orthodox Buddhists. In the Mahâ Vagga[1] it is said that during the first watch of the night following on Gotama's victory over the Evil One, he fixed his mind upon the Chain of Causation, during the second watch he did the same, and during the third watch he did the same—the only difference in the narrative being the verses with which in each of the three watches the meditation closed.

In the life of Gotama prefixed to the *G*âtakas[2], the simplicity of this account is improved away by saying that

[1] I, 1, 2–6.

[2] *G*âtaka I, 75, translated in 'Buddhist Birth Stories,' p. 102.

in the first watch he acquired the knowledge of Past Births (Pubbe-nivâsa-nâna, described in our § 17), in the second the knowledge of Present Births (Dibba-*k*akkhu, described in our § 19), and only in the third the knowledge of the Chain of Causation (Pati*kk*a-samuppâda). It is curious that in the corresponding passage of the northern Buddhist Sanskrit poem, the Lalita Vistara[1], we find precisely the same tradition, which must therefore have been current in both northern and southern churches before the fifth century of our era.

I think it is quite possible that at that time it had become part of the Buddhist theory that every Arahat possessed this supernatural insight; and as Gotama was supposed by the authors of these two later works to have acquired Arahatship by his victory over the Evil One, it naturally seemed to them proper to say that he then also acquired these particular powers. It is clear that even in the time when the Pi*t*akas were put into their present form it was considered that the Buddha had acquired them[2], and that they could be acquired by less exalted persons[3]. In the later literature several instances are given of particular persons who possessed one or other of them in a greater or less degree; but it is instructive to notice that these are always persons who lived long before the time of the writer who records the instances.

The early Buddhist doctrine as to witchcraft, astrology, omens, auguries, sacrifices, prophecies, and the like, will be found in the Mahâ Sîla (above, pp. 196–200), and in the Third Fetter (below, p. 222).

[1] Calcutta edition, pp. 440–448.

[2] See, for instance, the Tevi*gg*a-va*kkh*agotta Sutta.

[3] Sâma*ññ*a Phala Sutta, pp. 144–154.

IF HE SHOULD DESIRE—.

ÂKAṄKHEYYA-SUTTA.

1. Thus have I heard. The Blessed One was once staying at Sâvatthi in Anâtha Pi*nd*ika's park.

There the Blessed One addressed the Brethren, and said, 'Bhikkhus.' 'Yea, Lord!' said the Brethren, in assent, to the Blessed One.

Then spake the Blessed One:

2. 'Continue, Brethren, in the practice of Right Conduct[1], adhering to the Rules of the Order[2]; continue enclosed by the restraint of the Rules of the Order, devoted to uprightness in life[3]; train yourselves according to the Precepts[4], taking them upon you in the sense of the danger in the least offence.

3. 'If a Bhikkhu should desire, Brethren, to become beloved, popular, respected among his fellow-disciples, let him then fulfil all righteousness, let him be devoted to that quietude of heart which springs from within[5], let him not drive back the ecstasy of contemplation[6], let him look through things[7], let him be much alone!'

---

[1] Sîla. [2] Pâtimokkhâ.

[3] Â*k*âragoka*r*â. Comp. Tevigga Sutta I, 49.

[4] Sikkhâpadesu. The Buddhist Decalogue (given in 'Buddhism,' p. 160).

[5] Agg*h*attam *k*eto samatha*m*. [6] *Gh*âna.

[7] Vipassanâ: it is always used, in contrast to samatha

4. 'If a Bhikkhu should desire, Brethren, to receive the requisites—clothing, food, lodging, and medicine, and other necessaries for the sick—let him then fulfil all righteousness, let him be devoted to that quietude of heart which springs from within, let him not drive back the ecstasy of contemplation, let him look through things, let him be much alone!'

5. 'If a Bhikkhu should desire, Brethren, that to those people among whom he receives the requisites—clothing, food, lodging, and medicine, and other necessaries for the sick—that charity of theirs should redound to great fruit and great advantage, let him then fulfil all righteousness, let him be devoted to that quietude of heart which springs from within, let him not drive back the ecstasy of contemplation, let him look through things, let him be much alone!'

6. 'If a Bhikkhu should desire, Brethren, that those relatives of his, of one blood with him, dead and gone, who think of him with believing heart should find therein great fruit and great advantage[1], let him then fulfil all righteousness, let him be devoted to that quietude of heart which springs from within, let him not drive back the ecstasy of contemplation, let him look through things, let him be much alone!'

7. 'If a Bhikkhu should desire, Brethren, that he

(note 5), of insight into objective phenomena. These three qualities are constantly referred to as parts of Arahatship. The Rev. David da Silva makes vipassanâ identical with the sevenfold perception (saññâ, mentioned as conditions of the welfare of a community in the Book of the Great Decease, Chap. I, § 10).

[1] Even after death those who remember the Buddha, the Truth, or the Order with believing heart can reap spiritual advantage. Compare the Dhammapada commentary, p. 97.

should be victorious over discontent and lust [1], that discontent should never overpower him, that he should master and subdue any discontent that had sprung up within him, let him then fulfil all righteousness, let him be devoted to that quietude of heart which springs from within, let him not drive back the ecstasy of contemplation, let him look through things, let him be much alone!'

8. 'If a Bhikkhu should desire, Brethren, that he should be victorious over (spiritual) danger and dismay, that neither danger nor dismay should ever overcome him, that he should master and subdue every danger and dismay, let him then fulfil all righteousness, let him be devoted to that quietude of heart which springs from within, let him not drive back the ecstasy of contemplation, let him look through things, let him be much alone!'

9. 'If a Bhikkhu should desire, Brethren, to realise the hopes of those spiritual men who live in the bliss which comes, even in this present world, from the four *Gh*ânas, should he desire not to fall into the pains and difficulties (which they avoid), let him then fulfil all righteousness, let him be devoted to that quietude of heart which springs from within, let him not drive back the ecstasy of contemplation, let him look through things, let him be much alone [2]!'

10. 'If a Bhikkhu should desire, Brethren, to reach with his body and remain in those stages of deliverance which are incorporeal, and pass beyond

[1] Aratiratisaho. Arati is the disinclination to fulfil the duties of a Sama*n*a, discontent with the restrictions of the Order.

[2] The bliss here referred to, and described in detail below, Mahâ-Sudassana Sutta, Chap. III, is the 'ecstasy of contemplation' referred to in the refrain.

phenomena[1], let him then fulfil all righteousness, let him be devoted to that quietude of heart which springs from within, let him not drive back the ecstasy of contemplation, let him look through things, let him be much alone!'

11. 'If a Bhikkhu should desire, Brethren, by the complete destruction of the three Bonds to become converted, to be no longer liable to be reborn in a state of suffering, and to be assured of final salvation[2], let him then fulfil all righteousness, let him be devoted to that quietude of heart which springs from within, let him not drive back the ecstasy of contemplation, let him look through things, let him be much alone!'

12. 'If a Bhikkhu should desire, Brethren, by the complete destruction of the three Bonds, and by the reduction to a minimum of lust, hatred, and delusion, to become a Sakadâgâmin, and (thus) on his first return to this world to make an end of sorrow, let him then fulfil all righteousness, let him be devoted to that quietude of heart which springs from within, let him not drive back the ecstasy of contemplation, let him look through things, let him be much alone!'

13. 'If a Bhikkhu should desire, Brethren, by the complete destruction of the five Bonds which bind people to this earth, to become an inheritor of the highest heavens[3], there to pass entirely away, thence

---

[1] These are the eight Vimokkhâ, a list of which occurs in the Great Decease, Chap. III, §§ 33–42.

[2] On this and the two following sections compare Mahâparinibbâna Sutta II, 7, and on the Bonds or Fetters below, p. 222.

[3] Opapâtika. This is another of those words which, from their connoting Buddhist ideas unknown in Europe, are really untranslatable. It means a being who springs into existence without the intervention of parents, and therefore, as it were,

never to return, let him then fulfil all righteousness, let him be devoted to that quietude of heart which springs from within, let him not drive back the ecstasy of contemplation, let him look through things, let him be much alone!'

14.[1] 'If a Bhikkhu should desire, Brethren, to exercise one by one each of the different Iddhis, being one to become multiform, being multiform to become one; to become visible, or to become invisible; to go without being stopped to the further side of a wall, or a fence, or a mountain, as if through air; to penetrate up and down through solid ground, as if through water; to walk on the water without dividing it, as if on solid ground; to travel cross-legged through the sky, like the birds on wing; to touch and feel with the hand even the sun and the moon, mighty and powerful though they be; and to reach in the body even up to the heaven of Brahmâ; let him then fulfil all righteous-

uncaused, and seeming to appear by chance. All the higher devas (angels or gods) are opapâtika, there being no sex or birth in the highest heavens; and it is with especial allusion to this that the word is here used. There is of course from the Buddhist point of view (which admits of nothing without a cause) a very sufficient cause for the sudden appearance of an opapâtika in heaven, viz. the karma of a being who has past away somewhere else; but the Buddhist theory necessitated the choice of an expression which would give no countenance to the (heretical) idea of a soul flying away after the death of its body from one world to another.

In the expression 'which bind people to this world,' by world is meant the Rûpa-loka, or world of form, which include all those parts of the universe whose inhabitants have an outward form and are subject to lusts.

[1] With this paragraph compare Mahâparinibbâna Sutta III, 14, and Sâmañña Phala Sutta, p. 145.

ness, let him be devoted to that quietude of heart which springs from within, let him not drive back the ecstasy of contemplation, let him look through things, let him be much alone!'

15.[1] 'If a Bhikkhu should desire, Brethren, to hear with clear and heavenly ear, surpassing that of men, sounds both human and celestial, whether far or near, let him then fulfil all righteousness, let him be devoted to that quietude of heart which springs from within, let him not drive back the ecstasy of contemplation, let him look through things, let him be much alone!'

16.[2] 'If a Bhikkhu should desire, Brethren, to comprehend by his own heart the hearts of other beings and of other men; to discern the passionate mind to be passionate, and the calm mind calm; the angry mind to be angry, and the peaceable peaceable; the deluded mind to be deluded, and the wise mind wise; the concentrated thoughts to be concentrated, and the scattered to be scattered; the lofty mind to be lofty, and the narrow mind narrow; the sublime thoughts to be sublime, and the mean to be mean; the steadfast mind to be steadfast, and the wavering to be wavering; the free mind to be free, and the enslaved mind to be enslaved; let him then fulfil all righteousness, let him be devoted to that quietude of heart which springs from within, let him not drive back the ecstasy of contemplation, let him look through things, let him be much alone!'

17. 'If a Bhikkhu should desire, Brethren, to be able to call to mind his various temporary states in days gone by; such as one birth, two births,

---

[1] With this paragraph compare Sâmañña Phala Sutta, p. 146.

[2] Compare M. P. S. I, 16, and Sâmañña Phala Sutta, p. 147.

three, four, five, ten, twenty, thirty, forty, fifty, a hundred or a thousand, or a hundred thousand births[1]; his births in many an æon of destruction, in many an æon of renovation, in many an æon of both destruction and renovation[2]; (so as to be able to say), "In that place such was my name, such my family, such my caste[3], such my subsistence, such my experience of comfort or of pain, and such the limit of my life; and when I passed from thence, I took form again in that other place where my name was so and so, such my family, such my caste, such my subsistence, such my experience of comfort or of joy, and such my term of life; and when I fell from thence, I took form in such and such a place[4];"—should he desire thus to call to mind his temporary states in days gone by in all their modes and all their details let him then fulfil all righteousness, let him be devoted to that quietude of heart which springs from within, let him not drive back the ecstasy of contemplation, let him look through things, let him be much alone!'

18.[5] 'If a Bhikkhu should desire, Brethren, to see with pure and heavenly vision, surpassing that of

[1] The Lalita Vistara (p. 442) characteristically carries this enumeration further up into innumerable ko*t*is and niyutas of births.

[2] This is based on the Buddhist theory of the periodical destruction and renovation of the universe, each of which takes countless years to be accomplished.

[3] Va*nn*a, colour.

[4] The text of this clause recurs nearly word for word in the Brahma-*g*âla Sutta, pp. 17–21; and in the Lalita Vistara, Chap. XXII, p. 442; and exactly in the Sâma*ññ*a Phala Sutta, p. 148.

[5] This paragraph recurs in the Sâma*ññ*a Phala Sutta, p. 150, and in nearly the same words in the Lalita Vistara, Chap. XXII.

men, beings as they pass from one state of existence and take form in others; beings base or noble, good-looking or ill-favoured, happy or miserable, according to the karma they inherit—(if he should desire to be able to say), "These beings, reverend sirs, by their bad conduct in action, by their bad conduct in word, by their bad conduct in thought, by their speaking evil of the Noble Ones[1], by their adhesion to false doctrine, or by their acquiring the karma of false doctrine[2], have been reborn, on the dissolution of the body after death, in some unhappy state of suffering or woe[3]." "These beings, reverend sirs, by their good conduct in action, by their good conduct in word, by their good conduct in thought, by their not speaking evil of the Noble Ones, by their adhesion to right doctrine, by their acquiring the karma of right doctrine, have been reborn, on the dissolution of the body after death, into some happy state in heaven;"—should he desire thus to see with pure and heavenly vision, surpassing that of men, beings as they thus pass from one state of existence and take form in others; beings base or noble, good-looking or ill-favoured, happy or miserable, according to the karma they inherit; let him then fulfil all righteousness, let him be devoted to that quietude of heart which springs

---

[1] This is a collective term, meaning Buddhas, Pa*kk*eka Buddhas, Arahats, Anâgâmins, Sakadâgâmins, and Sotâpannas; that is, those who are walking in the Noble Eightfold Path.

[2] The Pâli is mi*kkh*â- (and below sammâ-) di*tth*i-kamma-samâdâna; the Lalita Vistara, whose other expressions are identical with the Pâli, has, very strangely, mithyâ- (and below samyag-) di*tth*i-karma-dharma-samâdâna.

[3] See note on M. P. S., Chap. I, § 23.

from within, let him not drive back the ecstasy of contemplation, let him look through things, let him be much alone!'

19.[1] 'If a Bhikkhu should desire, Brethren, by the destruction of the great evils (Âsavas[2]), by himself, and even in this very world, to know and realise and attain to Arahatship, to emancipation of heart, and emancipation of mind, let him then fulfil all righteousness, let him be devoted to that quietude of heart which springs from within, let him not drive back the ecstasy of contemplation, let him look through things, let him be much alone!'

20. 'Continue therefore, Brethren, in the practice of Right Conduct, adhering to the Rules of the Order; continue enclosed by the restraint of the Rules of the Order, devoted to uprightness in life; train yourselves according to the Precepts, taking them upon you in the sense of the danger in the least offence. For to this end alone has all, that has been said, been said!'

21. Thus spake the Blessed One. And those Brethren, delighted in heart, exalted the word of the Blessed One.

End of the Âkaṅkheyya Sutta.

---

[1] Compare Sâmañña Phala Sutta, p. 151; Mahâparinibbâna Sutta II, 7; and Lalita Vistara, Chap. XXII, p. 442.

[2] Sensuality, individuality, delusion, and ignorance.

*K*ETOKHILA-SUTTA.

INTRODUCTION

TO THE

*K*ETOKHILA SUTTA.

THE following translation has been made from a text, based on the Turnour and Phayre MSS. in the India Office, of which Dr. Morris was kind enough to allow me the use. The Suttas in the Ma*ggh*ima Nikâya are usually distinguished by the way in which a single thought or one or two allied thoughts are stated shortly at the commencement, and are then elaborated and repeated through a number of consecutive and carefully-balanced paragraphs arranged in a literary form that would now be considered monotonous and tiresome in the extreme. The repetitions in the Suttas of the Dîgha Nikâya are no doubt equally artificial, but the train of reasoning being longer and more varied, there is always the hope of a change in the form, or of a new departure in the thought, to sustain the reader's flagging interest.

The argument of this Sutta may be shortly stated thus. The means by which freedom from barrenness and bondage of heart can be reached are zeal and determined effort. But that zeal will be crippled in its struggle against barrenness by want of confidence in the teacher, his doctrine, his order, or his system of self-culture, and by want of concord with the brethren. And that zeal will be crippled in its struggle against bondage by sensuality, by sloth, or by a craving after a future life in any of its various forms. If the disciple be strenuously diligent in the struggle against these things he need not fear or doubt, he will never fail, but will assuredly reach even to the supreme security of Arahatship.

When I first read this Sutta I was irresistibly reminded of that passage in the New Testament where the exhortation to the disciple, 'giving all diligence' to add to his faith virtue, knowledge, temperance, patience, godliness, and brotherly kindness, is followed by the figure that these things will make him to be 'neither barren nor unfruitful;' and closes with the promise that if he do these things, giving diligence to make his calling and election sure, he shall never fall, but shall enter into that everlasting kingdom which is the supreme goal of the Christian life.

The analogy is sufficiently close to throw considerable light upon our Sutta, but it touches only the barrenness. The bondage is specially Buddhistic, and is allied with the doctrine of the Sanyo*g*anas, or fetters, which the pilgrim along the Noble Path has to break before he can reach the full fruit of Arahatship. It should be compared also with the fivefold bond mentioned in the Tevi*gg*a Sutta, Chap. I, §§ 26–28, the word there used being bandhana*m*, as against vinibandhana*m* here, and the fivefold bond being a fivefold division of our first bondage.

The ten fetters are—

1. The delusion of self (sakkâya-di*tth*i).
2. Doubt (vi*k*iki*kkh*â).
3. Reliance on the efficacy of rites and ceremonies (sîlabbata-parâmâsa).
4. The bodily lusts or passions (kâma).
5. Hatred, ill-feeling (patigha).
6. Desire for a future life in the worlds of form (rûparâga).
7. Desire for a future life in the formless worlds (arûparâga).
8. Pride (mâno).
9. Self-righteousness (uddha*kk*a).
10. Ignorance (avi*gg*â).

Here the 4th fetter is correlative to our first bondage; the 6th fetter to our 2nd and 3rd bondage; and part of the 3rd fetter to our 5th bondage.

The 2nd, 3rd, and 5th bondage are in fact but a new way of stating the fundamental Buddhist doctrine that good must be pursued without any ulterior motive; and that that man is not spiritually free in whom there is still the least hankering after any future life beyond the grave.

BARRENNESS AND BONDAGE.

*K*ETOKHILA-SUTTA.

1. Thus have I heard. The Blessed One was once dwelling at Sâvatthi, in the park of Anâtha Pi*nd*ika.

There the Blessed One addressed the brethren, saying, 'Brethren!'

'Yea, Lord!' said those brethren, in assent, to the Blessed One.

Then the Blessed One spake:

2. 'Whatsoever brother, O Bhikkhus, has not quite become free from the five kinds of spiritual barrenness[1], has not altogether broken through the five kinds of mental bondage[2]—that such a one should reach up to the full advantage of, should attain to the full growth in, to full breadth in, this doctrine and discipline[3]—that can in no wise be!'

---

3. 'And who has not become free from the five kinds of spiritual barrenness?'

'In the first place, O Bhikkhus, when a brother

---

[1] Pa*ñk*a *k*etokhilâ.

[2] Pa*ñk*a *k*etaso vinibandhâ.

[3] Dhamma-vinaye. On the disputed question as to whether this compound is a Dvanda or not, see Dr. Oldenberg, Mahâ Vagga, p. x. M. Léon Feer ('Études Bouddhiques,' p. 203) has taken it as Tatpurusha; and it would be hazardous to say that it is never used as such. Here I think it is a Dvandva.

doubts in the Teacher (Satthâ), is uncertain regarding him, has not confidence in him, and has not faith in him; then is his mind not inclined towards zeal, exertion, perseverance, and struggle.

'But whosesoever mind inclineth not towards zeal, exertion, perseverance, and struggle, he has not become free from this first spiritual barrenness.

4. 'And further, O Bhikkhus, when a brother doubts in the System of Belief (Dhamma), is uncertain regarding it, has not confidence in it, has not faith in it; then is his mind not inclined towards zeal, exertion, perseverance, and struggle.

'But whosesoever mind inclineth not towards zeal, exertion, perseverance, and struggle, he has not become free from this second spiritual barrenness.

5. 'And further, O Bhikkhus, when a brother has doubt in the Brotherhood (Saṅgha), is uncertain about it, has no confidence in it, has no faith in it; then is his mind not inclined towards zeal, exertion, perseverance, and struggle.

'But whosesoever mind inclineth not towards zeal, exertion, perseverance, and struggle, he has not become free from this third spiritual barrenness.

6. 'And further, O Bhikkhus, when a brother has doubt in the System of Self-culture (Sikkhâ), is uncertain about it, has no confidence in it, has no faith in it; then is his mind not inclined towards zeal, exertion, perseverance, and struggle.

'But whosesoever mind inclineth not towards zeal, exertion, perseverance, and struggle, he has not become free from this fourth spiritual barrenness.

7. 'And further, O Bhikkhus, when a brother is angry with his fellow-disciples, discontented with

them, excited against them, barren towards them, the mind of the brother, O Bhikkhus, thus angry with his fellow-disciples, discontented with them, excited against them, barren towards them does not incline towards zeal, exertion, perseverance, and struggle.

'But whosesoever mind inclineth not towards zeal, exertion, perseverance, and struggle, he has not become free from this fifth spiritual barrenness.

'It is such a one, O Bhikkhus, who is not free from the five kinds of spiritual barrenness.'

---

8. 'And who has not broken through the five kinds of spiritual bondage?'

'In the first place, O Bhikkhus, when a brother has not got rid of the passion for lusts (kâme), has not got rid of the desire after lusts, has not got rid of the attraction to lusts, has not got rid of the thirst for lusts, has not got rid of the fever of lust, has not got rid of the craving after lusts.—

'Whatsoever brother, O Bhikkhus, has not got rid of the passion for lusts, has not got rid of the desire after lusts, has not got rid of the attraction to lusts, has not got rid of the thirst for lusts, has not got rid of the fever of lust, has not got rid of the craving after lusts, his mind does not incline to zeal, exertion, perseverance, and struggle.

'But whosesoever mind inclineth not toward zeal, exertion, perseverance, and struggle, he has not broken through this first spiritual bondage.

9. 'And further, O Bhikkhus, when a brother has not got rid of the passion for a body[1] (kâye),

[1] It is possible that kâya may be used here in a technical sense, as the group or aggregate of qualities, apart from form, which go

has not got rid of the desire after a body, has not got rid of the attraction to a body, has not got rid of the thirst for a body, has not got rid of the fever of a body, has not got rid of the craving after a body.—

'Whatsoever brother, O Bhikkhus, has not got rid of the passion for a body, has not got rid of the desire after a body, has not got rid of the attraction to a body, has not got rid of the thirst for a body, has not got rid of the fever of a body, has not got rid of the craving after a body, his mind does not incline to zeal, exertion, perseverance, and struggle.

'But whosesoever mind inclineth not toward zeal, exertion, perseverance, and struggle, he has not broken through this second spiritual bondage.

10. 'And further, O Bhikkhus, when a brother has not got rid of the passion for a form (rûpe), has not got rid of the desire after a form, has not got rid of the attraction to a form, has not got rid of the thirst for a form, has not got rid of the fever of a form, has not got rid of the craving after a form.—

'Whatsoever brother, O Bhikkhus, has not got rid of the passion for a form, has not got rid of the desire after a form, has not got rid of the attraction to a form, has not got rid of the thirst for a form, has not got rid of the fever of a form, has not got rid of the craving after a form, his mind does not incline to zeal, exertion, perseverance, and struggle.

'But whosesoever mind inclineth not toward zeal, exertion, perseverance, and struggle, he has not broken through this third spiritual bondage.

---

to make up an individual. This paragraph would then correspond to the 7th Sa*m*yogana.

11. 'And further, O Bhikkhus, a brother may have eaten enough and to satiety, and begins to follow after the ease of sleep, the ease of softness, the ease of sloth.

'Whatsoever brother, O Bhikkhus, when he has eaten enough and to satiety, begins to follow after the ease of sleep, the ease of softness, the ease of sloth, his mind does not incline to zeal, exertion, perseverance, and struggle.

'But whosesoever mind inclineth not toward zeal, exertion, perseverance, and struggle, he has not broken through this fourth spiritual bondage.

12. 'And further, O Bhikkhus, a brother may have adopted the religious life in the aspiration of belonging to some one or other of the angel hosts[1], and thinking to himself: "By this morality, or by this observance, or by this austerity, or by this religious life, I shall become an angel, or one of the angels!"—

'Whatsoever brother, O Bhikkhus, may have adopted the religious life in the aspiration of belonging to some one or other of the angel hosts, and thinking to himself: "By this morality, or by this observance, or by this austerity, or by this religious life, I shall become an angel, or one of the angels!" his mind does not incline to zeal, exertion, perseverance, and struggle.

'But whosesoever mind inclineth not toward zeal, exertion, perseverance, and struggle, he has not broken through this fifth spiritual bondage.

'It is such a one, O Bhikkhus, who has not broken through the five kinds of mental bondage.

[1] *Aññataram* deva-nikâya*m*. Compare Mahâparinibbâna Sutta, Chap. I, § 11, Chap. II, § 9.

13. 'And whatsoever brother, O Bhikkhus, has not quite become free from the five kinds of spiritual barrenness, has not altogether broken through the five kinds of mental bondage—that such a one should reach up to the full advantage of, should attain to the full growth in, to full breadth in, this doctrine and discipline—that can in no wise be!

---

14. 'But whatsoever brother, O Bhikkhus, has become quite free from the five kinds of mental barrenness, has altogether broken through the five kinds of spiritual bondage—that such a one should reach up to the full advantage of, should attain to full growth in, to full breadth in, this doctrine and discipline—that can well be!'

15. 'And who has become free from the five kinds of spiritual barrenness?'

'In the first place, O Bhikkhus, when a brother does not doubt in the Teacher (Satthâ), is not uncertain regarding him, has confidence in him, and has faith in him; then his mind does incline to zeal, exertion, perseverance, and struggle.

'But whosesoever mind inclineth towards zeal, exertion, perseverance, and struggle, he has become free from this first spiritual barrenness.

16. 'And further, O Bhikkhus, when a brother does not doubt in the System of Belief (Dhamma), is not uncertain regarding it, has confidence in it, and has faith in it; then his mind does incline to zeal, exertion, perseverance, and struggle.

'But whosesoever mind inclineth towards zeal, exertion, perseverance, and struggle, he has become free from this second spiritual barrenness.

17. 'And further, O Bhikkhus, when a brother

does not doubt in the Brotherhood (Sangha), is not uncertain about it, has confidence in it, and has faith in it; then his mind does incline to zeal, exertion, perseverance, and struggle.

'But whosesoever mind inclineth towards zeal, exertion, perseverance, and struggle, he has become free from this third spiritual barrenness.

18. 'And further, O Bhikkhus, when a brother does not doubt in the System of Self-culture (Sikkhâ), is not uncertain about it, has confidence in it, and has faith in it; then his mind does incline to zeal, exertion, perseverance, and struggle.

'But whosesoever mind inclineth towards zeal, exertion, perseverance, and struggle, he has become free from this fourth spiritual barrenness.

19. 'And further, O Bhikkhus, when a brother is not angry with his fellow-disciples, is not discontented with them, is not excited against them, is not barren towards them, the mind of the brother, O Bhikkhus, who is thus not angry with his fellow-disciples, not discontented with them, not excited against them, not barren towards them, does incline toward zeal, exertion, perseverance, and struggle.

'But whosesoever mind inclineth towards zeal, exertion, perseverance, and struggle, he has become free from this fifth spiritual barrenness.'

---

20. 'And who has broken through the five kinds of spiritual bondage?'

'In the first place, O Bhikkhus, when a brother has got rid of the passion after lusts (kâme), has got rid of the desire after lusts, has got rid of the attraction to lusts, has got rid of the thirst for lusts, has got rid of the fever of lust, has got rid of the craving after lusts.—

'Whatsoever brother, O Bhikkhus, has got rid of the passion after lusts, has got rid of the desire after lusts, has got rid of the attraction to lusts, has got rid of the thirst for lusts, has got rid of the fever of lust, has got rid of the craving after lusts, his mind does incline to zeal, exertion, perseverance, and struggle.

'But whosesoever mind inclineth towards zeal, exertion, perseverance, and struggle, he has become free from this first spiritual bondage.

21. 'And, further, O Bhikkhus, when a brother has got rid of the passion after a body (kâye), has got rid of the desire after a body, has got rid of the attraction to a body, has got rid of the thirst for a body, has got rid of the fever of a body, has got rid of the craving after a body.—

'Whatsoever brother, O Bhikkhus, has got rid of the passion after a body, has got rid of the desire after a body, has got rid of the attraction to a body, has got rid of the thirst for a body, has got rid of the fever of a body, has got rid of the craving after a body, his mind does incline to zeal, exertion, perseverance, and struggle.

'But whosesoever mind inclineth towards zeal, exertion, perseverance, and struggle, he has become free from this second spiritual bondage

22. 'And further, O Bhikkhus, when a brother has got rid of the passion for a form (rûpe), has got rid of the desire after a form, has got rid of the attraction to a form, has got rid of the thirst for a form, has got rid of the fever of a form, has got rid of the craving after a form.—

'Whatsoever brother, O Bhikkhus, has got rid of the passion for a form, has got rid of the desire after a form, has got rid of the attraction to a form, has got rid of the thirst for a form, has got rid of the fever of a form, has got rid of the craving after a form, his mind does incline to zeal, exertion, perseverance, and struggle.

'But whosesoever mind inclineth towards zeal, exertion, perseverance, and struggle, he has become free from this third spiritual bondage.

23. 'And further, O Bhikkhus, when a brother does not, having eaten enough and to satiety, begin to follow after the ease of sleep, the ease of softness, the ease of sloth.

'Whatsoever brother, O Bhikkhus, does not, having eaten enough and to satiety, begin to follow after the ease of sleep, the ease of softness, the ease of sloth, his mind does incline to zeal, exertion, perseverance, and struggle.

'But whosesoever mind inclineth towards zeal, exertion, perseverance, and struggle, he has become free from this fourth spiritual bondage[1].

24. 'And further, O Bhikkhus, when a brother has not adopted the religious life in the aspiration of belonging to some one or other of the angel hosts, thinking to himself: "By this morality, or by this observance, or by this austerity, or by this religious life, I shall become an angel, or one of the angels!"—

'Whatsoever brother, O Bhikkhus, has not

---

[1] In this section, and in section 11, I have rendered sukha by ease, and not by happiness, as I think the former is always its more exact meaning in such passages.

adopted the religious life in the aspiration of belonging to some one or other of the angel hosts, thinking to himself: "By this morality, or by this observance, or by this austerity, or by this religious life, I shall become an angel, or one of the angels!" his mind does incline to zeal, exertion, perseverance, and struggle.

'But whosesoever mind inclineth towards zeal, exertion, perseverance, and struggle, he has become free from this fifth spiritual bondage.

'It is such a one, O Bhikkhus, who has broken through the five kinds of spiritual bondage.

25. 'Whatsoever brother, O Bhikkhus, has become quite free from the five kinds of mental barrenness, has altogether broken through the five kinds of spiritual bondage—that such a one should reach up to the full advantage of, should attain to full growth in, to full breadth in, this doctrine and discipline—that can well be!

---

26. 'He practises the (first) road to saintship[1], which is accompanied by the union of the will to acquire it with earnest contemplation, and with the struggle against sin. He practises the (second) road to saintship, which is accompanied by the union of exertion with earnest contemplation, and with the struggle against sin. He practises the (third) road to saintship, which is accompanied by the union of thought with earnest contemplation, and with the struggle against sin. He practises the (fourth) road to saintship, which is accompanied by the union of investigation with earnest con-

[1] Iddhipâda*m*. Here Iddhi must be (spiritual) welfare.

templation and the struggle against sin[1],—and strong determination too as a fifth.

27. 'The brother, O Bhikkhus, thus endowed with fifteenfold determination[2] becomes destined to come forth into the light, capable of the higher wisdom, sure of attaining to the supreme security[3].

28. 'Just, O Bhikkhus, as when a hen has eight or ten or twelve eggs, and the hen has properly brooded over them, properly sat upon them, properly sat herself round them, however much such a wish may arise on her heart as this, "O would that my little chickens should break open the egg-shell with the points of their claws, or with their beaks, and come forth into the light in safety!" yet all the while those little chickens are sure to break the egg-shell with the points of their claws, or with their beaks, and to come forth into the light in safety.

29. 'Just even so, a brother thus endowed with fifteenfold determination is sure to come forth into the light, sure to reach up to the higher wisdom, sure to attain to the supreme security[4]!'

---

[1] The text of this section, so far, will be found in Childers's dictionary, sub voce Iddhipâdo.

[2] That is, the four Iddhipâdas, and Ussolhi, each multiplied by three.

[3] Anuttarassa Yogakkhemassa; that is, Nirvâna. Compare Dhammapada, ver. 23 and p. 180.

[4] The tertium quid of the parable is the absolute certainty of the event which will follow on the hen having duly and diligently followed the law of her instinct, even though she, meanwhile, in her ignorance, be full of doubt and desire. The certainty of the delivery of a woman with child is not unfrequently used as a symbol of what can be absolutely depended upon. So of 'the word of the glorious Buddhas,' which endureth for ever, in 'Buddhist Birth Stories,' p. 18. I have attempted to imitate the play in the text upon the two words for the 'coming forth into the light,'

30. Thus spake the Blessed One. And those Brethren, delighted in heart, exalted the word of the Blessed One.

End of the Sutta, the sixth, on barrenness and bondage.

---

figuratively and literally, of the disciple and of the little chicken. The first is in Pâli bhabbo abhinibbidâya (from vid), the latter is aho vata . . . sotthinâ abhinibbhi*gg*eyyan (from bhid). On sammâ-paribhavitâni, here applied to the a*nd*âni, see above, Mahâparinibbâna Sutta, Chap. I, § 12, note.

MAHÂ-SUDASSANA-SUTTA.

INTRODUCTION

TO THE

MAHÂ-SUDASSANA SUTTA.

THE following translation is made from a text based on three MSS. from the same sources as those referred to at the commencement of the Tevi*gg*a Sutta, and referred to in my notes by the same letters.

This Sutta follows in the Dîgha Nikâya immediately after the Book of the Great Decease, and is based on the same legend as the Mahâ-Sudassana *G*âtaka, No. 95 in Mr. Fausböll's edition. As the latter differs in several important particulars from our Sutta, it is probably not taken directly from it, but is merely derived from the same source. To facilitate comparison between the two I add here a translation of the *G*âtaka, which has not been reached as yet in my 'Buddhist Birth Stories,' and which is very short.

The part enclosed in brackets [ ] is the comment, which was probably written in Ceylon in the fifth century of our era, and I have included that part of the comment which is explanatory of the words in the verse, as it is of more than usual interest. There is every reason to believe, for the reasons given in the Introduction to the 'Buddhist Birth Stories,' that the stories themselves belong to a very early period in the history of Buddhism; and we may be sure that if this particular story had been abstracted by the author of the commentary from our Sutta, he would not have ventured to introduce such serious changes into what he regarded as sacred writ.

MAHÂ-SUDASSANA *G*ÂTAKA.

THE GREAT KING OF GLORY.

['How transient are all component things.' This the Master told when lying on his death-couch, concerning that word of Ânanda the Thera, when he said, 'Do not, O Blessed One, die in this little town,' and so on.

When the Tathâgata was at the *G*etavana[1] he thought 'the Thera Sâriputta, who was born at Nâlagâma, has died, on the day of the full moon in the month of Kattika, in that very village[2]; and Mahâ Moggallâna in the latter, the dark half of that same month. As my two chief disciples are thus dead, I too will pass away at Kusinârâ.' Thereupon he proceeded straight on to that place, and lay down on the Uttara-sîsaka couch, between the twin Sâla trees, never to rise again.

Then the venerable Ânanda besought him, saying, 'Let

---

[1] It is not easy with our present materials to reconcile the apparently conflicting statements with regard to the Buddha's last journey. According to the Mâlâlankâra-vatthu this refers here to a residence at the *G*etavana, which took place between the end of § 30 in Chap. II, in the Book of the Great Decease, and the beginning of § 31. It will be noticed that § 31 speaks of 'the monastery,' which is apparently an undesigned confirmation of this tradition. (Such undesigned circumstances, however really undesigned, are very far, of course, from proving the actual truth of the tradition. They would only show that it was older than the time when the works in which they occur were put into their present shape.)

Mr. Fausböll, by his punctuation, includes these words in the following thought ascribed to the Blessed One, but I think they only describe the time at which the thought is supposed to have arisen.

[2] Or perhaps 'at Varaka.' I do not understand the word varaka, which has puzzled Mr. Fausböll. The modern name of the village, afterwards the site of the famous Buddhist university of Nâlanda, is Baragaon. The full-moon day in Kattika is the 1st of December. An account of the death of Sâriputta will be found in the Mâlâlankâra-vatthu (Bigandet, 'Legend,' &c., 3rd ed., II, 1–25), and of the murder of Moggallâna by the Niga*nth*as in the Dhammapada commentary (Fausböll, p. 298 seq.), of which Spence Hardy's account ('Manual of Buddhism,' p. 338) is nearly a translation; and Bigandet's account (loc. cit. pp. 25–27) is an abridgment.

not the Blessed One die in this little township[1], in this little town in the jungle, in this branch township. Let the Blessed One die in one of the other great cities, such as Râgagaha, and the rest!'

But the Master answered, 'Say not, Ânanda, that this is a little township, a little town in the jungle, a branch township. I was dwelling formerly in this town at the time when I was Sudassana, the king of kings; and then it was a great city, surrounded by a jewelled rampart, twelve leagues in length!'

And at the request of the Thera, he, telling the tale, uttered the Mahâ-Sudassana Sutta.]

Now on that occasion when Queen Subhaddâ saw Mahâ Sudassana, when he had come down out of the Palace of Righteousness, and was lying down, not far off, on the appropriate couch, spread out in the grove of the seven kinds of gems, and when she said: 'Thine, O king, are these four and eighty thousand cities, of which the chief is the royal city of Kusavâtî. Quicken thy desire after these!'

Then replied Mahâ Sudassana, 'Speak not thus, O queen! but exhort me rather, saying, "Cast away desire for these, long not after them[2]!"'

And when she asked, 'Why so, O king?' 'To-day my time is come, and I shall die!' was his reply[3].

Then the weeping queen, wiping her eyes, brought herself with difficulty and distress to address him accordingly. And having spoken, she wept, and lamented; and the other four and eighty thousand women wept too, and lamented; and of the attendant courtiers not one could restrain himself, but all also wept.

But the Bodisat stopped them all, saying, 'Enough my friends! Be still!' And he exhorted the queen, saying, 'Neither do thou, O queen, weep: neither do thou lament. For even unto a grain of sesamum fruit there is no such

[1] Khuddaka-nagarake. See the note on Mahâparinibbâna Sutta, ver. 60.

[2] Both these speeches are different from those given on the same occasion in the Sutta below.

[3] This question and answer are not in the Sutta.

thing as a compound which is permanent! All are transient, all have the inherent quality of dissolution!'

And when he had so said, he further uttered this stanza:

'How transient are all component things!
Growth is their nature and decay:
They are produced, they are dissolved again:
And then is best,—when they have sunk to rest[1]!'

[In these verses the words 'How transient are all component things!' mean 'Dear lady, Subhaddâ, wheresoever and by whatsoever causes made or come together, compounds[2],—that is, all those things which possess the essential constituents (whether material or mental) of existing things[3],—all these compounds are impermanence itself. For of these form[4] is impermanent, reason[5] is impermanent, the (mental) eye[6] is impermanent, and qualities[7] are impermanent. And whatever treasure there be, whether conscious or unconscious, that is transitory. Understand therefore "How transient are all component things!"

'And why? "Growth is their nature and decay." These, all, have the inherent quality of coming into (individual) existence, and have also the inherent quality of growing old; or (in other words) their very nature is to come into existence and to be broken up. Therefore should it be understood that they are impermanent.

'And since they are impermanent, when "they are produced, they are dissolved again." Having come into existence, having reached a state[8], they are surely dissolved. For all these things come into existence, taking an individual form; and are dissolved, being broken up. To them as soon as there is birth, there is what is called a state; as soon as there is a state, there is what is called

[1] All this is omitted in the Sutta. It is true the verse occurs there, but it is placed in the Sutta in the mouth of the Teacher, after the account of Mahâ Sudassana's death.

The last clause is literally, 'Blessed is their cessation,' where the word for cessation, upasamo, is derived from the word sam, 'to be calm, to be quiet,' and means cessation by sinking into rest. Compare below.

[2] Sankhârâ. [3] Khandâyatanâdayo. [4] Rûpam. [5] Viññânam. [6] *Kakkhum*. [7] Dhammâ. [8] Thiti.

disintegration[1]. For to the unborn there is no such thing as state, and there is no such thing as a state which is without disintegration. Thus are all compounds, having attained to the three characteristic marks (of impermanency, pain, and want of any abiding principle[2]), subject, in this way and in that way, to dissolution. All these component things therefore, without exception, are impermanent, momentary[3], despicable, unstable, disintegrating, trembling, quaking, unlasting, sure to depart[4], only for a time[5], and without substance;—as temporary[5] as a phantom, as the mirage, or as foam!

'How then in these, dear lady Subhaddâ, is there any sign of ease? Understand rather that "then is best, when they have sunk to rest;" but their sinking to rest, their cessation, comes from the cessation of the whole round (of life), and is the same as Nirvâ*n*a. That and this are one[6]. And hence there is no such thing as ease.']

And when Mahâ Sudassana had thus brought his discourse to a point with the ambrosial great Nirvâ*n*a, he made exhortation also to the rest of the great multitude, saying, 'Give gifts! Observe the precepts! Keep the sacred days[7]!' and became an inheritor of the world of the gods.

[When the Master had concluded this lesson in the truth, he summed up the *G*âtaka, saying, 'She who was then Subhaddâ the queen was the mother of Râhula, the great adviser was Râhula, the rest of the retinue the Buddha's retinue, and Mahâ Sudassana I myself.']

---

[1] Bhaṅgo.

[2] Ane*kk*a*m*, dukkha*m*, anatta*m*. See *G*âtaka I, 275; and, on the last, Mahâparinibbâna Sutta I, 10, and Mahâ Vagga I, vi, 38–47.

[3] Kha*n*ikâ. See Oldenberg's note on Dîpava*m*sa I, 53.

[4] Pâyâtâ, literally 'departed.' The forms payâti and payâto, given by Childers, should be corrected into pâyâti and pâyâto. See *G*âtaka I, 146.

[5] Tâvakâlikâ. See *G*âtaka I, 121, where the word is used of a cart let out on hire for a time only.

[6] Tad ev eka*m* eka*m*, which is not altogether without ambiguity.

[7] This paragraph, too, is omitted in the Sutta.

The word translated 'component things' or 'compounds' in this *G*âtaka is sankhârâ, literally confections, from kar, 'to do,' and sam, 'together.' It is a word very frequently used in Buddhist writings, and a word consequently of many different connotations; and there is, of course, no exactly corresponding word in English. 'Production' would often be very nearly correct, although it fails entirely to give the force of the preposition sam; but a greater objection to that word is the fact that it is generally used, not of things that have come into being of themselves, but of things that have been produced by some one else. It suggests, if it does not imply, a producer; which is contrary to the whole spirit of the Buddhist passages in which the word sankhârâ occurs. In this important respect the word 'compound' is a much more accurate translation, though it lays somewhat too much stress on the sam.

The term Confections (to coin a rendering) is sometimes used, as in the first line of these verses (as used in this connection), to denote all things which have been brought together, made up, by pre-existing causes; and in this sense it includes, as the commentator here points out, all those material or mental qualities which unite to form an individual, a separate thing or being, whether conscious or unconscious.

It is more usually used, with special reference to their origin from pre-existing causes, and with allusion to the wider class denoted by the same word, of the mental confections only, of all sentient beings generally, or of man alone. In this sense it forms by itself one of the five classes or aggregates (khandhâ) into which the material and mental qualities of each separate individual are divided in Buddhist writings—the class of dispositions, capabilities, and all that goes together to make what we call character. This class has naturally enough been again divided and subdivided; and a full list of the Confections in this sense, as now acknowledged by orthodox Buddhists, will be found in my manual 'Buddhism.' At the time when the Pâli Pi*t*akas reached their present form, no such elaborate list of Confections in detail seems to have been made; but the general sense of the word was, as is quite clear from the passages in which it occurs, the idea which these details together convey. It is this second and more usual meaning of the term which is more especially emphasised in the concluding verse of the above stanza.

I have ventured to dwell so far on the word Confections, because the commentator here says that the cessation of these Confections is the same thing as Nirvâ*n*a; and the question of Nirvâ*n*a engrosses so large a share of the attention of those who are interested in Buddhism.

Whether it is entitled to do so is open to serious question. The Buddhist salvation was held to consist in a change of heart, a modification of personal character, to be attained to in this world, and forming the subject of Gotama's first discourse, 'The Foundation of the Kingdom of Righteousness[1].' When looked at from different points of view this state of mind was denoted, in the very numerous passages in which it is mentioned or referred to, under a great variety of different names or epithets, suggestive of the different points of view from which it could be regarded. The term Nibbâna, or Nirvâ*n*a, is only one of those epithets; and it is a most significant fact, to which I would invite especial attention, that it is an epithet comparatively very seldom employed in the Pâli Pi*t*akas themselves. It is to the state of mind itself, the salvation which every Arahat has reached while yet alive, in a word, to Arahatship, that importance ought to be attached, rather than to that particular connotation of it suggested by the word Nirvâ*n*a.

One of the many ideas involved in Arahatship was the absolute dissolution of individuality. Gotama, whether rightly or wrongly is here of no importance, held that freedom from pain, absolute ease, happiness, was incompatible with existence as a distinct individual (whether animal, god, or man). The cessation of the Confections, so far from being a thing to be dreaded, was the inevitable result of the emancipation of heart and mind in Arahatship.

---

[1] The Dhamma-*k*akka-ppavattana Sutta, translated below.

But it was not a thing to be desired, and could not, in fact, be brought about apart from all the other things involved in Arahatship. The formation of these Confections ceases in Nirvâ*n*a, and in Nirvâ*n*a alone; and when the poet declares that their cessation is blessed, he is saying the same thing as if he had said 'Nirvâ*n*a is blessed[1].'

Turning now to the Sutta itself, we find that the portion of the legend omitted in the *G*âtaka throws an unexpected light upon the tale; for it commences with a long description of the riches and glory of Mahâ Sudassana, and reveals in its details the instructive fact that the legend is nothing more nor less than a spiritualist's sun-myth.

It cannot be disputed that the sun-myth theory has become greatly discredited, and with reason, by having been used too carelessly and freely as an explanation of religious legends of different times and countries which have really no historical connection with the earlier awe and reverence inspired by the sun. The very mention of the word sun-myth is apt to call forth a smile of incredulity, and the undubitable truth which is the basis of the theory has not sufficed to protect it from the shafts of ridicule. The 'Book of the Great King of Glory' seems to afford a useful example both of the extent to which the theory may be accepted, and of the limitations under which it should always be applied.

It must at once be admitted that whether the whole story is based on a sun-story, or whether certain parts or details of it are derived from things first spoken about the sun, or not, it is still essentially Buddhistic. A large proportion of its contents has nothing at all to do with the worship of the sun; and even that which has, had not, in

[1] In this respect it should be noticed that the very word here used for cessation, upasamo, is used as one among a string of epithets of Arahatship at Dhamma-*k*akka-ppavattana Sutta, § 3, = *G*âtaka I, 97, and again in Dhammapada, verses 368, 381. In this last passage the whole of the phrase in the last verse in our stanza recurs in the accusative case as an equivalent to Arahatship, and the comma inserted by Mr. Fausböll between sa*n*khârûpasama*m* and sukha*m* is, in both verses, unnecessary.

the mind of the author, when the book was put together. Whether indebted to a sun-myth or not, it is therefore perfectly true and valid evidence of the religious belief of the people among whom it was current; and no more shows that the Buddhists were unconscious sun worshippers than the story of Samson, under any theory of its possible origin, would prove the same of the Jews.

What we really have is a kind of wonderful fairy tale, a gorgeous poem, in which an attempt is made to describe in set terms the greatest possible glory and majesty of the greatest possible king, in order to show that all is vanity, save only righteousness—just such a poem as a Jewish prophet might have written of Solomon in all his glory. It would have been most strange, perhaps impossible, for the author to refrain from using the language of the only poets he knew, who had used their boldly figurative language in an attempt to describe the appearance of the sun.

To trace back all the rhetorical phrases of our Sutta to their earliest appearance in the Vedic hymns would be an interesting task of historical philology, though it would throw more light upon Buddhist forms of speech than upon Buddhist forms of belief. In M. Senart's valuable work, 'La Legende du Bouddha,' he has already done this with regard to the seven treasures (mentioned in the early part of the Sutta) on the basis of the corresponding passage in the later Buddhist Sanskrit poem called the Lalita Vistara. The description of the royal city and of its wondrous Palace of Righteousness have been probably originated by the author, though on the same lines; and it reminds one irresistibly, in many of its expressions, of the similar, but simpler and more beautiful poem in which a Jewish author, some three centuries afterwards, described the heavenly Jerusalem.

When the Northern Buddhists, long afterwards, had smothered the simple teaching of the founder of their religion under the subtleties of theological and metaphysical speculation, and had forgotten all about the Noble Path, their goal was no longer a change of heart in the Arahatship to be reached on earth, but a life of happiness, under a change of outward condition, in a heaven of bliss beyond the skies. One of the most popular books among the Buddhists of China and Japan is a description of this heavenly paradise of theirs, called the Sukhâvatî-vyûha, the 'Book of the Happy Country,' the Sanskrit text of which has been just published by Professor Max Müller in the volume of the Journal of the Royal Asiatic Society for the present year. It is instructive to find that several of the expressions used are word for word the same as the corresponding phrases in the 'Book of the Great King of Glory.'

THE GREAT KING OF GLORY[1].

MAHÂ-SUDASSANA-SUTTA.

CHAPTER I.

1. Thus have I heard. The Blessed One was once staying at Kusinârâ in the Upavattana, the Sâla grove of the Mallas, between the twin Sâla trees, at the time of his death.

2. Now the venerable Ânanda went up to the place where the Blessed One was, and bowed down before him, and took his seat respectfully on one side. And when he was so seated, the venerable Ânanda said to thc Blessed One:

[2] 'Let not the Blessed One die in this little wattel and daub town, in this town in the midst of the jungle, in this branch township. For, Lord, there are other great cities, such as *K*ampâ, Râ*g*agaha, Sâvatthi, Sâketa, Kosambi, and Benâres. Let the Blessed One die in one of them. There there are many wealthy nobles and Brâhmans and heads of houses, believers in the Tathâgata, who will pay due honour to the remains of the Tathâgata.'

3. 'Say not so, Ânanda! Say not so, Ânanda,

---

[1] Sudassana means 'beautiful to see, having a glorious appearance,' and is the name of many kings and heroes in Indian legend.

[2] From here down to the end of the next section is found also, nearly word for word, in the Mahâparinibbâna Sutta, above, pp. 99, 100. Compare also Mahâ-Sudassana *G*âtaka, No. 95.

that this is but a small wattel and daub town, a town in the midst of the jungle, a branch township. Long ago, Ânanda, there was a king, by name Mahâ-Sudassana, a king of kings, a righteous man who ruled in righteousness, an anointed Kshatriya[1], Lord of the four quarters of the earth, conqueror, the protector of his people, possessor of the seven royal treasures. This Kusinârâ, Ânanda, was the royal city of king Mahâ-Sudassana, under the name of Kusâvatî[2], and on the east and on the west it was twelve leagues in length, and on the north and on the south it was seven leagues in breadth. That royal city Kusâvatî, Ânanda, was mighty, and prosperous, and full of people, crowded with men, and provided with all things for food. Just, Ânanda, as the royal city of the gods, Â*l*akamandâ by name, is mighty, prosperous, and full of people, crowded with the gods, and provided with all kinds of food, so, Ânanda, was the royal city Kusâvatî mighty and prosperous, full of people, crowded with men, and provided with all kinds of food. Both by day and by night, Ânanda, the royal city Kusâvatî resounded

[1] Khattiyo muddhâvasitto, which does not occur in the Mahâparinibbâna Sutta, the Mahâpadhâna Sutta, the Lakkha*n*a Sutta, and other places where this stock description of a *K*akkavatti is found. It is omitted also in the Lalita Vistara. The Burmese Phayre MS. of the India Office reads here muddâbhisitto, but this is an unnecessary correction. So the name of the Hindu caste mentioned in the Sahyâdri Kha*nd*a of the Skanda Purâ*n*a is spelt both ways. The epithet is probably inserted here from § 12 below.

[2] Ku*s*âvatî was the name of a famous city mentioned as the capital of Southern Kusala in post-Buddhistic Sanskrit plays and epic poems. In the Mahâbhârata it is called Ku*s*avatî. It is said to have been so named after Ku*s*a, son of Râma, by whom it was built; and it is also called Ku*s*asthalî.

with the ten cries; that is to say, the noise of elephants, and the noise of horses, and the noise of chariots; the sounds of the drum, of the tabor, and of the lute; the sound of singing, and the sounds of the cymbal and of the gong; and lastly, with the cry, "Eat, drink, and be merry[1]!"

---

4. 'The royal city Kusâvatî, Ânanda, was surrounded by Seven Ramparts. Of these, one rampart was of gold, and one of silver, and one of beryl, and one of crystal, and one of agate, and one of coral, and one of all kinds of gems[2]!'

---

[1] This enumeration is found also at *G*âtaka, p. 3, only that the chank is added there—wrongly, for that makes the number of cries eleven.

[2] Beryl, agate, and coral are doubtful renderings of Pâli names of precious substances, the exact meaning of which has been discussed on the very slender evidence available (and hence, it seems to me, with very little certain result) by Burnouf in the 'Lotus de la Bonne Loi,' pp. 319–321; and Professor Max Müller has a further note in the Journal of the Royal Asiatic Society, 1880, p. 178. The Pâli words here are in the first column:

1. Sova*nn*amayo,	Suvar*n*asya;
2. Rûpimayo,	Rûpasya;
3. Ve*l*uriyamayo,	Vai*d*ûryasya;
4. Phalikamayo,	Spha*t*ikasya;
5. Lohitaṅkamayo,	Lohitamuktasya;
6. Masâragallamayo,	Asmagarbhasya;
7. Sabbaratanamayo,	Musâragalvasya:

those in the second being taken from the Sukhavatîvyûha in the passage corresponding to § 6 below. It is quite possible that the writers of these passages used the rarer words only as names of precious substances, without attaching any clearly distinct meaning to each (compare Rev. xxi. 19–21). The Pâli author seems to have been hard put to it to find enough names to fill up the sacred number seven; just as in the 'Seven Jewels' of the Dhamma, the sacred number seven is reached by giving to one jewel two distinct names (Pa*ñk*' indriyâni = pa*ñk*a balâni). At *K*ulla Vagga IX, 1, 4 we find the following enumeration of

5. 'To the royal city Kusâvatî, Ânanda, there were Four Gates. One gate was of gold, and one of silver, and one of jade, and one of crystal. At each gate seven pillars were fixed; in height as three times or as four times the height of a man. And one pillar was of gold, and one of silver, and one of beryl, and one of crystal, and one of agate, and one of coral, and one of all kinds of gems.

6. 'The royal city Kusâvatî, Ânanda, was surrounded by Seven Rows of Palm Trees. One row was of palms of gold, and one of silver, and one of beryl, and one of crystal, and one of agate, and one of coral, and one of all kinds of gems.

7. 'And the Golden Palms had trunks of gold, and leaves and fruits of silver. And the Silver Palms had trunks of silver, and leaves and fruits of gold. And the Palms of Beryl had trunks of beryl, and leaves and fruits of crystal. And the Crystal Palms had trunks of crystal, and leaves and fruits of beryl. And the Agate Palms had trunks of agate, and leaves and fruits of coral. And the Coral Palms had trunks of coral, and leaves and fruits of agate. And the Palms of every kind of Gem had trunks and leaves and fruits of every kind of gem.

8. [1]'And when those rows of palm trees, Ânanda,

---

ratanas as found in the ocean, though only Nos. 1, 4, 5, 6 are really produced there:

1. Mutta.
2. Ma*n*i.
3. Ve*l*uriyo.
4. Saṅkho.
5. Silâ.
6. Pavâ*l*a*m*.
7. Ragata*m*.
8. *G*âtarûpa*m*.
9. Lohitaṅko.
10. Masâragalla*m*.

[1] This section and § 9 should be compared with one in the Sukhavatîvyûha, translated by Professor Max Müller as follows (Journal of the Royal Asiatic Society, 1880, p. 170):

'And again, O *S*âriputra, when those rows of palm trees and were shaken by the wind, there arose a sound sweet, and pleasant, and charming, and intoxicating.

'Just, Ânanda, as the seven kind of instruments yield, when well played upon, to the skilful man, a sound sweet, and pleasant, and charming, and intoxicating—just even so, Ânanda, when those rows of palm trees were shaken by the wind, there arose a sound sweet, and pleasant, and charming, and intoxicating.

9. 'And whoever, Ânanda, in the royal city Kusâvatî were at that time gamblers, drunkards, and given to drink, they used to dance round together to the sound of those palms when shaken by the wind.

---

10. 'The Great King of Glory, Ânanda, was the possessor of Seven Precious Things, and was gifted with Four Marvellous Powers.'

'What are those seven?'

11. [1]'In the first place, Ânanda, when the Great King of Glory, on the Sabbath day[2], on the day of

---

strings of bells in that Buddha country are moved by the wind, a sweet and enrapturing sound proceeds from them. Yes, O *S*âriputra, as from a heavenly musical instrument consisting of a hundred thousand ko*t*is of sounds, when played by Âryas, a sweet and enrapturing sound proceeds; a sweet and enrapturing sound proceeds from those rows of palm trees and strings of bells moved by the wind.

'And when the men there hear that sound, reflection on Buddha arises in their body, reflection on the Law, reflection on the Assembly.'

Compare also below, § 81, and *G*âtaka I, 32.

[1] The following enumeration is found word for word in several other Pâli Suttas, and occurs also, in almost identical terms, in the Lalita Vistara (Calcutta edition, pp. 14–19).

[2] Uposatha, a weekly sacred day; being full-moon day, new-moon day, and the two equidistant intermediate days. Comp. § 21.

the full moon, had purified himself, and had gone up into the upper story of his palace to keep the sacred day, there then appeared to him the heavenly Treasure of the Wheel[1], with its nave, its tire, and all its thousand spokes complete.

12. 'When he beheld it the Great King of Glory thought:

'"This saying have I heard, 'When a king of the warrior race, an anointed king, has purified himself on the Sabbath day, on the day of the full moon, and has gone up into the upper story of his palace to keep the sacred day; if there appear to him the heavenly Treasure of the Wheel, with its nave, its tire, and all its thousand spokes complete—that king becomes a king of kings invincible.' May I, then, become a king of kings invincible[2]."

13. 'Then, Ânanda, the Great King of Glory rose from his seat, and reverently uncovering from one shoulder his robe, he held in his left hand a pitcher, and with his right hand he sprinkled water up over the Wheel, as he said:

'"Roll onward, O my Lord, the Wheel! O my Lord, go forth and overcome!"

14. 'Then the wondrous Wheel, Ânanda, rolled onwards towards the region of the East, and after it went the Great King of Glory[3], and with him his

[1] *K*akka-ratana*m*, where the *k*akka is the disk of the sun.

[2] *K*akkavattirâ*g*â.

[3] Atha kho *k*akka-ratana*m* puratthima*m* disa*m* pavatti anvad eva râ*g*â Mahâsudassano, &c. Here anvad must be the Sanskrit anva*ñk*. The Lalita Vistara has anveti in the corresponding passage, and the (Phayre Burmese) MS. here reads anud eva. The verb in the second clause must be supplied, as

army, horses, and chariots, and elephants, and men. And in whatever place, Ânanda, the Wheel stopped, there the Great King of Glory took up his abode, and with him his army, horses, and chariots, and elephants, and men.

15. 'Then, Ânanda, all the rival kings in the region of the East came to the Great King of Glory and said:

'"Come, O mighty king! Welcome, O mighty king! All is thine, O mighty king! Do thou, O mighty king, be a Teacher to us!"

16. 'Thus spake the Great King of Glory:

'"Ye shall slay no living thing.

'"Ye shall not take that which has not been given.

'"Ye shall not act wrongly touching the bodily desires.

'"Ye shall speak no lie.

'"Ye shall drink no maddening drink.

'"Ye shall eat as ye have eaten [1]."

17. 'Then, Ânanda, all the rival kings in the region of the East became subject unto the Great King of Glory.

18. 'But the wondrous Wheel, Ânanda, having plunged down into the great waters in the East, rose up out again, and rolled onward to the region of the South [and there all happened as had hap-

---

is the case in the one or two other passages where I have met with this phrase.

[1] Yathâbhuttam bhuñgatha. Buddhaghosa has no comment on this. I suppose it means, 'Observe the rules current among you regarding clean and unclean meats.' If so, the Great King of Glory disregards the teaching of the Âmagandha Sutta, quoted in 'Buddhism,' p. 131.

pened in the region of the East. And in like manner the wondrous Wheel rolled onward to the extremest boundary of the West and of the North; and there, too, all happened as had happened in the region of the East].

19. 'Now when the wondrous Wheel, Ânanda, had gone forth conquering and to conquer o'er the whole earth to its very ocean boundary, it returned back again to the royal city of Kusâvatî and remained fixed on the open terrace in front of the entrance to the inner apartments of the Great King of Glory, as a glorious adornment to the inner apartments of the Great King of Glory.

20. 'Such, Ânanda, was the wondrous Wheel which appeared to the Great King of Glory.

---

21. 'Now further, Ânanda, there appeared to the Great King of Glory the Elephant Treasure[1], all white, sevenfold firm[2], wonderful in power, flying through the sky—the Elephant-King, whose name was "The Changes of the Moon[3]."

22. 'When he beheld it the Great King of Glory was pleased at heart at the thought:

---

[1] Hatthi-ratana.

[2] Satta-ppatittho, that is, perhaps, in regard to its four legs, two tusks, and trunk. The expression is curious, and Buddhaghosa has no note upon it. It is quite possible that it merely signifies 'exceeding firm,' the number seven being used without any hard and fast interpretation.

[3] Uposatho. In the Lalita Vistara its name is 'Wisdom' (Bodhi). Uposatha is the name for the sacred day of the moon's changes—first, and more especially the full-moon day; next, the new-moon day; and lastly, the days equidistant between these two. It was therefore a weekly sacred day, and, as Childers says, may often be well rendered 'Sabbath.'

'"Auspicious were it to ride upon that Elephant, if only it would submit to be controlled!"

23. 'Then, Ânanda, the wondrous Elephant—like a fine elephant of noble blood long since well trained—submitted to control.

24. 'When as before, Ânanda, the Great King of Glory, to test that wondrous Elephant, mounted on to it early in the morning, it passed over along the broad earth to its very ocean boundary, and then returned again, in time for the morning meal, to the royal city of Kusâvatî[1].

25. 'Such, Ânanda, was the wondrous Elephant that appeared to the Great King of Glory.

---

26. 'Now further, Ânanda, there appeared to the Great King of Glory the Horse Treasure[2], all white with a black head, and a dark mane, wonderful in power, flying through the sky—the Charger-King, whose name was "Thunder-cloud[3]."

27. 'When he beheld it, the Great King of Glory was pleased at heart at the thought:

'"Auspicious were it to ride upon that Horse if only it would submit to be controlled!"

28. 'Then, Ânanda, the wondrous Horse—like

[1] Compare on this and § 29 my 'Buddhist Birth Stories,' p. 85, where a similar phrase is used of Kanthaka.

[2] Assa-ratana*m*.

[3] Valâhako. Compare the Valâhassa *G*âtaka (Fausböll, No. 196, called in the Burmese MS. Valâhakassa *G*âtaka), of which the Chinese story translated by Mr. Beal at pp. 332–340 of his 'Romantic History,' &c., is an expanded and altered version. In the Valâhaka Sa*m*yutta of the Sa*m*yutta Nikâya the spirits of the skies are divided into U*n*ha-valâhakâ Devâ, Sîta-valâhakâ Devâ, Abbha-valâhakâ Devâ, Vâta-valâhakâ Devâ, and Vassa-valâhakâ Devâ, that is, the cloud-spirits of cold, heat, air, wind, and rain respectively.

a fine horse of the best blood long since well trained—submitted to control.

29. 'When as before, Ânanda, the Great King of Glory, to test that wondrous Horse, mounted on to it early in the morning, it passed over along the broad earth to its very ocean boundary, and then returned again, in time for the morning meal, to the royal city of Kusâvatî.

30. 'Such, Ânanda, was the wondrous Horse that appeared to the Great King of Glory.

---

31. 'Now further, Ânanda, there appeared to the Great King of Glory the Gem-Treasure[1]. That Gem was the Ve*l*uriya, bright, of the finest species, with eight facets, excellently wrought, clear, transparent, perfect in every way.

32. 'The splendour, Ânanda, of that wondrous Gem spread round about a league on every side.

33. 'When as before, Ânanda, the Great King of Glory, to test that wondrous Gem, set all his fourfold army in array and raised aloft the Gem upon his standard top, he was able to march out in the gloom and darkness of the night.

34. 'And then too, Ânanda, all the dwellers in the villages, round about, set about their daily work, thinking, "The daylight hath appeared."

35. 'Such, Ânanda, was the wondrous Gem that appeared to the Great King of Glory.

---

36. 'Now further, Ânanda, there appeared to the Great King of Glory the Woman-Treasure[2], graceful in figure, beautiful in appearance, charming in manner, and of the most fine complexion; neither

---

[1] Ma*n*i-ratana*m*.

[2] Itthi-ratana*m*.

very tall, nor very short; neither very stout, nor very slim; neither very dark, nor very fair; surpassing human beauty, she had attained unto the beauty of the gods[1].

37. 'The touch too, Ânanda, of the skin of that wondrous Woman was as the touch of cotton or of cotton wool: in the cold her limbs were warm, in the heat her limbs were cool; while from her body was wafted the perfume of sandal wood and from her mouth the perfume of the lotus.

38. 'That Pearl among Women too, Ânanda, used to rise up before the Great King of Glory, and after him retire to rest; pleasant was she in speech, and ever on the watch to hear what she might do in order so to act as to give him pleasure.

39. 'That Pearl among Women too, Ânanda, was never, even in thought, unfaithful to the Great King of Glory—how much less then could she be so with the body!

40. 'Such, Ânanda, was the Pearl among Women who appeared to the Great King of Glory.

---

41. 'Now further, Ânanda, there appeared unto the Great King of Glory a Wonderful Treasurer[2], possessed, through good deeds done in a

[1] The above description of an ideally beautiful woman is of frequent occurrence.

[2] Gahapati-ratanam. The word gahapati has been hitherto usually rendered 'householder,' but this may often, and would certainly here, convey a wrong impression. There is no single word in English which is an adequate rendering of the term, for it connotes a social condition now no longer known among us. The gahapati was the head of a family, the representative in a village community of a family, the pater familias. So the god of fire, with allusion to the sacred fire maintained in each household, is called in the Rig-veda the *gri*hapati, the pater familias,

former birth, of a marvellous power of vision by which he could discover treasure, whether it had an owner or whether it had not.

42. 'He went up to the Great King of Glory, and said:

'"Do thou, O King, take thine ease! I will deal with thy wealth even as wealth should be dealt with."

43. 'Then, as before, Ânanda, the Great King of Glory, to test that wonderful Treasurer, went on board a boat, and had it pushed out into the current in the midst of the river Ganges. Then he said to the wonderful steward:

'"I have need, O Treasurer, of yellow gold!"

'"Let the ship then, O Great King, go alongside either of the banks."

'"It is here, O Treasurer, that I have need of yellow gold."

44. 'Then the wonderful Treasurer reached down to the water with both his hands, and drew up a jar

---

of the human race. Thence it is often used in opposition to brâhmana very much as we might use 'yeoman' in opposition to 'clerk' (*G*âtaka I, 83, and below, § 53); and the two combined are used in opposition to people of other ranks and callings held to be less honourable than that of clerk or yeoman (*G*âtaka I, 218). In this respect the term gahapati is nearly equivalent, though from a different point of view, to the Kshatriyas and Vaisyas of the Hindu caste division; but the compound brâhmana-gahapatikâ as a collective term comes to be about equivalent to 'priests and laymen' (see, for instance, below, § 53, and Mahâ Vagga I, 22; 3, 4, &c.) Then again the gahapati is distinct from the subordinate members of the family, who had not the control and management of the common property (Sâmañña Phala Sutta, 133, = Tevi*gg*a Sutta I, 47); and it is this implication of the term that is emphasised in the text. Buddhaghosa uses, as an explanatory phrase, the words se*tth*i-gahapati. See further the passages quoted in the index to the *K*ulla Vagga (p. 354).

full of yellow gold, and said to the Great King of Glory:

'"Is that enough, O Great King? Have I done enough, O Great King?"

'And the Great King of Glory replied:

'"It is enough, O Treasurer. You have done enough, O Treasurer. You have offered me enough, O Treasurer!"

45. 'Such was the wonderful Treasurer, Ânanda, who appeared to the Great King of Glory.

---

46. 'Now further, Ânanda, there appeared to the Great King of Glory a Wonderful Adviser[1], learned, clever, and wise; and qualified to lead the Great King of Glory to undertake what he ought to undertake, and to leave undone what he ought to leave undone.

47. 'He went up to the Great King of Glory, and said:

'"Do thou, O King, take thine ease! I will be thy guide."

48. 'Such, Ânanda, was the wonderful Adviser who appeared to the Great King of Glory.

'The Great King of Glory was possessed of these Seven Precious Things.

---

49. 'Now further, Ânanda, the Great King of Glory was gifted with Four Marvellous Gifts[2].'

'What are the Four Marvellous Gifts?'

---

[1] Pari*n*âyaka-ratana*m*. Buddhaghosa says that he was the eldest son of the king; but this is probably a mere putting back into the Sutta of a later idea derived from the summary in the *G*âtaka. The Lalita Vistara makes him a general.

[2] *K*atûhi iddhîhi. Here again, as elsewhere, it will be noticed that there is nothing supernatural about these four Iddhis. See

50. 'In the first place, Ânanda, the Great King of Glory was graceful in figure, handsome in appearance, pleasing in manner, and of most beautiful complexion, beyond what other men are.

'The Great King of Glory, Ânanda, was endowed with this First Marvellous Gift.

51. 'And besides that, Ânanda, the Great King of Glory was of long life, and of many years, beyond those of other men.

'The Great King of Glory, Ânanda, was endowed with this Second Marvellous Gift.

52. 'And besides that, Ânanda, the Great King of Glory was free from disease, and free from bodily suffering; and his internal fire was neither too hot nor too cold, but such as to promote good digestion, beyond that of other men [1].

---

the notes above on the 'Book of the Great Decease,' I, 1; III, 2. They are merely attributes accompanying or forming part of the majesty (iddhi) of the *K*akkavatti.

[1] Samavepâkiniyâ gaha*n*iyâ samannâgato nâtisîtâya nâ*kk*u*n*hâya. The same thing is said of Ra*tth*apâla in the Ra*tth*apâla Sutta, where Gogerly renders the whole passage, 'Ra*tth*apâla is healthy, free from pain, having a good digestion and appetite, being troubled with no excess of either heat or cold' (Journal of the Ceylon Asiatic Society, 1847–1848, p. 98). The gaha*n*i is a supposed particular organ or function situate at the junction of the stomach and intestines. Moggallâna explains it, udare tu tathâ pâ*k*analasmi*m* gaha*n*i (Abhidhâna-ppadîpikâ, 972), where Subhûti's Sinhalese version is 'kukshi, pâkâgni,' and his English version, 'the belly, the internal fire which promotes digestion.' Buddhaghosa explains samavipâkiyâ kamma*g*â-te*g*o-dhâtuyâ, and adds, 'If a man's food is dissolved the moment he has eaten it, or if it remains like a lump, he has not the samavepâkini gaha*n*i, but he who has appetite (bhatta*k*-*kh*ando) when the time for food comes round again, he has the samavepâkini gaha*n*i,'—which is delightfully naïve.

'The Great King of Glory, Ânanda, was endowed with this Third Marvellous Gift.

53. 'And besides that, Ânanda, the Great King of Glory was beloved and popular with Brâhmans and with laymen alike[1]. Just, Ânanda, as a father is near and dear to his own sons, just so, Ânanda, was the Great King of Glory beloved and popular with Brâhmans and with laymen alike. And just, Ânanda, as his sons are near and dear to a father, just so, Ânanda, were Brâhmans and laymen alike near and dear to the Great King of Glory.

54. 'Once, Ânanda, the Great King of Glory marched out with all his fourfold army to the pleasure ground. There, Ânanda, the Brâhmans and laymen went up to the Great King of Glory, and said:

'"O King, pass slowly by, that we may look upon thee for a longer time!"

'But the Great King of Glory, Ânanda, addressed his charioteer, and said:

'"Drive on the chariot slowly, charioteer, that I may look upon my people (Brâhmans and laymen) for a longer time!"

55. 'This was the Fourth Marvellous Gift, Ânanda, with which the Great King of Glory was endowed.

56. 'These are the Four Marvellous Gifts, Ânanda, with which the Great King of Glory was endowed.

---

57. 'Now to the Great King of Glory, Ânanda, there occurred the thought:

'"Suppose, now, I were to make Lotus-ponds

---

[1] Brâhma*n*a-gahapatikâna*m*. See the note on § 41.

in the spaces between these palms, at every hundred bow lengths."

'Then, Ânanda, the Great King of Glory, in the spaces between those palms, at distances of a hundred bow lengths, made Lotus-ponds.

58. 'And those Lotus-ponds, Ânanda, were faced with tiles of four kinds. One kind of tile was of gold, and one of silver, and one of beryl, and one of crystal.

59. 'And to each of those Lotus-ponds, Ânanda, there were four flights of steps, of four different kinds. One flight of steps was of gold, and one of silver, and one of beryl, and one of crystal. The flight of golden steps had balustrades of gold, with the cross bars and the figure head of silver. The flight of silver steps had balustrades of silver, with the cross bars and the figure head of gold. The flight of beryl steps had balustrades of beryl, with the cross bars and the figure head of crystal. The flight of crystal steps had balustrades of crystal, with cross bars and figure head of beryl.

60. 'And round those Lotus-ponds there ran, Ânanda, a double railing. One railing was of gold, and one was of silver. The golden railing had its posts of gold, and its cross bars and its capitals of silver. The silver railing had its posts of silver, and its cross bars and its capitals of gold[1].

---

[1] Pokkhara*n*i, the word translated Lotus-pond, is an artificial pool or small lake for water plants. There are some which are probably nearly as old as this passage still in good preservation in Anurâdhapuru in Ceylon. Each is oblong, and has its tiles and its four flights of steps, and some had railings. The balustrades, cross bars, figure head, and railing are in Pâli thambhâ, sû*k*iyo, unhîsa*m*, and vedikâ, of the exact meaning of which I am not quite confident. They do not occur in the description

61. 'Now, to the Great King of Glory, Ânanda, there occurred the thought:

'"Suppose, now, I were to have flowers of every season planted in those Lotus-ponds for the use of all the people—to wit, blue water lilies and blue lotuses, white lotuses and white water lilies."

'Then, Ânanda, the Great King of Glory had flowers of every season planted in those Lotus-ponds for the use of all the people—to wit, blue water lilies and blue lotuses, white lotuses and white water lilies.

62. 'Now, to the Great King of Glory, Ânanda, occurred the thought:

'"Suppose, now, I were to place bathing-men on the banks of those Lotus-ponds, to bathe such of the people as come there from time to time."

'Then, Ânanda, the Great King of Glory placed bathing-men on the banks of those Lotus-ponds, to bathe such of the people as come there from time to time.

63. 'Now, to the Great King of Glory, Ânanda, occurred the thought:

'"Suppose, now, I were to establish a perpetual grant by the banks of those Lotus-ponds—to wit, food for the hungry, drink for the thirsty, raiment for the naked, means of conveyance for those who have need of it, couches for the tired, wives for

---

of the Lotus-lakes in Sukhavatî. General Cunningham says that the cross bars of the Buddhist railings are called **sûkiyo** in the inscriptions at Bharhut (The Stupa of Bharhut, p. 127). Buddhaghosa, who is good enough to tell us the exact number of the ponds—to wit, 84,000, has no explanation of these words, merely saying that of the two **vedikâs** one was at the limit of the tiles and one at the limit of the **parive*n*a**. The phrases in the text are repeated below, §§ 73–87, of the Palace of Righteousness.

those who want wives, gold for the poor, and money for those who are in want."

'Then, Ânanda, the Great King of Glory established a perpetual grant by the banks of those Lotus-ponds—to wit, food for the hungry, drink for the thirsty, raiment for the naked, means of conveyance for those who needed it, couches for the tired, wives for those who wanted wives, gold for the poor, and money for those who were in want.

---

64. 'Now, Ânanda, the people (Brâhmans and laymen) went to the Great King of Glory, taking with them much wealth. And they said:

'"This abundant wealth, O King, have we brought here for the use of the King of Kings. Let the King accept it of us!"

'"I have enough wealth, my friends, laid up for myself, the produce of righteous taxation. Do you keep this, and take away more with you!"

65. 'When those men were thus refused by the King they went aside and considered together, saying:

'"It would not beseem us now, were we to take back this wealth to our own houses. Suppose, now, we were to build a mansion for the Great King of Glory."

66. 'Then they went to the Great King of Glory, and said:

'"A mansion would we build for thee, O King!"'

'"Then, Ânanda, the Great King of Glory signified, by silence, his consent.

---

67. 'Now, Ânanda, when Sakka, the king of the gods, became aware in his mind of the thoughts that

were in the heart of the Great King of Glory, he addressed Vissakamma the god[1], and said:

'"Come now, Vissakamma, create me a mansion for the Great King of Glory—a palace which shall be called 'Righteousness[2].'"

68. '"Even so, Lord!" said Vissakamma, in assent, Ânanda, to Sakka, the king of the gods. And as instantaneously as a strong man might stretch forth his folded arm, or draw in his arm again when it was stretched forth, so quickly did he vanish from the heaven of the Great Thirty-Three, and appeared before the Great King of Glory.

69. 'Then, Ânanda, Vissakamma the god said to the Great King of Glory:

'"I would create for thee, O King, a mansion—a palace which shall be called 'Righteousness!'"

'Then, Ânanda, the Great King of Glory signified, by silence, his consent.

---

70. 'So Vissakamma the god, Ânanda, created for the Great King of Glory a mansion—a palace to be called "Righteousness."

71. 'The Palace of Righteousness, Ânanda, was on the east and on the west a league in length, and on the north and on the south half a league in breadth.

72. 'The ground-floor, Ânanda, of the Palace of Righteousness[3], in height as three times the height to which a man can reach, was built of bricks, of four kinds. One kind of brick was of gold, and one of silver, and one of beryl, and one of crystal.

---

[1] Vissakammam devaputtam, where devaputtam means not 'son of a god,' but 'belonging to, born into the class of, the gods.'

[2] Dhammam nâma Pâsâdam.

[3] Dhammassa pâsâdassa vatthum.

73. 'To the Palace of Righteousness, Ânanda, there were eighty-four thousand pillars of four kinds. One kind of pillar was of gold, and one of silver, and one of beryl, and one of crystal.

74. 'The Palace of Righteousness, Ânanda, was fitted up with seats of four kinds. One kind of seat was of gold, and one of silver, and one of beryl, and one of crystal.

75. 'In the Palace of Righteousness, Ânanda, there were twenty-four staircases of four kinds. One staircase was of gold, and one of silver, and one of beryl, and one of crystal. The staircase of gold had balustrades of gold, with the cross bars and the figure head of silver. The staircase of silver had balustrades of silver, with the cross bars and the figure head of gold. The staircase of beryl had balustrades of beryl, with the cross bars and the figure head of crystal. The staircase of crystal had balustrades of crystal, with cross bars and figure head of beryl.

76. 'In the Palace of Righteousness, Ânanda, there were eighty-four thousand chambers of four kinds. One kind of chamber was of gold, and one of silver, and one of beryl, and one of crystal.

'In the golden chamber a silver couch was spread; in the silver chamber a golden couch; in the beryl chamber a couch of ivory; and in the crystal chamber a couch of coral.

'At the door of the golden chamber there stood a palm tree of silver; and its trunk was of silver, and its leaves and fruits of gold.

'At the door of the silver chamber there stood a palm tree of gold; and its trunk was of gold, and its leaves and fruits of silver.

'At the door of the beryl chamber there stood a palm tree of crystal; and its trunk was of crystal, and its leaves and fruits of beryl.

'At the door of the crystal chamber there stood a palm tree of beryl; and its trunk was of beryl, and its leaves and fruits of crystal.

---

77. 'Now there occurred, Ânanda, to the Great King of Glory this thought:

'"Suppose, now, I were to make a grove of palm trees, all of gold, at the entrance to the chamber of the Great Complex[1], under the shade of which I may pass the heat of the day."

'Then, Ânanda, the Great King of Glory made a grove of palm trees, all of gold, at the entrance to the chamber of the Great Complex, under the shade of which he might pass the heat of the day.

78. 'The Palace of Righteousness, Ânanda, was surrounded by a double railing. One railing was of gold, and one was of silver. The golden railing had its posts of gold, and its cross bars and its figure head of silver. The silver railing had its posts of silver, and its cross bars and its figure head of gold[2].

79. 'The Palace of Righteousness, Ânanda, was hung round with two networks of bells. One network of bells was of gold, and one was of silver.

---

[1] Mahâvyûhassa ku*t*âgârassa dvâre. The 'Great Complex' contains a double allusion, in the same spirit in which the whole legend has been worked out: 1. To the Great Complex as a name of the Sun-God regarded as a unity of the four mythological deities, Vasudeva, Sankarsha*n*a, Pragumna, and Aniruddha; and 2. To the Great Complex as a name of a particular kind of deep religious meditation or speculation.

[2] See above, § 60, and the note on § 54.

The golden network had bells of silver, and the silver network had bells of gold.

80. 'And when those networks of bells, Ânanda, were shaken by the wind there arose a sound sweet, and pleasant, and charming, and intoxicating.

'Just, Ânanda, as the seven kind of instruments yield, when well played upon, to the skilful man, a sound sweet, and pleasant, and charming, and intoxicating—just even so, Ânanda, when those networks of bells were shaken by the wind, there arose a sound sweet, and pleasant, and charming, and intoxicating.

81. 'And whoever, Ânanda, in the royal city Kusâvatî were at that time gamblers, drunkards, and given to drink, they used to dance round together to the sound of those networks of bells when shaken by the wind.

---

82. 'When the Palace of Righteousness, Ânanda, was finished it was hard to look at, destructive to the eyes. Just, Ânanda, as in the last month of the rains in the autumn time, when the sky has become clear and the clouds have vanished away, the sun, springing up along the heavens, is hard to look at, and destructive to the eyes,—just so, Ânanda, when the Palace of Righteousness was finished was it hard to look at, and destructive to the eyes.

---

83. 'Now there occurred, Ânanda, to the Great King of Glory this thought:

'"Suppose, now, in front of the Palace of Righteousness, I were to make a Lotus-lake to bear the name of 'Righteousness.'"

'Then, Ânanda, the Great King of Glory made a Lotus-lake to bear the name of "Righteousness."

84. 'The Lake of Righteousness, Ânanda, was on the east and on the west a league in length, and on the north and on the south half a league in breadth.

85. 'The Lake of Righteousness, Ânanda, was faced with tiles of four kinds. One kind of tile was of gold, and one of silver, and one of beryl, and one of crystal.

86. 'The Lake of Righteousness, Ânanda, had four and twenty flights of steps, of four different kinds. One flight of steps was of gold, and one of silver, and one of beryl, and one of crystal. The flight of golden steps had balustrades of gold, with the cross bars and the figure head of silver. The flight of silver steps had balustrades of silver, with the cross bars and the figure head of gold. The flight of beryl steps had balustrades of beryl, with the cross bars and the figure head of crystal. The flight of crystal steps had balustrades of crystal, with cross bars and figure head of beryl.

87. 'Round the Lake of Righteousness, Ânanda, there ran a double railing. One railing was of gold, and one was of silver. The golden railing had its posts of gold, and its cross bars and its capitals of silver. The silver railing had its posts of silver, and its cross bars and its capitals of gold.

88. 'The Lake of Righteousness, Ânanda, was surrounded by seven rows of palm trees. One row was of palms of gold, and one of silver, and one of beryl, and one of crystal, and one of agate, and one of coral, and one of all kinds of gems.

89. 'And the golden palms had trunks of gold, and leaves and fruits of silver. And the silver palms had trunks of silver, and leaves and fruits of gold. And the palms of beryl had trunks of beryl,

and leaves and fruits of crystal. And the crystal palms had trunks of crystal, and leaves and fruits of beryl. And the agate palms had trunks of agate, and leaves and fruits of coral. And the coral palms had trunks of coral, and leaves and fruits of agate. And the palms of every kind of gem had trunks and leaves and fruits of every kind of gem.

90. 'And when those rows of palm trees, Ânanda, were shaken by the wind, there arose a sound sweet, and pleasant, and charming, and intoxicating.

'Just, Ânanda, as the seven kind of instruments yield, when well played upon, to the skilful man, a sound sweet, and pleasant, and charming, and intoxicating,—just even so, Ânanda, when those rows of palm trees were shaken by the wind, there arose a sound sweet, and pleasant, and charming, and intoxicating.

91. 'And whoever, Ânanda[1], in the royal city Kusâvatî were at that time gamblers, drunkards, and given to drink, they used to dance round together to the sound of those palms when shaken by the wind.

---

92. 'When the Palace of Righteousness, Ânanda, was finished, and the Lotus-lake of Righteousness was finished, the Great King of Glory entertained with all good things those of the Sama*n*as who, at that time, were held in high esteem, and those of the Brâhmans who, at that time, were held in high esteem. Then he ascended up into the Palace of Righteousness.'

End of the First Portion for Recitation.

---

[1] This paragraph is perhaps repeated by mistake; but it is scarcely less in harmony with its context at § 8 than it is here. It is more probable that § 92 followed, originally, immediately after § 82, with the Lotus-lake clause omitted.

Chapter II.

1. 'Now there occurred, Ânanda, this thought to the Great King of Glory:

'"Of what previous character, now, may this be the fruit, of what previous character the result, that I am now so mighty and so great?"

2. 'And then occurred, Ânanda, to the Great King of Glory this thought:

'"Of three qualities is this the fruit, of three qualities the result, that I am now so mighty and so great,—that is to say, of giving, of self-conquest, and of self-control[1]."

---

3. 'Now the Great King of Glory, Ânanda, ascended up into the chamber of the Great Complex; and when he had come there he stood at the door, and there he broke out into a cry of intense emotion:

'"Stay here, O thoughts of lust!

'"Stay here, O thoughts of ill-will!

'"Stay here, O thoughts of hatred!

'"Thus far only, O thoughts of lust!

'"Thus far only, O thoughts of ill-will!

'"Thus far only, O thoughts of hatred!"

4. 'And when, Ânanda, the Great King of Glory had entered the chamber of the Great Complex,

---

[1] I have here translated kamma by 'previous character' and by 'quality.' The easiest plan would, no doubt, have been, to preserve in the translation the technical term karma, which is explained at some length in 'Buddhism,' pp. 99–106.

and had seated himself upon the couch of gold, having put away all passion and all unrighteousness, he entered into, and remained in, the First *Gh*âna, —a state of joy and ease, born of seclusion, full of reflection, full of investigation.

5. 'By suppressing reflection and investigation, he entered into, and remained in, the Second *Gh*âna, —a state of joy and ease, born of serenity, without reflection, without investigation, a state of elevation of mind, of internal calm.

6. 'By absence of the longing after joy, he remained indifferent, conscious, self-possessed, experiencing in his body that ease which the noble ones announce, saying, "The man indifferent and self-possessed is well at ease," and thus he entered into, and remained in, the Third *Gh*âna.

7. 'By putting away ease, by putting away pain, by the previous dying away both of gladness and of sorrow, he entered into, and remained in, the Fourth *Gh*âna,—a state of purified self-possession and equanimity, without ease, and without pain [1].

---

8. 'Then, Ânanda, the Great King of Glory went out from the chamber of the Great Complex, and entered the golden chamber and sat himself down on the silver couch. And he let his mind pervade

[1] The above paragraphs are an endeavour to express the inmost feelings when they are first strung to the uttermost by the intense effects of deep religious emotion, and then feel the effects of what may be called, for want of a better word, the reaction. Most deeply religious natures have passed through such a crisis; and though the feelings are perhaps really indescribable, this passage is dealing, not with a vain mockery, but with a very real event in spiritual experience.

one quarter of the world with thoughts of Love; and so the second quarter, and so the third, and so the fourth. And thus the whole wide world, above, below, around, and everywhere, did he continue to pervade with heart of Love, far-reaching, grown great, and beyond measure, free from the least trace of anger or ill-will.

9. 'And he let his mind pervade one quarter of the world with thoughts of Pity; and so the second quarter, and so the third, and so the fourth. And thus the whole wide world, above, below, around, and everywhere, did he continue to pervade with heart of Pity, far-reaching, grown great, and beyond measure, free from the least trace of anger or ill-will.

10. 'And he let his mind pervade one quarter of the world with thoughts of Sympathy; and so the second quarter, and so the third, and so the fourth. And thus the whole wide world, above, below, around, and everywhere, did he continue to pervade with heart of Sympathy, far-reaching, grown great, and beyond measure, free from the least trace of anger or ill-will.

11. 'And he let his mind pervade one quarter of the world with thoughts of Equanimity[1]; and so the second quarter, and so the third, and so the fourth. And thus the whole wide world, above, below, around, and everywhere, did he continue to pervade with heart of Equanimity, far-reaching, grown great, and beyond measure, free from the least trace of anger or ill-will.

---

[1] These are the four Appama*ññ*âs or infinite feelings, also called (e.g. below, § II, 36) the four Brahma-vihâras. They are here very appropriately represented to follow immediately after

12. 'The Great King of Glory, Ânanda, had four and eighty thousand cities, the chief of which was the royal city of Kusâvatî:

'Four and eighty thousand palaces, the chief of which was the Palace of Righteousness:

'Four and eighty thousand chambers, the chief of which was the chamber of the Great Complex:

'Four and eighty thousand divans, of gold, and silver, and ivory, and sandal wood, spread with long-haired rugs, and cloths embroidered with flowers, and magnificent antelope skins; covered with lofty canopies; and provided at both ends with purple cushions:

'Four and eighty thousand state elephants, with trappings of gold, and gilded flags, and golden coverings of network,—of which the king of elephants, called "the Changes of the Moon," was chief:

'Four and eighty thousand state horses, with trappings of gold, and gilded flags, and golden coverings of network,—of which "Thunder-cloud," the king of horses, was the chief:

'Four and eighty thousand chariots, with coverings of the skins of lions, and of tigers, and of panthers,—of which the chariot called "the Flag of Victory" was the chief:

'Four and eighty thousand gems, of which the Wondrous Gem was the chief:

'Four and eighty thousand wives, of whom the Queen of Glory was the chief:

---

the state of feeling described in the *G*h*â*nas; but they ought to be the constant companions of a good Buddhist (see Khaggavisâna Sutta 8; and compare also Tevi*gg*a Sutta III, 7; *G*âtaka, vol. i. p. 246; and the Araka *G*âtaka, No. 169).

'Four and eighty thousand yeomen, of whom the Wonderful Steward was the chief:

'Four and eighty thousand nobles, of whom the Wonderful Adviser was the chief:

'Four and eighty thousand cows, with jute trappings, and horns tipped with bronze:

'Four and eighty thousand myriads of garments, of delicate textures, of flax, and cotton, and silk, and wool:

'Four and eighty thousand dishes, in which, in the evening and in the morning, rice was served[1].

---

13. 'Now at that time, Ânanda, the four and eighty thousand state elephants used to come every evening and every morning to be of service to the Great King of Glory.

14. 'And this thought occurred to the Great King of Glory:

'"These eighty thousand elephants come every evening and every morning to be of service to me. Suppose, now, I were to let the elephants come in alternate forty thousands, once each, every alternate hundred years!"

15. 'Then, Ânanda, the Great King of Glory said to the Great Adviser:

'"O, my friend, the Great Adviser! these eighty thousand elephants come every evening and every morning to be of service to me. Now, let the elephants come, O my friend, the Great Adviser, in

---

[1] Most of the trappings and cloths here mentioned are the same as those referred to in the Ma*ggh*ima Sîla, §§ 5, 6, 7 recurring in the Tevi*gg*a Sutta, and in the Brahma*g*âla Sutta. The whole paragraph is four times repeated below, §§ 29, 31, 33, 37.

alternate forty thousands, once each, every alternate hundred years!"

'"Even so, Lord!" said the Wonderful Adviser, in assent, to the Great King of Glory.

16. 'From that time forth, Ânanda, the elephants came in alternate forty thousands, once each, every alternate hundred years.

---

17. 'Now, Ânanda, after the lapse of many years, of many hundred years, of many thousand years, there occurred to the Queen of Glory[1] this thought:

'"'Tis long since I have beheld the Great King of Glory. Suppose, now, I were to go and visit the Great King of Glory."

18. 'Then, Ânanda, the Queen of Glory said to the women of the harem:

'"Arise now, dress your hair, and clad yourselves in fresh raiment. 'Tis long since we have beheld the Great King of Glory. Let us go and visit the Great King of Glory!"

19. '"Even so, Lady!" said the women of the harem, Ânanda, in assent, to the Queen of Glory. And they dressed their hair, and clad themselves in fresh raiment, and came near to the Queen of Glory.

20. 'Then, Ânanda, the Queen of Glory said to the Great Adviser:

'"Arrange, O Great Adviser, the fourfold army in array. 'Tis long since I have beheld the Great King of Glory. I am about to go to visit the Great King of Glory."

---

[1] Subhaddâ Devî. Subhadda, 'glorious, magnificent,' is a not uncommon name both for men and women in Buddhist and post-Buddhistic Hindu literature.

21. '"Even so, O Queen!" said the Great Adviser, Ânanda, in assent, to the Queen of Glory. And he set the fourfold army in array, and had the fact announced to the Queen of Glory in the words:

'"The fourfold army, O Queen, is set for thee in array. Do now whatever seemeth to thee fit."

22. 'Then, Ânanda, the Queen of Glory, with the fourfold army, repaired, with the women of the harem, to the Palace of Righteousness. And when she had arrived there she mounted up into the Palace of Righteousness, and went on to the chamber of the Great Complex. And when she had reached it, she stopped and lent against the side of the door.

23. 'When, Ânanda, the Great King of Glory heard the noise he thought:

'"What, now, may this noise, as of a great multitude of people, mean?"

24. 'And going out from the chamber of the Great Complex, he beheld the Queen of Glory standing leaning up against the side of the door. And when he beheld her, he said to the Queen of Glory:

'"Stop there, O Queen! Enter not!"

---

25. 'Then the Great King of Glory, Ânanda, said to one of his attendants:

'"Arise, good man! take the golden couch out of the chamber of the Great Complex, and make it ready under that grove of palm trees which is all of gold."

26. '"Even so, Lord!" said the man, in assent, to the Great King of Glory. And he took the golden couch out of the chamber of the Great Complex, and made it ready under that grove of palm trees which was all of gold.

27. 'Then, Ânanda, the Great King of Glory laid himself down in the dignified way a lion does; and lay with one leg resting on the other, calm and self-possessed.

---

28. 'Then, Ânanda, there occurred to the Queen of Glory this thought:

'"How calm are all the limbs of the Great King of Glory! How clear and bright is his appearance! O may it not be that the Great King of Glory is dead[1]!"

29. 'And she said to the Great King of Glory:

'"Thine, O King, are those four and eighty thousand cities, the chief of which is the royal city of Kusâvatî. Arise, O King, re-awaken thy desire for these! quicken thy longing after life!

'"Thine, O King, are those four and eighty thousand palaces, the chief of which is the Palace of Righteousness. Arise, O King, re-awaken thy desire for these! quicken thy longing after life!

'"Thine, O King, are those four and eighty thousand chambers, the chief of which is the chamber of the Great Complex. Arise, O King, re-awaken thy desire for these! quicken thy longing after life!

'"Thine, O King, are those four and eighty thousand divans, of gold, and silver, and ivory, and sandal wood, spread with long-haired rugs, and cloths embroidered with flowers, and magnificent antelope skins; covered with lofty canopies; and provided at both ends with purple cushions. Arise,

---

[1] The rather curious connexion between these clauses is worthy of notice in comparison with the legend of the 'Transfiguration' just before the Buddha's death (above, pp. 80–82).

O King, re-awaken thy desire for these! quicken thy longing after life!

'"Thine, O King, are those four and eighty thousand state elephants, with trappings of gold, and gilded flags, and golden coverings of network,—of which the king of elephants, called 'the Changes of the Moon,' is chief. Arise, O King, re-awaken thy desire for these! quicken thy longing after life!

'"Thine, O King, are those four and eighty thousand state horses, with trappings of gold, and gilded flags, and golden coverings of network,—of which 'Thunder-cloud,' the king of horses, is the chief. Arise, O King, re-awaken thy desire for these! quicken thy longing after life!

'"Thine, O King, are those four and eighty thousand chariots, with coverings of the skins of lions, and of tigers, and of panthers,—of which the chariot called 'the Flag of Victory' is the chief. Arise, O King, re-awaken thy desire for these! quicken thy longing after life!

'"Thine, O King, are those four and eighty thousand gems, of which the Wondrous Gem is the chief. Arise, O King, re-awaken thy desire for these! quicken thy longing after life!

'"Thine, O King, are those four and eighty thousand wives, of whom the Queen of Glory is the chief. Arise, O King, re-awaken thy desire for these! quicken thy longing after life!

'"Thine, O King, are those four and eighty thousand yeomen, of whom the Wonderful Steward is the chief. Arise, O King, re-awaken thy desire for these! quicken thy longing after life!

'"Thine, O King, are those four and eighty thousand nobles, of whom the Wonderful Adviser is the chief. Arise, O King, re-awaken thy desire for these! quicken thy longing after life!

'"Thine, O King, are those four and eighty thousand cows, with jute trappings, and horns tipped with bronze. Arise, O King, re-awaken thy desire for these! quicken thy longing after life!

'"Thine, O King, are those four and eighty thousand myriads of garments, of delicate textures, of flax, and cotton, and silk, and wool. Arise, O King, re-awaken thy desire for these! quicken thy longing after life!

'"Thine, O King, are those four and eighty thousand dishes, in which, in the evening and in the morning, rice is served. Arise, O King, re-awaken thy desire for these! quicken thy longing after life!"

---

30. 'When she had thus spoken, Ânanda, the Great King of Glory said to the Queen of Glory:

'"Long hast thou addressed me, O Queen, in pleasant words, much to be desired, and sweet. Yet now in this last time you speak in words unpleasant, disagreeable, not to be desired."

31. '"How then, O King, shall I address thee?"

'"Thus, O Queen, shouldst thou address me:—The nature of all things near and dear to us, O King, is such that we must leave them, divide ourselves from them, separate ourselves from them[1]. Pass not away, O King, with longing in thy heart. Sad is the death of him who longs, unworthy is the death of him who longs[2]. Thine, O King, are these

[1] The Pâli words are the same as those at the beginning of the constantly repeated longer phrase to the same effect in the Book of the Great Decease.

[2] Compare *Gâtaka*, No. 34.

four and eighty thousand cities, the chief of which is the royal city of Kusâvatî. Cast away desire for these! long not after life!

'"Thine, O King, are these four and eighty thousand palaces, the chief of which is the Palace of Righteousness. Cast away desire for these! long not after life!

'"Thine, O King, are these four and eighty thousand chambers, the chief of which is the chamber of the Great Complex. Cast away desire for these! long not after life!

'"Thine, O King, are these four and eighty thousand divans, of gold, and silver, and ivory, and sandal wood, spread with long-haired rugs, and cloths embroidered with flowers, and magnificent antelope skins; covered with lofty canopies; and provided at both ends with purple cushions. Cast away desire for these! long not after life!

'"Thine, O King, are these four and eighty thousand state elephants, with trappings of gold, and gilded flags, and golden coverings of network,—of which the king of elephants, called 'the Changes of the Moon,' is chief. Cast away desire for these! long not after life!

'"Thine, O King, are these four and eighty thousand state horses, with trappings of gold, and gilded flags, and golden coverings of network,—of which 'Thunder-cloud,' the king of horses, is the chief. Cast away desire for these! long not after life!

'"Thine, O King, are these four and eighty thousand chariots, with coverings of the skins of lions, and of tigers, and of panthers,—of which the chariot called 'the Flag of Victory' is the chief. Cast away desire for these! long not after life!

'"Thine, O King, are these four and eighty thousand gems, of which the Wondrous Gem is the chief. Cast away desire for these! long not after life!

'"Thine, O King, are these four and eighty thousand wives, of whom the Queen of Glory is the chief. Cast away desire for these! long not after life!

'"Thine, O King, are these four and eighty thousand yeoman, of whom the Wonderful Steward is the chief. Cast away desire for these! long not after life!

'"Thine, O King, are these four and eighty thousand nobles, of whom the Wonderful Adviser is the chief. Cast away desire for these! long not after life!

'"Thine, O King, are these four and eighty thousand cows, with jute trappings, and horns tipped with bronze. Cast away desire for these! long not after life!

'"Thine, O King, are these four and eighty thousand myriads of garments, of delicate textures, of flax, and cotton, and silk, and wool. Cast away desire for these! long not after life!

'"Thine, O King, are these four and eighty thousand dishes, in which, in the evening and in the morning, rice is served. Cast away desire for these! long not after life!"

---

32. 'When he thus spake, Ânanda, the Queen of Glory wept and poured forth tears.

33. 'Then, Ânanda, the Queen of Glory wiped away her tears, and addressed the Great King of Glory, and said:

'"The nature of all things near and dear to us, O King, is such that we must leave them, divide ourselves from them, separate ourselves from them. Pass not away, O King, with longing in thy heart. Sad is the death of him who longs, unworthy is the death of him who longs. Thine, O King, are these four and eighty thousand cities, the chief of which is the royal city of Kusâvatî. Cast away desire for these! long not after life!

'"Thine, O King, are these four and eighty thousand palaces, the chief of which is the Palace of Righteousness. Cast away desire for these! long not after life!

'"Thine, O King, are these four and eighty thousand chambers, the chief of which is the chamber of the Great Complex. Cast away desire for these! long not after life!

'"Thine, O King, are these four and eighty thousand divans, of gold, and silver, and ivory, and sandal wood, spread with long-haired rugs, and cloths embroidered with flowers, and magnificent antelope skins; covered with lofty canopies; and provided at both ends with purple cushions. Cast away desire for these! long not after life!

'"Thine, O King, are these four and eighty thousand state elephants, with trappings of gold, and gilded flags, and golden coverings of network,—of which the king of elephants, called 'the Changes of the Moon,' is chief. Cast away desire for these! long not after life!

'"Thine, O King, are these four and eighty thousand state horses, with trappings of gold, and gilded flags, and golden coverings of network,—of which 'Thunder-cloud,' the king of horses, is the chief. Cast away desire for these! long not after life!

'"Thine, O King, are these four and eighty thousand chariots, with coverings of the skins of lions, and of tigers, and of panthers,—of which the chariot called 'the Flag of Victory' is the chief. Cast away desire for these! long not after life!

'"Thine, O King, are these four and eighty thousand gems, of which the Wondrous Gem is the chief. Cast away desire for these! long not after life!

'"Thine, O King, are these four and eighty thousand wives, of whom the Queen of Glory is the chief. Cast away desire for these! long not after life!

'"Thine, O King, are these four and eighty thousand yeomen, of whom the Wonderful Steward is the chief. Cast away desire for these! long not after life!

'"Thine, O King, are these four and eighty thousand nobles, of whom the Wonderful Adviser is the chief. Cast away desire for these! long not after life!

'"Thine, O King, are these four and eighty thousand cows, with jute trappings, and horns tipped with bronze. Cast away desire for these! long not after life!

'"Thine, O King, are these four and eighty thousand myriads of garments, of delicate textures, of flax, and cotton, and silk, and wool. Cast away desire for these! long not after life!

'"Thine, O King, are these four and eighty thousand dishes, in which, in the evening and in the morning, rice is served. Cast away desire for these! long not after life!"

---

34. 'Then immediately, Ânanda, the Great King of Glory died. Just, Ânanda, as when a yeoman has eaten a hearty meal he becomes all drowsy,

just so were the feelings he experienced, Ânanda, as death came upon the Great King of Glory.

35. 'When the Great King of Glory, Ânanda, had died, he came to life again in the happy world of Brahmâ.

36. 'For eight and forty thousand years, Ânanda, the Great King of Glory lived the happy life of a prince; for eight and forty thousand years he was viceroy and heir-apparent; for eight and forty thousand years he ruled the kingdom; and for eight and forty thousand years he lived, as a layman, the noble life in the Palace of Righteousness. And then, when full of noble thoughts, he died; he entered, after the dissolution of the body, the noble world of Brahma[1].

---

37. 'Now it may be, Ânanda, that you may think "The Great King of Glory of that time was another person." But, Ânanda, you should not view the matter thus. I at that time was the Great King of Glory.

'Mine at that time were the four and eighty thousand cities, of which the chief was the royal city of Kusâvatî.

'Mine were the four and eighty thousand palaces, of which the chief was the Palace of Righteousness.

'Mine were the four and eighty thousand chambers, of which the chief was the chamber of the Great Complex.

'Mine were the four and eighty thousand divans,

---

[1] The 'noble thoughts' are the Brahma-vihâras, described above, Chap. II, §§ 8–11. The 'noble life' is the Brahmakariyam, which does not mean the same as it does in Sanskrit. The adjective Brahma may have reference here also to the subsequent (and consequent?) rebirth in the Brahma-loka.

of gold, and silver, and ivory, and sandal wood, spread with long-haired rugs, and cloths embroidered with flowers, and magnificent antelope skins; covered with lofty canopies; and provided at both ends with purple cushions.

'Mine were the four and eighty thousand state elephants, with trappings of gold, and gilded flags, and golden coverings of network,—of which the king of elephants, called "the Changes of the Moon," was chief.

'Mine were the four and eighty thousand state horses, with trappings of gold, and gilded flags, and golden coverings of network,—of which "Thunder-cloud," the king of horses, was the chief.

'Mine were the four and eighty thousand chariots, with coverings of the skins of lions, and of tigers, and of panthers,—of which the chariot called "the Flag of Victory" was the chief.

'Mine were the four and eighty thousand gems, of which the Wondrous Gem was the chief.

'Mine were the four and eighty thousand wives, of whom the Queen of Glory was the chief.

'Mine were the four and eighty thousand yeomen, of whom the Wonderful Steward was the chief.

'Mine were the four and eighty thousand nobles, of whom the Wonderful Adviser was the chief.

'Mine were the four and eighty thousand cows, with jute trappings, and horns tipped with bronze.

'Mine were the four and eighty thousand myriads of garments, of delicate textures, of flax, and cotton, and silk, and wool.

'Mine were the four and eighty thousand dishes, in which, in the evening and in the morning, rice was served.

---

38. 'Of those four and eighty thousand cities, Ânanda, one was that city in which, at that time, I used to dwell—to wit, the royal city of Kusâvatî.

'Of those four and eighty thousand palaces too, Ânanda, one was that palace in which, at that time, I used to dwell—to wit, the Palace of Righteousness.

'Of those four and eighty thousand chambers too, Ânanda, one was that chamber in which, at that time, I used to dwell—to wit, the chamber of the Great Complex.

'Of those four and eighty thousand divans too, Ânanda, one was that divan which, at that time, I used to occupy—to wit, one of gold, or one of silver, or one of ivory, or one of sandal wood.

'Of those four and eighty thousand state elephants too, Ânanda, one was that elephant which, at that time, I used to ride—to wit, the king of elephants, "the Changes of the Moon."

'Of those four and eighty thousand horses too, Ânanda, one was that horse which, at that time, I used to ride—to wit, the king of horses, "the Thunder-cloud."

'Of those four and eighty thousand chariots too, Ânanda, one was that chariot in which, at that time, I used to ride—to wit, the chariot called "the Flag of Victory."

'Of those four and eighty thousand wives too, Ânanda, one was that wife who, at that time, used to wait upon me—to wit, either a lady of noble birth, or a Velâmikânî.

'Of those four and eighty thousand myriads of suits of apparel too, Ânanda, one was the suit of apparel which, at that time, I wore—to wit, one of delicate texture, of linen, or cotton, or silk, or wool.

'Of those four and eighty thousand dishes too, Ânanda, one was that dish from which, at that time, I ate a measure of rice and the curry suitable thereto.

---

39. 'See, Ânanda, how all these things are now past, are ended, have vanished away. Thus impermanent, Ânanda, are component things; thus transitory, Ânanda, are component things; thus untrustworthy, Ânanda, are component things. Insomuch, Ânanda, is it meet to be weary of, is it meet to be estranged from, is it meet to be set quite free from the bondage of all component things!

---

40. 'Now I call to mind, Ânanda, how in this spot my body had been six times buried. And when I was dwelling here as the righteous king who ruled in righteousness, the lord of the four regions of the earth, the conqueror, the protector of his people, the possessor of the seven royal treasures—that was the seventh time.

41. 'But I behold not any spot, Ânanda, in the world of men and gods, nor in the world of Mâra, nor in the world of Brahmâ,—no, not among the race of Sama*n*as or Brâhmans, of gods or men,—where the Tathâgata for the eighth time will lay aside his body[1].'

---

[1] The whole of this conversation between the Great King of Glory and the Queen is very much shorter in the *G*âtaka, the enumeration of the possessions of the Great King being omitted (except the first clause referring to the four and eighty thousand cities), and clauses 34–38, 40, and 41 being also left out, § 39 and the concluding being placed in the mouth of the King immediately after § 33. This may be perhaps partly explained by the narrative style in which the *G*âtakas are composed—a style incompatible

42. Thus spake the Blessed One; and when the Happy One had thus spoken, once again the Teacher said:

'How transient are all component things!
Growth is their nature and decay:
They are produced, they are dissolved again:
And then is best, when they have sunk to rest[1]!'

End of the Mahâ-Sudassana Sutta.

---

with the repetitions of the Suttas, and confined to the facts of the story.

But I think that no one can read this Sutta in comparison with the short passage found in the Book of the Great Decease (above, pp. 99–101) without feeling that the latter is the more original of the two, and that the legend had not, when the Book of the Great Decease was composed, attained to its present extended form.

We seem therefore really to have three stages of the legend before us, and though the *G*âtaka story was actually put into its present shape at a known date (the fifth century of our era) long after the latest possible date for the Book of the Great King of Glory, it has probably preserved for us a reminiscence of what the legend was at the time when the Book of the Great Decease was composed.

[1] On this celebrated verse, see the note at Mahâparinibbâna Sutta VI, 16, where it is put into the mouth of Sakka, the king of the gods, and the discussion in the Introduction to this Sutta.

SABBÂSAVA-SUTTA.

INTRODUCTION

TO THE

SABBÂSAVA SUTTA.

DR. MORRIS, who had borrowed the Phayre and Turnour MSS. of the Ma*ggh*ima Nikâya from the India Office Library, has been good enough to transcribe the text of this Sutta for me.

I had hoped from the Rev. David da Silva's analysis of the Sutta in the Ceylon Friend for 1872, that it would determine the exact meaning of the difficult word Âsava as used in the theory of Arahatship, and in the important passage (the Faith, Reason, and Works paragraph) repeated so often in the Mahâparinibbâna Sutta. It will be seen that this is scarcely the case, but as it does throw light on the ideas wrapped up in the word, and contains a very interesting passage [1] on the especial value attached in Buddhism to the mental habit we should now call agnosticism, I have adhered to the intention of including it in this volume.

The word Âsava seems in this Sutta to be used in a general sense,—not confined only to the Âsavas of sensuality, individuality, delusion, and ignorance, but including the more various defilements or imperfections of mind, out of which those especial defilements will proceed.

Incidentally reference is made to the well-known Buddhist doctrine, that the right thing is to seek after the Nirvâ*n*a of a perfect life in Arahatship, and not to trouble and confuse oneself by the discussion of speculative questions as to past or future existence, or even as to the

---

[1] §§ 9, 10.

presence within the body of a soul. Buddhism is not only independent of the theory of soul, but regards the consideration of that theory as worse than profitless, as the source of manifold delusions and superstitions. Practically this comes, however, to much the same thing as the denial of the existence of the soul; just as agnosticism is, at best, but an earnest and modest sort of atheism. And we have seen above that anatta*m*, the absence of a soul or self as abiding principle, is one of the three parts of Buddhist wisdom (vi*gg*â)[1] and of Buddhist perception (sa*ññ*â)[2]. The reconciliation of these two doctrines, of the agnosticism and of the denial, is, I think, that the absence of soul is only predicated of those five Aggregates of parts and powers to which a good Buddhist should confine his attention. These alone he should consider; and he does wrong to care whether beyond and beside them a soul has, or has not, any real existence.

I may add that the importance of the Âsavas appears from the fact that elsewhere the knowledge of them, of their origin, of their cessation, and of the way that leads to their cessation is placed on the road to Arahatship immediately after, and parallel to, the knowledge of Suffering, of its origin, of its cessation, and of the way that leads to its cessation—the knowledge, that is, of the four Noble Truths[3].

The Âsavas there meant are sensuality, individuality (or life), and ignorance; and the expressions 'to him who knows, to him who sees' (*g*ânato passato) are used there much in the same way as they are in our § 3. Perhaps this was the passage which Burnouf had in his mind when he wrongly said[4] that he had found in the Mahâparinibbâna Sutta an enumeration of three classes of Âsavas, whereas that Sutta always divides them into four classes.

I am unable to suggest any good translation of the term itself—simple though it is. It means literally 'a running or flowing,' or (thence) 'a leak;' but as that figure is not

[1] See above, p. 162.

[2] See above, p. 9.

[3] Samañña Phala Sutta, p. 152.

[4] Lotus de la Bonne Loi, p. 823.

used in English in a spiritual sense, it is necessary to choose some other figure; and it is not easy to find one that is appropriate. 'Sin' would be very misleading, the Christian idea of sin being inconsistent with Buddhist ethics. A 'fault' in the geological use of the word comes somewhat nearer. 'Imperfection' is too long, and for 'stain' the Pâli has a different word[1]. In the Book of the Great Decease I have chosen 'evil;' here I leave the word untranslated.

[1] *Rago*. See the verses translated in 'Buddhist Birth Stories,' p. 164.

ALL THE ÂSAVAS.

SABBÂSAVA-SUTTA.

1. Thus have I heard. The Blessed One was once staying at Sâvatthi, at the *G*etavana, in Anâtha Pi*nd*ika's park.

There the Blessed One addressed the brethren, and said, 'Bhikkhus.'

'Yea, Lord!' said those brethren, in assent, to the Blessed One.

Then the Blessed One spake:

2. 'I will teach you, O brethren, the lesson of the subjugation of all the Âsavas. Listen well, and attend, and I will speak!'

'Even so, Lord!' said the brethren, in assent, to the Blessed One.

Then the Blessed One spake:

'I say that there is destruction of the Âsavas, brethren, to him who knows, to him who sees; not to him who knows not, to him who sees not. And what do I say, brethren, is the destruction of the Âsavas to him who knows, to him who sees? It is (a matter of) wise consideration, and of foolish consideration.

3. 'In him, brethren, who considers unwisely, Âsavas which have not arisen spring up, and Âsavas which have arisen are increased. In him, brethren, who considers wisely, Âsavas which have not arisen

spring not up, and Âsavas which have arisen do not increase.

---

4. 'There are Âsavas which should be abandoned, brethren, by insight, there are Âsavas which should be abandoned by subjugation, there are Âsavas which should be abandoned by right use, there are Âsavas which should be abandoned by endurance, there are Âsavas which should be abandoned by avoidance, there are Âsavas which should be abandoned by removal, there are Âsavas which should be abandoned by cultivation.

---

5. 'And which, brethren, are the Âsavas which should be abandoned by insight[1]?

'In the first place, brethren, the ignorant unconverted man, who perceives not the Noble Ones, who comprehends not, nor is trained according to the doctrine of the noble ones; who perceives not good men, who comprehends not, nor is trained according to the doctrine of good men; he neither understands what things ought to be considered, nor what things ought not to be considered; the things that ought not to be considered, those he considers; and the things that ought to be considered, those he does not consider.

6. 'And which, brethren, are those things which he should not consider, which he nevertheless considers?

'There are things which, when a man considers them, the Âsava of Lust springs up within him, which had not sprung up before; and the Âsava of Lust, which had sprung up, grows great; the Âsava of

---

[1] Dassanâ.

Life springs up within him, which had not sprung up before; and the Âsava of Life, which had sprung up, grows great; the Âsava of Ignorance springs up within him, which had not sprung up before; and the Âsava of Ignorance, which had sprung up, grows great.

'These are the things which ought not to be considered, things which he considers.

7. 'And which, brethren, are those things which should be considered, which he nevertheless does not consider?

'There are things, brethren, which, when a man considers them, the Âsava of Lust, if it had not sprung up before, springs not up within him; and the Âsava of Lust, which had sprung up, is put away; the Âsava of Life, if it had not sprung up before, springs not up within him; and the Âsava of Life, which had sprung up, is put away; the Âsava of Ignorance, if it had not sprung up before, springs not up within him; and the Âsava of Ignorance, which had sprung up, is put away.

'These are the things which ought to be considered, things which he does not consider.

8. 'It is by his consideration of those things, which ought not to be considered; and by his non-consideration of those things, which ought to be considered, that Âsavas arise within him which had not sprung up; and Âsavas which had sprung up, grow great.'

---

9. 'Unwisely doth he consider thus:

'"Have I existed during the ages that are past, or have I not? What was I during the ages that are past? How was I during the ages that are past? Having been what, what did I become in the ages that are past? Shall I exist during the ages of the future, or shall I not? What shall I be during the ages of the future? How shall I be during the ages of the future? Having been what, what shall I become during the ages of the future?"

'Or he debates within himself as to the present: "Do I after all exist, or am I not? How am I? This is a being; whence now did it come, and whither will it go?"

10. 'In him, thus unwisely considering, there springs up one or other of the six (absurd) notions[1].

'As something true and real he gets the notion, "I have a self!"

'As something true and real he gets the notion, "I have not a self!"

'As something true and real he gets the notion, "By my self, I am conscious of my self!"

'As something true and real he gets the notion, "By myself I am conscious of my non-self!"

'Or, again, he gets the notion, "This soul of mine can be perceived, it has experienced the result of good and evil actions committed here and there: now this soul of mine is permanent, lasting, eternal, has the inherent quality of never changing, and will continue for ever and ever!"

11. 'This, brethren, is called the walking in delusion, the jungle of delusion[2], the wilderness of delusion, the puppet show of delusion, the writhing of delusion, the fetter of delusion.

12. 'Bound, brethren, with this fetter of delusion,

---

[1] *Kh*anna*m* di*tth*înam.

[2] Di*tth*i-gahana*m*, with allusion, doubtless, if the reading is correct, to gaha*n*a*m*.

the ignorant unconverted man becomes not freed from birth, decay, and death, from sorrows, lamentations, pains, and griefs, and from expedients[1]—he does not become free, I say, from pain.

---

13. 'But the wise man, brethren, the disciple walking in the Noble Path, who perceives the noble ones; who comprehends, and is trained according to, the doctrine of the Noble Ones; who perceives good men, who comprehends, and is trained according to, the doctrine of good men; he understands both what things ought to be considered, and what things ought not to be considered—and thus understanding, the things that ought to be considered those he considers; and the things that ought not to be considered, those he does not consider.

14. 'And which, brethren, are those things which ought not to be considered, and which he does not consider?

'There are things which, when a man considers them, the Âsava of Lust springs up within him, which had not sprung up before; and the Âsava of Lust, which had sprung up, grows great; the Âsava of Life springs up within him, which had not sprung up before; and the Âsava of Life, which had sprung up, grows great; the Âsava of Ignorance springs up within him, which had not sprung up before; and the Âsava of Ignorance, which had sprung up, grows great.

'These are the things which ought not to be considered, things which he considers.

---

[1] That is, the practice of rites and ceremonies and the worship of Gods.

15. 'And which, brethren, are those things which should be considered, and which he does consider?

'There are things, brethren, which, when a man considers them, the Âsava of Lust, if it had not sprung up before, springs not up within him; and the Âsava of Lust, which had sprung up, is put away; the Âsava of Life, if it had not sprung up before, springs not up within him; and the Âsava of Life, which had sprung up, is put away; the Âsava of Ignorance, if it had not sprung up before, springs not up within him; and the Âsava of Ignorance, which had sprung up, is put away.

'These are the things which ought to be considered, things which he does not consider.

16. 'It is by his not considering those things which ought to be considered, and by his considering those things which ought not to be considered, that Âsavas which had not sprung up within him spring not up, and Âsavas which had sprung up are put away.

17. 'He considers, "This is suffering." He considers, "This is the origin of suffering." He considers, "This is the cessation of suffering." He considers, "This is the way which leads to the cessation of suffering." And from him, thus considering, the three fetters fall away—the delusion of self, hesitation, and the dependence on rites and ceremonies.

'These are the Âsavas, brethren, which are to be abandoned by insight.

---

18. 'And which are the Âsavas to be abandoned by subjugation (samvarâ)?

'Herein, brethren, a Bhikkhu, wisely reflecting,

remains shut in by the subjugation of the organ of Sight. For whereas to the man not shut in by the subjugation of the organ of sight Âsavas may arise, full of vexation and distress, to the man shut in by the subjugation of the organ of sight the Âsavas, full of vexation and distress, are not.

19. 'Wisely reflecting, he remains shut in by the subjugation of the organ of Hearing. For whereas to the man not shut in by the subjugation of the organ of hearing Âsavas may arise, full of vexation and distress, to the man shut in by the subjugation of the organ of hearing the Âsavas, full of vexation and distress, are not.

20. 'Wisely reflecting, he remains shut in by the subjugation of the organ of Smell. For whereas to the man not shut in by the subjugation of the organ of smell Âsavas may arise, full of vexation and distress, to the man shut in by the subjugation of the organ of smell the Âsavas, full of vexation and distress, are not.

21. 'Wisely reflecting, he remains shut in by the subjugation of the organ of Taste. For whereas to the man not shut in by the subjugation of the organ of taste Âsavas may arise, full of vexation and distress, to the man shut in by the subjugation of the organ of taste the Âsavas, full of vexation and distress, are not.

22. 'Wisely reflecting, he remains shut in by the subjugation of the organ of Touch. For whereas to the man not shut in by the subjugation of the organ of touch Âsavas may arise, full of vexation and distress, to the man shut in by the subjugation of the organ of touch the Âsavas, full of vexation and distress, are not.

23. 'Wisely reflecting, he remains shut in by the subjugation of the organ of Mind. For whereas to the man not shut in by the subjugation of the organ of mind Âsavas may arise, full of vexation and distress, to the man shut in by the subjugation of the organ of mind the Âsavas, full of vexation and distress, are not.

'These, brethren, are called the Âsavas to be abandoned by subjugation.

---

24. 'And which are the Âsavas to be abandoned by right use[1]?

'Herein, brethren, a Bhikkhu, wisely reflecting, makes use of his robes for the purpose only of warding off the cold, of warding off the heat, of warding off the contact of gad-flies and mosquitoes, of wind and sun, and snakes; and of covering his nakedness[2].

25. 'Wisely reflecting, he makes use of alms, not for sport or sensual enjoyment, not for adorning or beautifying himself, but solely to sustain the body in life, to prevent its being injured, to aid himself in the practice of a holy life—thinking the while, "Thus shall I overcome the old pain, and shall incur no new; and everywhere shall I be at ease, and free from blame."

26. 'Wisely reflecting, he makes use of an abode; only to ward off cold, to ward off heat, to ward off the contact of gad-flies and mosquitoes, of wind and sun, and snakes; only to avoid the dangers of the climate, and to secure the delight of privacy.

---

[1] Pa*t*isevanâ.

[2] Compare Dickson's Kammavâ*k*â, p. 7, where the reading, however, is wrong.

27. 'Wisely reflecting, he makes use of medicine and other necessaries for the sick; only to ward off the pain that causes injury, and to preserve his health.

28. 'For whereas, brethren, to the man not making such right use, Âsavas may arise, full of vexation and distress; to the man making such right use, the Âsavas, full of vexation and distress, are not.

'These, brethren, are called the Âsavas to be abandoned by right use.

---

29. 'And which, brethren, are the Âsavas to be abandoned by endurance[1]?

'Herein, brethren, a Bhikkhu, wisely reflecting, is patient under cold and heat, under hunger and thirst, under the contact of gad-flies and mosquitoes, of wind and sun, and snakes; he is enduring under abusive words, under bodily suffering, under pains however sharp, rough, severe, unpleasant, disagreeable, and destructive even to life.

30. 'For whereas, brethren, to the man who endureth not, Âsavas may arise, full of vexation and distress; to him who endures, the Âsavas, full of vexation and distress, are not.

'These, brethren, are called the Âsavas to be abandoned by endurance.

---

31. 'And which, brethren, are the Âsavas to be abandoned by avoidance[2]?

'Herein, brethren, a Bhikkhu wisely reflecting, avoids a rogue elephant, he avoids a furious horse, he avoids a wild bull, he avoids a mad dog, a snake, a stump in the path, a thorny bramble, a pit, a precipice, a dirty tank or pool. When tempted to

---

[1] Adhivâsanâ.

[2] Parivaggana̧.

sit in a place where one should not sit, or to walk where one should not walk, or to cultivate the acquaintance of bad companions, he is skilled to shun the evil: and wisely reflecting he avoids that, as a place whereon one should not sit, that, as a place wherein one should not walk, those men, as companions that are bad.

32. 'For whereas, brethren, to the man who avoideth not, Âsavas may arise, full of vexation and distress; to him who avoids, the Âsavas, full of vexation and distress, are not.

'These, brethren, are called the Âsavas to be abandoned by avoidance.

---

33. 'And which, brethren, are the Âsavas to be abandoned by removal[1]?

'Herein, brethren, a Bhikkhu, wisely reflecting, when there has sprung up within him a lustful thought, that he endureth not, he puts it away, he removes it, he destroys it, he makes it not to be; when there has sprung up within him an angry thought, a malicious thought, some sinful, wrong disposition, that he endureth not, he puts it away, he removes it, he destroys it, he makes it not to be.

34. 'For whereas, brethren, to the man who removeth not, Âsavas may arise, full of vexation and distress; to him who removes, the Âsavas, full of vexation and distress, are not.

'These, brethren, are called the Âsavas to be abandoned by removal.

---

35. 'And which, brethren, are the Âsavas to be abandoned by cultivation[2]?

---

[1] Vinodanâ. [2] Bhâvanâ.

'[1] Herein, brethren, a Bhikkhu, wisely reflecting, cultivates that part of the higher wisdom called Mindfulness, dependent on seclusion, dependent on passionlessness, dependent on the utter ecstasy of contemplation, resulting in the passing off of thoughtlessness.

36. 'He cultivates that part of the higher wisdom called Search after Truth, he cultivates that part of the higher wisdom called Energy, he cultivates that part of the higher wisdom called Joy, he cultivates that part of the higher wisdom called Peace, he cultivates that part of the higher wisdom called Earnest Contemplation, he cultivates that part of the higher wisdom called Equanimity—each dependent on seclusion, dependent on passionlessness, dependent on the utter ecstasy of contemplation, resulting in the passing off of thoughtlessness.

37. 'For whereas, brethren, to the man who cultivateth not, Âsavas may arise, full of vexation and distress; to him who cultivates, the Âsavas, full of vexation and distress, are not.

'These, brethren, are called the Âsavas to be abandoned by cultivation.

---

38. 'And then when a Bhikkhu has by insight put away the Âsavas to be abandoned by insight, and by subjugation has put away the Âsavas to be abandoned by subjugation, and by right use has put away the Âsavas to be abandoned by right use, and by endurance has put away the Âsavas to be abandoned by endurance, and by avoidance has put away the Âsavas to be abandoned by avoidance,

---

[1] Compare Mahâparinibbâna Sutta I, 9.

and by removal has put away the Âsavas to be abandoned by removal, and by cultivation has put away the Âsavas to be abandoned by cultivation—that Bhikkhu, brethren, remains shut in by the subjugation of the Âsavas, he has destroyed that Craving Thirst, by thorough penetration of mind he has rolled away every Fetter, and he has made an end of Pain.'

---

39. Thus spake the Blessed One; and those Bhikkhus, glad at heart, exalted the word of the Blessed One.

End of the Sabbâsava Sutta.

INDEX.

ADDENDA ET CORRIGENDA.

Mahâ-parinibbâna Sutta I, 23, 24. The 'nobles' (khattiyas) should come before the 'Brâhmans,' as in III, 21, and in the Tevi*gg*a Sutta I, 19. The sentiment of I, 24 recurs in a passage given by Mr. Beal from the Chinese in the 'Indian Antiquary,' IV, 96.

— II, 31. 'Went out from the monastery' (vihâra). There is no mention of a vihâra in the previous sections. The following conversation seems therefore to have been originally recorded in some other connection.

— III, 20. Add at the end, 'These, Ânanda, are the eight causes, proximate and remote, of the appearance of a mighty earthquake.'

— V, 10 (note p. 88). The passage here quoted from Buddhaghosa, about angels on the point of a gimlet, recurs in the Aṅguttara Nikâya, Duka Nipâta.

— V, 52. The words 'who was not a believer' should be in brackets. They are inserted to give the full force of the word paribbâgako, as the translation 'mendicant' might convey the impression that Subhadda was a Buddhist mendicant.

— VI, 26. Compare *G*âtaka I, 60, line 17.

TRANSLITERATION OF ORIENTAL ALPHABETS ADOPTED FOR THE TRANSLATIONS OF THE SACRED BOOKS OF THE EAST.

CONSONANTS.	MISSIONARY ALPHABET.			Sanskrit.	Zend.	Pehlevi.	Persian.	Arabic.	Hebrew.	Chinese.
	I Class.	II Class.	III Class.							
Gutturales.										
1 Tenuis	k	...	...	क	𐬐	𐭪	ک	ك	כּ	k
2 „ aspirata	kh	...	...	ख	𐬑	𐭧	...	...	כ	kh
3 Media	g	...	...	ग	𐬔	𐭢	گ	...	גּ	...
4 „ aspirata	gh	...	...	घ	𐬖	𐭢	...	...	ג	...
5 Gutturo-labialis	q	...	...	...	...	...	ق	ق	ק	...
6 Nasalis	ṅ (ng)	...	...	ङ	{𐬣 (ng) / 𐬧 (N)}	...	...	...	...	...
7 Spiritus asper	h	...	...	ह	𐬵 (𐬷 hv)	𐭤	ه	ه	ה	h, hs
8 „ lenis	'	...	...	...	...	...	ا	ا	א	...
9 „ asper faucalis	‛h	...	...	...	...	...	ح	ح	ח	...
10 „ lenis faucalis	'h	...	...	...	...	...	ع	ع	ע	...
11 „ asper fricatus	...	‛*h*	...	...	...	...	خ	خ	ח	...
12 „ lenis fricatus	...	'*h*	...	...	...	...	...	...	...	...
Gutturales modificatae (palatales, &c.)										
13 Tenuis	...	*k*	...	च	𐬗	𐭰	چ	...	...	*k*
14 „ aspirata	...	*kh*	...	छ	...	...	...	...	...	*kh*
15 Media	...	*g*	...	ज	𐬘	𐭩	ج	ج	...	...
16 „ aspirata	...	*gh*	...	झ	...	...	غ	غ	...	...
17 „ Nasalis	...	*ñ*	...	ञ	...	...	...	...	...	...

CONSONANTS (*continued*).	MISSIONARY ALPHABET. I Class.	II Class.	III Class.	Sanskrit.	Zend.	Pehlevi.	Persian.	Arabic.	Hebrew.	Chinese.
18 Semivocalis	y	...	...	य	[illegible] init.	[illegible]	ي	ي	י	y
19 Spiritus asper	...	(ẙ)	...	...	...	...	...	...	...	...
20 „ lenis	...	(ẙ)	...	...	...	...	...	...	...	...
21 „ asper assibilatus	...	*s*	...	श	[illegible]	[illegible]	ش	ش	...	...
22 „ lenis assibilatus	...	*z*	...	...	[illegible]	[illegible]	ژ	...	...	*z*
Dentales.										
23 Tenuis	t	...	...	त	[illegible]	[illegible]	ت	ت	תּ	t
24 „ aspirata	th	...	...	थ	[illegible]	...	...	...	ת	th
25 „ assibilata	...	...	TH	...	...	...	ث	ث	...	...
26 Media	d	...	...	द	[illegible]	[illegible]	د	د	דּ	...
27 „ aspirata	dh	...	...	ध	[illegible]	...	...	...	ד	...
28 „ assibilata	...	...	DH	...	...	...	ذ	ذ	...	...
29 Nasalis	n	...	...	न	[illegible]	[illegible]	ن	ن	נ	n
30 Semivocalis	l	...	...	ल	...	[illegible]	ل	ل	ל	l
31 „ mollis 1	...	*l*	...	ळ	...	...	...	...	...	...
32 „ mollis 2	...	...	L	...	...	...	...	...	...	...
33 Spiritus asper 1	s	...	...	स	[illegible]	[illegible]	س(ث)	س	שׂ	s
34 „ asper 2	...	...	s (ʃ)	...	...	...	...	...	ס	...
35 „ lenis	z	...	...	...	[illegible]	[illegible]	ز (ذ)	ز	ז	z
36 „ asperrimus 1	...	...	z (ʒ)	...	...	...	ص	ص	צ	ʒ, ʒh
37 „ asperrimus 2	...	...	ẓ (ʒ̣)	...	...	...	ض	...	...	...

Dentales modificatae (linguales, &c.)										
38 Tenuis	...	*t*	....	ट	....	...	ط	ط	ט	...
39 „ aspirata	...	*th*	....	ठ	....	...	ظ	ظ	...	...
40 Media	...	*d*	....	ड	[illegible]	[illegible]	...	...	...	...
41 „ aspirata	...	*dh*	....	ढ	....	...	...	ض	...	...
42 Nasalis	...	*n*	....	ण	[illegible]	...	...	...	...	...
43 Semivocalis	r	...	....	र	[illegible]	[illegible]	ر	ر	ר	...
44 „ fricata	...	*r*	....	...	....	...	...	...	...	*r*
45 „ diacritica	...	...	R	...	....	...	...	...	...	...
46 Spiritus asper	sh	...	....	ष	[illegible]	[illegible]	...	...	...	sh
47 „ lenis	zh	...	....	...	....	...	...	...	...	...
Labiales.										
48 Tenuis	p	...	....	प	[illegible]	[illegible]	پ	...	פּ	p
49 „ aspirata	ph	...	....	फ	....	...	...	...	פ	ph
50 Media	b	...	....	ब	[illegible]	[illegible]	ب	ب	בּ	...
51 „ aspirata	bh	...	....	भ	....	...	...	...	ב	...
52 Tenuissima	...	*p*	....	...	....	...	...	...	...	...
53 Nasalis	m	...	....	म	[illegible]	[illegible]	م	م	מ	m
54 Semivocalis	w	...	....	...	[illegible]	...	...	...	...	w
55 „ aspirata	hw	...	....	...	....	...	...	...	...	...
56 Spiritus asper	f	...	....	...	[illegible]	[illegible]	ف	ف	...	f
57 „ lenis	v	...	....	व	[illegible]	[illegible]	و	و	ו	...
58 Anusvâra	...	*m̃*	....	अं	[illegible] ã	...	...	...	...	...
59 Visarga	...	*h*	....	अः	....	...	...	...	...	...

VOWELS.	MISSIONARY ALPHABET. I Class.	II Class.	III Class.	Sanskrit.	Zend.	Pehlevi.	Persian.	Arabic.	Hebrew.	Chinese.
1 Neutralis	0	...	....	...	....	...	...	...	ְ	ă
2 Laryngo-palatalis	ĕ	...	....	...	....	...	...	...	...	...
3 " labialis	ŏ	...	....	...	....	ı fin.	...	...	...	...
4 Gutturalis brevis	a	...	....	अ	𐬀	𐭠 init.	ـَ	ـَ	ַ	a
5 " longa	â	(a)	....	आ	𐬁	𐭠	ـَا	ـَا	ָ	â
6 Palatalis brevis	i	...	....	इ	𐬌	...	ـِ	ـِ	ִ	i
7 " longa	î	(i)	....	ई	𐬍	𐭩	ـِي	ـِي	ִי	î
8 Dentalis brevis	*li*	...	....	ऌ	....	...	...	...	...	...
9 " longa	*lî*	...	....	ॡ	....	...	...	...	...	...
10 Lingualis brevis	*ri*	...	....	ऋ	....	...	...	...	...	...
11 " longa	*rî*	...	....	ॠ	....	...	...	...	...	...
12 Labialis brevis	u	...	....	उ	𐬎	...	ـُ	ـُ	ֻ	u
13 " longa	û	(u)	....	ऊ	𐬏	𐭥	ـُو	ـُو	וּ	û
14 Gutturo-palatalis brevis	e	...	....	...	𐬈(e) 𐬆(e)	...	...	...	ֶ	e
15 " longa	ê (ai)	(e)	....	ए	𐬉, 𐬇	𐭩	...	...	ֵ	ê
16 Diphthongus gutturo-palatalis	âi	(ai)	....	ऐ	....	...	ـَيْ	ـَيْ	...	âi
17 " "	ei (ĕi)	...	....	...	....	...	...	...	...	ei, êi
18 " "	oi (ŏu)	...	....	...	....	...	...	...	...	...
19 Gutturo-labialis brevis	o	...	....	...	𐬊	...	...	...	ָ	o
20 " longa	ô (au)	(o)	....	ओ	𐬋	𐭥	...	...	וֹ	...
21 Diphthongus gutturo-labialis	âu	(au)	....	औ	𐬃𐬎 (au)	...	ـَوْ	ـَوْ	...	âu
22 " "	eu (ĕu)	...	....	...	....	...	...	...	...	...
23 " "	ou (ŏu)	...	....	...	....	...	...	...	...	...
24 Gutturalis fracta	ä	...	....	...	....	...	...	...	...	...
25 Palatalis fracta	ï	...	....	...	....	...	...	...	...	...
26 Labialis fracta	ü	...	....	...	....	...	...	...	...	ü
27 Gutturo-labialis fracta	ö	...	....	...	....	...	...	...	...	...

SACRED BOOKS OF THE EAST

TRANSLATED BY VARIOUS ORIENTAL SCHOLARS

AND EDITED BY

THE RIGHT HON. F. MAX MÜLLER.

*** *This Series is published with the sanction and co-operation of the Secretary of State for India in Council.*

REPORT presented to the ACADÉMIE DES INSCRIPTIONS, May 11, 1883, by M. ERNEST RENAN.

'M. Renan présente trois nouveaux volumes de la grande collection des "Livres sacrés de l'Orient" (Sacred Books of the East), que dirige à Oxford, avec une si vaste érudition et une critique si sûre, le savant associé de l'Académie des Inscriptions, M. Max Müller. . . . La première série de ce beau recueil, composée de 24 volumes, est presque achevée. M. Max Müller se propose d'en publier une seconde, dont l'intérêt historique et religieux ne sera pas moindre. M. Max Müller a su se procurer la collaboration des savans les plus éminens d'Europe et d'Asie. L'Université d'Oxford, que cette grande publication honore au plus haut degré, doit tenir à continuer dans les plus larges proportions une œuvre aussi philosophiquement conçue que savamment exécutée.'

EXTRACT from the QUARTERLY REVIEW.

'We rejoice to notice that a second series of these translations has been announced and has actually begun to appear. The stones, at least, out of which a stately edifice may hereafter arise, are here being brought together. Prof. Max Müller has deserved well of scientific history. Not a few minds owe to his enticing words their first attraction to this branch of study. But no work of his, not even the great edition of the Rig-Veda, can compare in importance or in usefulness with this English translation of the Sacred Books of the East, which has been devised by his foresight, successfully brought so far by his persuasive and organising power, and will, we trust, by the assistance of the distinguished scholars he has gathered round him, be carried in due time to a happy completion.'

Professor E. HARDY, Inaugural Lecture in the University of Freiburg, 1887.

'Die allgemeine vergleichende Religionswissenschaft datirt von jenem grossartigen, in seiner Art einzig dastehenden Unternehmen, zu welchem auf Anregung Max Müllers im Jahre 1874 auf dem internationalen Orientalistencongress in London der Grundstein gelegt worden war, die Übersetzung der heiligen Bücher des Ostens' (*the Sacred Books of the East*).

The Hon. ALBERT S. G. CANNING, 'Words on Existing Religions.'

'The recent publication of the "Sacred Books of the East" in English is surely a great event in the annals of theological literature.'

Oxford

AT THE CLARENDON PRESS

LONDON: HENRY FROWDE

OXFORD UNIVERSITY PRESS WAREHOUSE, AMEN CORNER, E.C.

FIRST SERIES.

VOL. I. The Upanishads.

Translated by F. MAX MÜLLER. Part I. The *Kh*ândogya-upanishad, The Talavakâra-upanishad, The Aitareya-âra*n*yaka, The Kaushîtaki-brâhma*n*a-upanishad, and The Vâgasaneyi-sa*m*hitâ-upanishad. *Second Edition.* 8vo, cloth, 10*s.* 6*d.*

The Upanishads contain the philosophy of the Veda. They have become the foundation of the later Vedânta doctrines, and indirectly of Buddhism. Schopenhauer, speaking of the Upanishads, says: 'In the whole world there is no study so beneficial and so elevating as that of the Upanishads. It has been the solace of my life, it will be the solace of my death.'

[See also Vol. XV.]

VOL. II. The Sacred Laws of the Âryas,

As taught in the Schools of Âpastamba, Gautama, Vâsish*th*a, and Baudhâyana. Translated by GEORG BÜHLER. Part I. Âpastamba and Gautama. *Second Edition.* 8vo, cloth, 10*s.* 6*d.*

The Sacred Laws of the Âryas contain the original treatises on which the Laws of Manu and other lawgivers were founded.

[See also Vol. XIV.]

VOL. III. The Sacred Books of China.

The Texts of Confucianism. Translated by JAMES LEGGE. Part I. The Shû King, The Religious Portions of the Shih King, and The Hsiâo King. 8vo, cloth, 12*s.* 6*d.*

Confucius was a collector of ancient traditions, not the founder of a new religion. As he lived in the sixth and fifth centuries B.C. his works are of unique interest for the study of Ethology.

[See also Vols. XVI, XXVII, XXVIII, XXXIX, and XL.]

VOL. IV. The Zend-Avesta.

Translated by JAMES DARMESTETER. Part I. The Vendîdâd. *Second Edition.* 8vo, cloth, 14*s.*

The Zend-Avesta contains the relics of what was the religion of Cyrus, Darius, and Xerxes, and, but for the battle of Marathon, might have become the religion of Europe. It forms to the present day the sacred book of the Parsis, the so-called fire-worshippers.

[See also Vols. XXIII and XXXI.]

VOL. V. Pahlavi Texts.

Translated by E. W. WEST. Part I. The Bundahis, Bahman Yast, and Shâyast lâ-shâyast. 8vo, cloth, 12*s.* 6*d.*

The Pahlavi Texts comprise the theological literature of the revival of Zoroaster's religion, beginning with the Sassanian dynasty. They are important for a study of Gnosticism.

[See also Vols. XVIII, XXIV, XXXVII, and XLVII.]

VOLS. VI AND IX. The Qur'ân.

Parts I and II. Translated by E. H. PALMER. 8vo, cloth, 21*s.*

This translation, carried out according to his own peculiar views of the origin of the Qur'ân, was the last great work of E. H. Palmer, before he was murdered in Egypt.

VOL. VII. The Institutes of Vishnu.

Translated by JULIUS JOLLY. 8vo, cloth, 10*s.* 6*d.*

A collection of legal aphorisms, closely connected with one of the oldest Vedic schools, the Kathas, *but considerably added to in later time. Of importance for a critical study of the Laws of Manu.*

VOL. VIII. The Bhagavadgîtâ, with The Sanatsugâtîya, and The Anugîtâ.

Translated by KÂSHINÂTH TRIMBAK TELANG. *Second Edition.* 8vo, cloth, 10*s.* 6*d.*

The earliest philosophical and religious poem of India. It has been paraphrased in Arnold's 'Song Celestial.'

VOL. X. The Dhammapada,

Translated from Pâli by F. MAX MÜLLER; and

The Sutta-Nipâta,

Translated from Pâli by V. FAUSBÖLL; being Canonical Books of the Buddhists. *Second Edition.* 8vo, cloth, 10*s.* 6*d.*

The Dhammapada contains the quintessence of Buddhist morality. The Sutta-Nipâta gives the authentic teaching of Buddha on some of the fundamental principles of religion.

VOL. XI. Buddhist Suttas.

Translated from Pâli by T. W. RHYS DAVIDS. 1. The Mahâ-parinibbâna Suttanta; 2. The Dhamma-*k*akka-ppavattana Sutta. 3. The Tevi*gg*a Suttanta; 4. The Âkaṅkheyya Sutta; 5. The *K*etokhila Sutta; 6. The Mahâ-sudassana Suttanta; 7. The Sabbâsava Sutta. 8vo, cloth, 10*s*. 6*d*.

A collection of the most important religious, moral, and philosophical discourses taken from the sacred canon of the Buddhists.

VOL. XII. The *S*atapatha-Brâhma*n*a, according to the Text of the Mâdhyandina School.

Translated by JULIUS EGGELING. Part I. Books I and II. 8vo, cloth, 12*s*. 6*d*.

A minute account of the sacrificial ceremonies of the Vedic age. It contains the earliest account of the Deluge in India.

[See also Vols. XXVI, XLI, XLIII, and XLIV.]

VOL. XIII. Vinaya Texts.

Translated from the Pâli by T. W. RHYS DAVIDS and HERMANN OLDENBERG. Part I. The Pâtimokkha. The Mahâvagga, I–IV. 8vo, cloth, 10*s*. 6*d*.

The Vinaya Texts give for the first time a translation of the moral code of the Buddhist religion as settled in the third century B.C.

[See also Vols. XVII and XX.]

VOL. XIV. The Sacred Laws of the Âryas,

As taught in the Schools of Âpastamba, Gautama, Vâsish*th*a, and Baudhâyana. Translated by GEORG BÜHLER. Part II. Vâsish*th*a and Baudhâyana. 8vo, cloth, 10*s*. 6*d*.

VOL. XV. The Upanishads.

Translated by F. MAX MÜLLER. Part II. The Ka*th*a-upanishad, The Mu*nd*aka-upanishad, The Taittirîyaka-upanishad, The B*ri*hadâra*n*yaka-upanishad, The *S*vetâ*s*vatara-upanishad, The Pra*s*ña-upanishad, and The Maitrâya*n*a-brâhma*n*a-upanishad. 8vo, cloth, 10*s*. 6*d*.

[*** Vol. XV can only be supplied as part of a complete set of the First Series.]

VOL. XVI. The Sacred Books of China.

The Texts of Confucianism. Translated by JAMES LEGGE. Part II. The Yî King. 8vo, cloth, 10*s*. 6*d*.

[See also Vols. XXVII, XXVIII.]

VOL. XVII. Vinaya Texts.

Translated from the Pâli by T. W. RHYS DAVIDS and HERMANN OLDENBERG. Part II. The Mahâvagga, V–X. The *K*ullavagga, I–III. 8vo, cloth. 10*s*. 6*d*.

Vol. XVIII. Pahlavi Texts.

Translated by E. W. West. Part II. The Dâdistân-î Dînîk and The Epistles of Mânûskîhar. 8vo, cloth, 12*s*. 6*d*.

Vol. XIX. The Fo-sho-hing-tsan-king.

A Life of Buddha by Asvaghosha Bodhisattva, translated from Sanskrit into Chinese by Dharmaraksha, A.D. 420, and from Chinese into English by Samuel Beal. 8vo, cloth, 10*s*. 6*d*.

This life of Buddha was translated from Sanskrit into Chinese, A.D. 420. It contains many legends, some of which show a certain similarity to the Evangelium infantiae, &c.

Vol. XX. Vinaya Texts.

Translated from the Pâli by T. W. Rhys Davids and Hermann Oldenberg. Part III. The Kullavagga, IV–XII. 8vo, cloth, 10*s*. 6*d*.

Vol. XXI. The Saddharma-pundarîka; or, The Lotus of the True Law.

Translated by H. Kern. 8vo, cloth, 12*s*. 6*d*.

'The Lotus of the True Law,' a canonical book of the Northern Buddhists, translated from Sanskrit. There is a Chinese translation of this book which was finished as early as the year 286 *A.D.*

Vol. XXII. Gaina-Sûtras.

Translated from Prâkrit by Hermann Jacobi. Part I. The Âkârânga-Sûtra and The Kalpa-Sûtra. 8vo, cloth, 10*s*. 6*d*.

The religion of the Gainas was founded by a contemporary of Buddha. It still counts numerous adherents in India, while there are no Buddhists left in India proper.

[See Vol. XLV.]

Vol. XXIII. The Zend-Avesta.

Translated by James Darmesteter. Part II. The Sîrôzahs, Yasts, and Nyâyis. 8vo, cloth, 10*s*. 6*d*.

Vol. XXIV. Pahlavi Texts.

Translated by E. W. West. Part III. Dînâ-î Maînôg-Khirad, Sikand-gûmânîk Vigâr, and Sad Dar. 8vo, cloth, 10*s*. 6*d*.

SECOND SERIES.

VOL. XXV. Manu.

Translated by GEORG BÜHLER. 8vo, cloth, 21*s*.

This translation is founded on that of Sir William Jones, which has been carefully revised and corrected with the help of seven native Commentaries. An Appendix contains all the quotations from Manu which are found in the Hindu Law-books, translated for the use of the Law Courts in India. Another Appendix gives a synopsis of parallel passages from the six Dharma-sûtras, the other Smritis, the Upanishads, the Mahâbhârata, &c.

VOL. XXVI. The *S*atapatha-Brâhma*n*a.

Translated by JULIUS EGGELING. Part II. Books III and IV. 8vo, cloth, 12*s*. 6*d*.

VOLS. XXVII AND XXVIII. The Sacred Books of China.

The Texts of Confucianism. Translated by JAMES LEGGE. Parts III and IV. The Lî *K*î, or Collection of Treatises on the Rules of Propriety, or Ceremonial Usages. 8vo, cloth, 25*s*.

VOL. XXIX. The G*ri*hya-Sûtras, Rules of Vedic Domestic Ceremonies.

Part I. *S*âṅkhâyana, Â*s*valâyana, Pâraskara, Khâdira. Translated by HERMANN OLDENBERG. 8vo, cloth, 12*s*. 6*d*.

VOL. XXX. The G*ri*hya-Sûtras, Rules of Vedic Domestic Ceremonies.

Part II. Gobhila, Hira*n*yake*s*in, Âpastamba. Translated by HERMANN OLDENBERG. Âpastamba, Yagña-paribhâshâ-sûtras. Translated by F. MAX MÜLLER. 8vo, cloth, 12*s*. 6*d*.

These rules of Domestic Ceremonies describe the home life of the ancient Âryas with a completeness and accuracy unmatched in any other literature. Some of these rules have been incorporated in the ancient Law-books.

VOL. XXXI. The Zend-Avesta.

Part III. The Yasna, Visparad, Âfrînagân, Gâhs, and Miscellaneous Fragments. Translated by L. H. MILLS. 8vo, cloth, 12*s*. 6*d*.

VOL. XXXII. Vedic Hymns.

Translated by F. MAX MÜLLER. Part I. 8vo, cloth, 18*s*. 6*d*.

[See also Vol. XLVI.]

VOL. XXXIII. The Minor Law-books.

Translated by JULIUS JOLLY. Part I. Nârada, B*ri*haspati. 8vo, cloth, 10*s*. 6*d*.

Vol. XXXIV. The Vedânta-Sûtras, with the Commentary by *S*aṅkarâ*k*ârya. Part I.

Translated by G. Thibaut. 8vo, cloth, 12*s.* 6*d.*

[See also Vol. XXXVIII.]

Vols. XXXV and XXXVI. The Questions of King Milinda.

Translated from the Pâli by T. W. Rhys Davids. Part I. 8vo, cloth, 10*s.* 6*d.* Part II. 8vo, cloth, 12*s.* 6*d.*

Vol. XXXVII. Pahlavi Texts.

Translated by E. W. West. Part IV. The Contents of the Nasks, as stated in the Eighth and Ninth Books of the Dînka*r*d. 15*s.*

Vol. XXXVIII. The Vedânta-Sûtras. Part II. 8vo, cloth, with full Index to both Parts, 12*s.* 6*d.*

Vols. XXXIX and XL. The Sacred Books of China. The Texts of Tâoism. Translated by James Legge. 8vo, cloth, 21*s.*

Vol. XLI. The *S*atapatha-Brâhma*n*a. Part III.

Translated by Julius Eggeling. 8vo, cloth, 12*s.* 6*d.*

Vol. XLII. Hymns of the Atharva-veda.

Translated by M. Bloomfield. 8vo, cloth, 21*s.*

Vol. XLIII. The *S*atapatha-Brâhma*n*a.

Translated by Julius Eggeling. Part IV. Books VIII, IX, and X. 12*s.* 6*d.*

Vol. XLIV. The *S*atapatha-Brâhma*n*a. Part V. [*Nearly ready.*]

Vol. XLV. The *G*aina-Sûtras.

Translated from Prak*r*it, by Hermann Jacobi. Part II. The Uttarâdhyayana Sûtra, The Sûtrak*r*itâṅga Sûtra. 8vo, cloth, 12*s.* 6*d.*

Vol. XLVI. Vedic Hymns. Part II. 8vo, cloth, 14*s.*

Vol. XLVII. Pahlavi Texts.

Translated by E. W. West. Part V. Marvels of Zoroastrianism. 8*s.* 6*d.*

Vol. XLVIII. The Vedânta-Sûtras, with Râmânu*g*a's *S*rîbhâshya.

Translated by G. Thibaut. [*In the Press.*]

Vol. XLIX. Buddhist Mahâyâna Texts. Buddha*k*arita, translated by E. B. Cowell. Sukhâvatî-vyûha, Va*g*ra*kkh*edikâ, &c., translated by F. Max Müller. Amitâyur-Dhyâna-Sûtra, translated by J. Takakusu. 8vo, cloth, 12*s.* 6*d.*

Anecdota Oxoniensia.

ARYAN SERIES.

Buddhist Texts from Japan. I. Vagra*kkh*edikâ; *The Diamond-Cutter.*

Edited by F. MAX MÜLLER, M.A. Small 4to, 3*s.* 6*d.*

One of the most famous metaphysical treatises of the Mahâyâna Buddhists.

Buddhist Texts from Japan. II. Sukhâvatî-Vyûha: *Description of Sukhâvatî, the Land of Bliss.*

Edited by F. MAX MÜLLER, M.A., and BUNYIU NANJIO. With two Appendices: (1) Text and Translation of Sanghavarman's Chinese Version of the Poetical Portions of the Sukhâvatî-Vyûha; (2) Sanskrit Text of the Smaller Sukhâvatî-Vyûha. Small 4to, 7*s.* 6*d.*

The *editio princeps* of the Sacred Book of one of the largest and most influential sects of Buddhism, numbering more than ten millions of followers in Japan alone.

Buddhist Texts from Japan. III. *The Ancient Palm-Leaves containing the* Pragñâ-Pâramitâ-H*ri*daya-Sûtra *and the* Ushnîsha-Vigaya-Dhâra*n*î.

Edited by F. MAX MÜLLER, M.A., and BUNYIU NANJIO, M.A. With an Appendix by G. BÜHLER, C.I.E. With many Plates. Small 4to, 10*s.*

Contains facsimiles of the oldest Sanskrit MS. at present known.

Dharma-Sa*m*graha, *an Ancient Collection of Buddhist Technical Terms.*

Prepared for publication by KENJIU KASAWARA, a Buddhist Priest from Japan, and, after his death, edited by F. MAX MÜLLER and H. WENZEL. Small 4to, 7*s.* 6*d.*

Kâtyâyana's Sarvânukrama*n*î of the *Ri*gveda.

With Extracts from Sha*d*guru*s*ishya's Commentary entitled Vedârthadîpikâ. Edited by A. A. MACDONELL, M.A., Ph.D. 16*s.*

The Buddha-*K*arita of A*s*vaghosha.

Edited, from three MSS., by E. B. COWELL, M.A. 12*s.* 6*d.*

The Mantrapāṭha, or the Prayer Book of the Āpastambins.

Edited, together with the Commentary of Haradatta, and translated by M. WINTERNITZ, Ph.D. *First Part.* Introduction, Sanskrit Text, Varietas Lectionis, and Appendices. Small quarto, 10*s.* 6*d.*

Oxford

AT THE CLARENDON PRESS

LONDON: HENRY FROWDE

OXFORD UNIVERSITY PRESS WAREHOUSE, AMEN CORNER, E.C.